"Paul Capetz takes us on a deep journey into the theology of interpreting the Bible from Luther and Calvin to Schleiermacher, Barth, Bultmann, and the present day. Along the way, he shows why appeals to biblical authority alone are never sufficient for Christian theology and ethics, and why progressives who want to proclaim the gospel should engage the Reformation heritage. It's a trip no serious contemporary Protestant thinker should miss."

—Douglas F. Ottati
Davidson College

"Paul Capetz argues that proclamation of the Christian message can and must be compatible with commonsense canons of reason and logic, and scientific and historical knowledge. At the center of his case is Protestantism's 'original insight'—the distinction between the Bible and the witness within it to the 'good news' that Jesus is the decisive representation of God's pure, unconditional love. This insight is key to a response to both 'evangelical' despisers of human intellect and cultural despisers of Christianity."

—David J. Lull
Wartburg Theological Seminary

"Drawing on decades of experience as a historical theologian, teacher, and pastor, Paul Capetz zeroes in on the problem of biblical authority that has long divided American Protestantism and now even threatens our republic. This is a rare and full-throated defense of Luther's 'original insight' and its continuing significance by a scholar too well-versed in the Christian theological tradition to let the currently fashionable dismissals of historical-critical exegesis—on the postmodern left as well as the atavistic right—go unchallenged."

—Brent W. Sockness
Stanford University

"Here Paul Capetz makes a provocative argument about untapped resources of the Protestant Reformation and how they can be utilized by contemporary Christians to transcend trenchant liberal/conservative divides in order to proclaim the gospel. Returning to Luther's original insight that proclamation of the gospel is not synonymous with proclaiming scripture, Capetz demonstrates, can counter anti-intellectual tendencies in contemporary American Christianity and speak in more compelling ways to the issues of our day."

—Deanna A. Thompson
St. Olaf College

"Paul Capetz is telling us not to run from critical thinking. But he is not running from the Bible or tradition. He's leaning in with the conviction that Luther's take on scripture is precisely what progressive Protestants need if they are to avoid falling into cultural irrelevancy. This set of deeply informed and precisely reasoned essays should convince you that he might just be right."

—Stephen Patterson
Willamette University

Recovering Protestantism's Original Insight

For Hans Dieter Betz,
   with deep respect for your scholarship and much gratitude for all that I have learned from it.

Paul Cyril

Recovering Protestantism's Original Insight

Luther's Heritage and Theological Criticism of the Bible

PAUL E. CAPETZ

CASCADE Books · Eugene, Oregon

RECOVERING PROTESTANTISM'S ORIGINAL INSIGHT
Luther's Heritage and Theological Criticism of the Bible

Copyright © 2023 Paul E. Capetz. All rights reserved. Except for brief quotations in critical publications or reviews, no part of this book may be reproduced in any manner without prior written permission from the publisher. Write: Permissions, Wipf and Stock Publishers, 199 W. 8th Ave., Suite 3, Eugene, OR 97401.

Cascade Books
An Imprint of Wipf and Stock Publishers
199 W. 8th Ave., Suite 3
Eugene, OR 97401

www.wipfandstock.com

PAPERBACK ISBN: 978-1-6667-3747-9
HARDCOVER ISBN: 978-1-6667-9695-7
EBOOK ISBN: 978-1-6667-9696-4

Cataloging-in-Publication data:

Names: Capetz, Paul E., author.

Title: Recovering Protestantism's original insight : Luther's heritage and theological criticism of the Bible / Paul E. Capetz.

Description: Eugene, OR: Cascade Books, 2023. | Includes bibliographical references and index.

Identifiers: ISBN: 978-1-6667-3747-9 (paperback). | ISBN: 978-1-6667-9695-7 (hardcover). | ISBN: 978-1-6667-9696-4 (ebook).

Subjects: LCSH: Bible—Hermeneutics. | Bible—Criticism, interpretation, etc. | Luther, Martin, 1483–1546. | Calvin, Jean, 1509–1564. |Schleiermacher, Friedrich, 1768–1834. | Barth, Karl, 1886–1968. | Bultmann, Rudolf, 1884–1976.

Classification: BS543 C37 2023 (print). | BS543 (epub).

Unless otherwise noted, Scripture quotations are taken from the New Revised Standard Version Bible, copyright © 1989 National Council of the Churches of Christ in the United States of America. Used by permission. All rights reserved worldwide.

VERSION NUMBER 053123

In memory of my father

"It has required all the impact of modern scientific, literary, and historical criticism to drive Protestantism back to its original insight."

—B. A. Gerrish[1]

---

1. "The Word of God and the Words of Scripture: Luther and Calvin on Biblical Authority," in *The Old Protestantism and the New: Essays on the Reformation Heritage* (Chicago: University of Chicago Press, 1982) 51–68 at 65.

Contents

Acknowledgments | ix

Introduction | 1

1 Luther's Heritage and Theological Criticism of the Bible | 13
2 Theology and the Historical-Critical Study of the Bible | 70
3 Friedrich Schleiermacher on the Old Testament as Jewish Scripture | 105
4 Karl Barth on the Old Testament as Christian Scripture | 139

Index | 173

Acknowledgments

THE ESSAYS IN THIS volume were originally published as articles in journals. I gratefully acknowledge that permission to reprint them has been granted by their original publishers:

Chapter 1 was originally published under the title "Reformation Heritage and the Question of *Sachkritik*: Theological Criticism of the Bible," *Currents in Mission and Theology: The Theological Journal of the Lutheran School of Theology at Chicago and Wartburg Theological Seminary* 45.4 (2018) 41–62. Permission to reprint granted by the co-editors of the journal.

Chapter 2 was originally published under the title "Theology and the Historical-Critical Study of the Bible," *Harvard Theological Review* 104.4 (2011) 459–88. Reproduced with permission of Cambridge University Press through PLSclear.

Chapter 3 was originally published under the title "Friedrich Schleiermacher on the Old Testament," *Harvard Theological Review* 102.3 (2009) 297–326. Reproduced with permission of Cambridge University Press through PLSclear.

Chapter 4 was originally published under the title "The Old Testament as a Witness to Jesus Christ: Historical Criticism and Theological Exegesis of the Bible according to Karl Barth," *Journal of Religion* 90.4 (2010) 475–506. Reproduced with permission of the University of Chicago Press.

Additionally, I wish to express my sincere gratitude to three persons who assisted me in preparing the manuscript for publication: K. C. Hanson, my editor at Cascade Books, for his enthusiasm for this project and his patient help at every step along the way in seeing it to completion; Dale Dobias, reference librarian at Luther Seminary in St. Paul, Minnesota, for his willingness to answer many bibliographical questions; and to Ashley Raper, office manager at Christ Church by the Sea in Newport Beach, California, for her expert assistance with stylistic matters that helped me to improve many sentences.

Introduction

THE FOUR ESSAYS COLLECTED here within the covers of this volume address various aspects of a single topic: Protestant theology's relation to the historical-critical study of the Bible. The lead essay, from which the subtitle of the volume as a whole is drawn, concerns itself directly with the normative theological question of the kind of authority the Bible can properly be said to have in the light of its thoroughgoing historical interpretation. Although historical-critical study of the Bible came into its own only after the Enlightenment had laid the foundations of a distinctively modern culture, its antecedents lay in the humanistic scholarship of the Renaissance, from which the Protestant Reformers of the sixteenth century drew heavily, and apart from which there would have been no Reformation at all. Five hundred years after Martin Luther undertook to reform the church by reforming its doctrine, his approach to the Bible still has much to teach all who claim to be his heirs, especially since many of his best lessons appear to have been forgotten or ignored. Of particular significance is his insight into the relation of the canon of scripture as a whole to the gospel: the Christian message about Jesus' decisive significance for human existence. For more than two centuries now, historical-critical scholarship has posed a serious challenge to the intellectual and moral credibility of certain traditional views about the Bible and its authority—views widely held by many (perhaps even by most) Protestants in America today. Yet Luther's pivotal insight offers the possibility of a vigorous theological engagement with the religious substance of scripture's witness to the gospel without shortchanging the results of historical-critical study.

These are not merely academic issues. The future of the Protestant ministry—its preaching and teaching—depends on how we address them. The mainline Protestant churches, which trace their origin by various routes back to Luther's reforming work, are currently in danger of losing the ability to engage our culture religiously and morally in a way that combines deep intellectual conviction with existential profundity. For large segments of our society, the Bible is now entirely identified with the reactionary agenda of the Religious Right that seeks political power for the sake of enforcing its own version of evangelical Christianity upon the nation as a whole. The Bible has thus become the symbolic possession of right-wing Christians who oppose many of the hard-won achievements of modernity in the name of fidelity to the Bible itself. While some evangelicals have been able to accept the results of historical-critical exegesis in very limited doses, fundamentalists reject it entirely just as they refuse to accept any conclusions of modern science that contradict their interpretation of the Bible. Recently these right-wing Christians have demonstrated their willingness to sacrifice our democratic form of government for authoritarian rule provided that it cloaks its designs in appeal to the Bible. Their mantra that the United States was founded on "biblical principles" and should be an officially Christian nation poses a grave threat to America's historic guarantee of religious freedom for all. Yet precisely on account of the Bible's captivity to this reactionary agenda in the popular mind, increasing numbers of Americans, especially among the younger generations, are leaving the churches in droves since they have come to believe that Christians are opposed to the progressive values of modern civilization. As a friend of mine who works in advertising puts it, Christianity is "a damaged brand." Mainline Protestantism no longer defines what it means to be a Protestant Christian in America today. Sadly, our public voice has been rendered mute.

My experience as the pastor of a mainline congregation corroborates the truth of this observation. On the one hand, very conservative Christians quickly lose interest in our church as soon as they learn that we do not uphold an evangelical doctrine of scripture that gives sanction to the moral and political agenda of the Religious Right. Such Christians assume that any departure from this approach to the Bible is a violation of everything that Protestantism has historically stood for. On the other hand, those persons who are opposed to the agenda of the Religious Right reject us out of hand simply because we are a "Christian" church. They cannot imagine a church that is open to the truth of science without reservation, progressive in its moral and political values, committed to our nation's religious freedom for all, supportive of the equal rights of sexual and gender minorities, and concerned about issues of social justice and ecology. Between these polarized extremes our church has a difficult time with evangelism and outreach since our Christian faith is deeply misunderstood by people on both sides.

How did the Bible become a weapon with which to hurt people? Or a symbol of cultural obscurantism and political reaction? The troubling question posed to his contemporaries by Schleiermacher almost two centuries ago has taken on new urgency in our time: "Shall the tangle of history so unravel that Christianity becomes identified with barbarism and science with unbelief?"[1] Schleiermacher famously attempted to address the cultured despisers of religion in his own time, but today we are also up against the religious despisers of culture. While the Religious Right may have lost the so-called culture wars that have divided our nation in the past four decades, it certainly seems to have won the religious war of defining what it means to be a Christian in the minds of both believers and unbelievers. By contrast, mainline Protestants, who once mediated the heritage of the Reformation to American culture, have been pushed to the sidelines by right-wing Christians and progressive secularists alike. In the face of this challenge, we have to ask, How can the gospel become "good news" again? There can be no doubt that the question of the Bible is urgent if mainline Protestantism ever hopes to regain its public voice.

Nothing could be more antithetical to this right-wing usurpation of the Bible than the genuine legacy of Luther. His crucial insight needs to be recovered since it holds the key to a contemporary approach to the Bible that is characterized by intellectual and moral integrity. Indeed, Schleiermacher was certain that the best way to prevent the alliance of Protestant religion with barbarism that he so feared lay in gaining a deeper understanding of our Reformation heritage.

> Unless the Reformation from which our church first emerged endeavors to establish an eternal covenant between the living Christian faith and completely free, independent scientific inquiry, so that faith does not hinder science and science does not exclude faith, it fails to meet adequately the needs of our time and we need another one, no matter what it takes to establish it. Yet it is my firm conviction that the basis for such a covenant was already established in the Reformation.[2]

What Schleiermacher says about science in this context applies not merely to natural science but also to humanistic learning in general, such as historical study of the Bible. Unfortunately, few Protestants in America today know the Reformation heritage well enough to understand what Schleiermacher meant by suggesting that there are untapped resources bequeathed to us by the Reformers that could assist us in solving some of our vexing contemporary dilemmas. The anti-intellectualism and historical amnesia

---

1. Friedrich Schleiermacher, *On the Glaubenslehre: Two Letters to Dr. Lücke*, trans. James Duke and Francis Fiorenza, Texts and Translation Series—American Academy of Religion 3 (Chico, CA: Scholars, 1981) 61.

2. Schleiermacher, *On the Glaubenslehre*, 64.

that infect so much American religion make it exceedingly difficult to get a hearing for an understanding of the Bible's proper role that is based in the theology of the first Protestant. It is surely ironic that in spite of their historic insistence that Roman Catholic tradition not be allowed to obscure the message of the Bible, Protestants have often failed to acknowledge the role their own theological traditions play in determining how *they* approach the Bible. For the truth of the matter is that many Protestant views *about* the Bible are not derived *from* the Bible. They are, rather, the product of our traditions that have taught us to think about the Bible and its authority in a particular way. Furthermore, the legacy we have inherited from the Reformers is far more complex than many Protestants have been taught to believe. As a careful historical analysis of the Reformation demonstrates, Protestants have actually inherited two contrasting approaches to the Bible that stand in significant tension to one another. Although Luther's approach has been less influential in the subsequent history of Protestantism, it signifies a far greater break with the medieval theological tradition criticized by the Reformers than the alternative approach represented by John Calvin. It also offers the promise for revitalizing mainline Protestantism today by taking the Bible back from its evangelical usurpers.

Luther's distinctive and original contribution to Christian theology includes his profound insight as to how we should think about the relation of the Bible as the received canon of scripture to the message of the gospel to which scripture bears witness. In making this crucial distinction, Luther recognized the necessity of theological criticism of the Bible, later to be called *Sachkritik* (content criticism) by Barth and Bultmann, who together explored—sometimes in agreement and at other times in disagreement with one another—how to recover a robust theological interpretation of scripture's message while steering clear of the Scylla of biblicism that views the Bible as a supernaturally inspired text and the Charybdis of historicism that views the Bible as a mere artifact of antiquity. Indeed, the amazing freedom with which Luther felt emboldened to criticize the Bible would certainly come as a surprise to many of his heirs for whom any criticism of scripture is tantamount to blasphemy. Yet the truth is that Luther not only called for a return to the Bible in order that the authentic meaning of Christian faith might be recovered but also criticized portions of the Bible that, in his judgment, failed to give adequate expression to the proper understanding of this faith. It is my conviction that if mainline Protestantism is ever to recover its public voice, it must retrieve Luther's innovative proposal since it alone can allow the gospel to be proclaimed and heard again as good news apart from doctrines of biblical authority that have long been shown to be intellectually untenable and morally problematic in the light of a thoroughgoing historical exegesis of scripture. In this manner we will confirm the wisdom of Schleiermacher's suggestion that a fuller acquaintance with our Reformation heritage can lead us to find unanticipated theological resources there with which to address some of the most difficult challenges facing us today.

In making my case for the superiority of Luther's original insight over its more popular alternative in English-speaking Protestantism, I do not wish to be misunderstood as endorsing Luther's theology in every respect. I am not a Lutheran in the denominational sense. My own religious background is Presbyterian and Methodist. Yet Luther's heritage is not the property of Lutherans alone. Neither Calvin nor Wesley would have been the Protestant theologians they were had it not been for their deep—though not uncritical—indebtedness to Luther. Like them, I too am critical of aspects of Luther's legacy. But for both Calvin and Wesley, Luther laid the indispensable foundation on the basis of which others might carry forward his work of reforming church and doctrine. While Protestants should pay more attention to their own theological traditions than they are usually wont to do, a genuine Protestant must always be ready to criticize these traditions for the sake of the same cause that led Luther to his reformation of medieval doctrine: the gospel. We see examples of precisely this Protestant criticism of Protestant tradition in Calvin's relation to Luther and Wesley's relation to Calvin. All I seek to propose is that Luther's groundbreaking insight into the relation of the gospel to the canon of scripture deserves to be recovered by the disciples of Calvin and Wesley as well as by other Protestants since it alone can best assist the cause of the gospel in our time, which was the same cause to which all three Reformers were loyal in their time and by which they wanted their own partial and imperfect efforts to be judged by those who came after them. Presbyterians have a memorable way of making just this point: "the church that has once been reformed in the past stands ever in need of further reformation today" (*ecclesia reformata, semper reformanda*).

While there have been some very fine theologians in mainline Protestantism since the Religious Right began its rise to public prominence, they have not exerted the kind of broader cultural influence that Reinhold Niebuhr or Paul Tillich once did.[3] David A. Hollinger, a historian who has examined the crisis of the mainline Protestant churches in some depth, draws attention to the fact that during this same period of time "theology itself was rapidly losing standing in the public culture of the nation."[4] In the

---

3. Paul Tillich spoke of the importance for both church and society of "an honest theology of high cultural standing." *Systematic Theology*, 3 vols. (Chicago: University of Chicago Press, 1951, 1957, 1963) 1:7.

4. David A. Hollinger, *Christianity's American Fate: How Religion Became More Conservative and Society More Secular* (Princeton: Princeton University Press, 2022)

face of the rising tide of the Religious Right, mainline Protestantism has lacked widely recognized intellectual leaders who "might have spoken with unique authority and sophistication" to our society at large about a "cluster of fundamental issues" concerning the proper interpretation of the Bible, "how it should be read, and how it could guide conduct in today's society."[5] In the decades of their steepest decline, what mainline Protestants most needed were articulate "voices in the public arena" who could explain "why their own perspective on the Bible was superior to that of their evangelical counterparts."[6] Unfortunately, this loss of a public voice for mainline Protestant theology "facilitated the transferal of Christianity's symbolic capital into the hands of the evangelicals" so that the Bible now belongs to them "more than ever" in the minds of most Americans.[7] The irony, as Hollinger indicates in the subtitle of his book, is that American religion has become much more conservative while American society as a whole has become far more secular.

Nobody objects when historical-critical methods are applied to the texts of Luther and Calvin so as to make possible a fully historical understanding of the Reformation. But the Bible is a different matter! Yet surely one of the greatest achievements of modern Protestant theology has been the development and further refinement of historical-critical methods for understanding the Bible as a document of the ancient world. Indeed, it is a testimony to the relentless honesty of their quest for truth that the most brilliant leaders of Protestant theology in the nineteenth and twentieth centuries fully embraced these methods and applied them without reservation to the church's scriptures while wrestling with the difficult normative questions of theology that a fully historicized approach to the interpretation of Christian religion inevitably raises for serious thinking. Nevertheless, the difficulties for theological reflection occasioned by modern historical thinking have at times called forth a negative reaction even from some quarters that have had to grant the validity of historical criticism in principle. In their view, historical-critical scholarship has to be kept within very strict limits so that it does not transgress upon theology's proper terrain, especially when it comes to what has been called a "theological exegesis" of the Bible.

Since such reservations have been voiced by certain theologians and biblical scholars in our time as well, I attempt to reply to some of their theological objections to historical criticism in the second essay reprinted

---

138.

    5. Hollinger, *Christianity's American Fate*, 149.

    6. Hollinger, *Christianity's American Fate*, 149.

    7. Hollinger, *Christianity's American Fate*, 151.

in this volume. I disagree with their initial premise that an authentically theological engagement with the Bible is only possible once we leave historical modes of thinking behind. The problem for a theological exegesis of the Bible does not lie with historical-critical method or its results. The problem, rather, is the inability or unwillingness to think theologically in a manner that takes full account of the new vistas on biblical history and literature that have been opened up for us by historical-critical biblical scholarship. For this reason, I am opposed to any conception of a theological exegesis of the Bible that minimizes or curtails the significance of historical-critical modes of interpretation. While a theological question about a biblical text is logically distinct from a historical question about the same text, it is unnecessary to pit these two types of questions against one another by claiming that the more we think historically about the Bible, the less we will be able to think theologically about it. This is an instance of the kind of false dichotomy that is so prevalent in the theological academy today and, like all false dichotomies, it prevents us from perceiving the full range of options available for any theological thinking that is historically informed. To use a nontheological example, no serious philosopher would pit a correct historical understanding of Plato against a normative philosophical engagement with Plato's ideas. Indeed, the former is the indispensable condition of the possibility of the latter. Why should this be any different in our theological engagement with the ideas of the biblical authors? If we would take seriously the theological ideas of the apostle Paul, do we not require the best historical understanding of them that is available to us today? What we most need, then, is not less history but better thinking.[8] Yet the theological critics of historical criticism are intent on insulating the Bible from the relativizing implications of a thoroughgoing historical approach to religion and theology. But this is futile for, as Troeltsch pointed out long ago, genuine historical thinking in theology works like leaven in dough: it transforms all our previous modes of theological thinking and leaves nothing unaffected.[9]

Whereas the focus in the lead essay is on the interpretation of the New Testament, the third and fourth essays in this volume address the theological

---

8. In this connection, I am reminded of Albert Schweitzer's complaint about the failure of theology in his day to absorb fully the insights of the historical-critical study of the Bible: "We have not yet arrived at any reconciliation between history and modern thought—only between half-way history and half-way thought." *The Quest of the Historical Jesus: A Critical Study of Its Progress from Reimarus to Wrede*, trans. W. Montgomery with an introduction by James M. Robinson (New York: Macmillan, 1968; originally published in 1906) 1.

9. Ernst Troeltsch, "Historical and Dogmatic Method in Theology," in *Religion in History*, trans. James Luther Adams and Walter F. Bense (Minneapolis: Fortress, 1991) 11–32 at 12.

question of the Old Testament in the light of its historical-critical interpretation. Here the contrasting views of Schleiermacher and Barth are examined in detail because their proposals for executing the theological task have been widely viewed as representing diametrically opposed alternatives for carrying forward the legacy of the Reformation after the Enlightenment. The comparison of their views on the Old Testament is particularly instructive since it illustrates how historical-critical exegesis of the Bible required modern Protestants to make a fundamental choice between two aspects of their inheritance from the Reformers that had now been set in opposition to one another.

Although the Reformers rejected spiritualizing modes of exegesis such as allegory and insisted upon a literal exegesis of both the Old and New Testaments in order to claim the entire Bible for their side in the debate with Roman Catholicism, with the advent of historical criticism the traditional christological exegesis of the Old Testament that the Reformers shared with their medieval forebears was fundamentally called into question. Since this christological exegesis had served as the warrant for the church's claim to sole possession of the Old Testament against the synagogue's counterclaim to it, historical-critical exegesis threatened to vindicate the cause of the Jews against that of the Christians in the question of Israel's scriptures. In this new situation, Schleiermacher clearly grasped the implications of the historical-critical exegesis of the Old Testament for Christian theology; as a result, he broke with the classical Christian tradition, including his own Protestant heritage, and argued that the Old Testament is Jewish scripture that rightfully belongs to the synagogue. Accordingly, it should no longer be considered as canonical by the church, no matter how much Christians may still continue to learn about the historical background of Jesus and his first disciples from study of the Old Testament literature.

In this question Schleiermacher championed the view of Marcion, who, prior to the development of a New Testament canon, had argued against retention of the Jewish scriptures in the church on the grounds that Judaism and Christianity are different religions. Since Marcion rejected every spiritualizing mode of exegesis and instead pressed for a literal exegesis of the Old Testament, his provocative challenge was never directly answered on his own terms by the proto-orthodox church that denounced him as a heretic. Indeed, in its effort to secure the Christian claim to the Old Testament against the Jews, the anti-Marcionite church availed itself of precisely those exegetical methods that had been explicitly repudiated by Marcion. Even though the Reformers of the sixteenth century continued this anti-Marcionite legacy of the classical Christian tradition, Schleiermacher rightly perceived that historical study of the Bible in his time had begun to undermine the theological unity of the two testaments that had been an unquestioned presupposition of both Luther and Calvin, and he endeavored to draw what he took to be the consistent consequences of the newer biblical scholarship for modern Protestants. Unfortunately, Schleiermacher's argument has rarely been taken seriously as it surely deserves to be. After the Holocaust, it has too easily been dismissed as an expression of anti-Semitism, which it is not. For the corollary of his argument about the Jewish character of the Old Testament is his recognition—hitherto unprecedented for a major Christian theologian—that Judaism is a religion with its own integrity that is entitled to be understood on its own terms and therefore should not be viewed as a *preparatio evangelica* that finds its inevitable fulfillment in the New Testament. It is at least arguable that the plight of the Jews throughout the long history of Christendom might have been far less difficult had the church not rejected Marcion's proposal.[10]

Against Schleiermacher's argument, Barth defended the Old Testament as Christian scripture. In the face of historical criticism, he sought to restore the unified canon of Old and New Testaments as the foundation of his own approach to theology that consciously modeled itself after the Reformers' way of reading the Bible theologically. But his defense of the Old Testament as Christian scripture also represented his effort to protect the church against the inroads of anti-Semitic propaganda that had seduced large segments of German Protestantism during the Nazi era. In this context, Barth made the important observation that not only the Old Testament but also much of the New Testament reflects Jewish influence. Nonetheless, Barth's heroic defense of the Old Testament against the attacks of anti-Semites does not recognize the right of post-Christian Judaism to possess this body of scripture for itself (Tanakh). For him, the Old Testament can be read and understood properly only in the light of its christological referent in the New Testament, that is, as a witness to Jesus Christ. Even though Barth always denied that he was opposed to historical criticism, he consistently minimized its value in his exegesis of the Old Testament. In fact, he tacitly conceded Schleiermacher's main point that historical-critical exegesis lends greater plausibility to the synagogue's claim to Israel's scriptural legacy than to that of the church. For this reason, Barth's defense of the Old Testament is ambiguous.

In this comparison of Schleiermacher and Barth, we see how these two giants of modern Protestant theology seized upon differing aspects of their

---

10. This point has been well made by Heikki Räisänen, "Attacking the Book, Not the People: Marcion and the Jewish Roots of Christianity," in *Marcion, Muhammad and the Mahatma: Exegetical Perspectives on the Encounter of Cultures and Faiths* (London: SCM, 1997) 64–80.

legacy from the Reformers. Schleiermacher embraced historical-critical exegesis in order to let the Old Testament speak in its own voice apart from the preconceived notions of theological tradition, even if the result undermined the theological preconceptions of Luther and Calvin about the unity of the Bible. By contrast, Barth minimized the importance of historical-critical study in order to restore the theological unity of the Bible and to base his theology upon a way of reading it that emulated that of Luther and Calvin, even if his theological exegesis of the Old Testament stands in significant tension with the results of historical-critical biblical scholarship. The question that this comparison of the opposing viewpoints of Schleiermacher and Barth raises is whether there is any theological rationale for inclusion of the Old Testament within the canon of the Christian Bible that does not minimize the valid insights of historical criticism. Is it possible to do justice to the legitimate concerns of both Schleiermacher and Barth? Can a theological case be made for the religious importance of the Old Testament in the Christian Bible while fully incorporating what historical criticism teaches us about the history and literature of ancient Israel?

I believe that it is possible to make this case. Such a theological justification for the place of the Old Testament in the Christian Bible can also enable the church to recognize the full legitimacy of the synagogue's claim to Israel's scriptural legacy. Moreover, it can give Marcion his belated due for having correctly perceived an acute theological problem that those Christians who denounced him as a heretic refused to recognize as honestly as he did. Even if, as I believe, there were good reasons for rejecting his proposal to jettison the Old Testament from the emerging canon of Christian scripture, Marcion's challenge deserves to be met on its own terms.[11] A Christian Bible without the Old Testament would have entailed a tremendous historical and religious impoverishment of the Christian church. This does not mean, however, that there is an unproblematic theological unity of the canon of Old and New Testaments, as premodern theologians assumed. Furthermore, if we admit the necessity of theological criticism of the Bible as Luther exercised in relation to the New Testament, then we will have to be willing to admit the same necessity of theological criticism in relation to the Old Testament. But in the case of the Old Testament, we cannot apply an

---

11. Hermann Gunkel put it well when he wrote: "With good reason, the church resisted this temptation and clung to its Old Testament, in spite of the serious difficulties presented by the task of interpreting it . . . The interpretation of the Old Testament may change, but the right of the Old Testament to its place in the church is indisputable." Gunkel, "Why Engage the Old Testament?" in *Water for a Thirsty Land: Israelite Literature and Religion*, ed. K. C. Hanson, trans. A. K. Dallas and James Schaaf, Fortress Classics in Biblical Studies (Minneapolis: Fortress 2001) 1–30 at 14.

external theological criterion derived from the New Testament; rather, the proper measure for criticizing Old Testament texts can only be internal to the Old Testament itself. This remains an unresolved problem of Old Testament theology.[12]

There is an inescapable ethical dimension to our interpretations of the Bible to which we must pay attention if we would be moral human beings. The truth is that historical-critical exegesis has finally allowed the Old Testament to come into its own within the church so that it can be heard speaking in its distinctive voice apart from the filter of the New Testament. I take this to be a rich gain for the church's understanding of its scripture, even if it requires repentance and humility on our part: repentance for past sins against the Jews and humility as we recognize our indebtedness to ancient Israel and early Judaism for much that is of essential value within our Christian tradition. In this sense, historical-critical scholarship of the Old Testament has fulfilled the Reformers' aspiration to let the Bible speak for itself apart from the lens of later tradition.

A fully historical understanding of the Bible can no longer allow for a sharp distinction to be made between scripture and the postbiblical tradition, as the Reformers made. In this regard, we have to admit the truth in Roman Catholic criticisms of the Reformation. Henceforth, we must look upon the Bible as reflecting the earliest and foundational layers of Christian tradition. Nonetheless, there remains something quintessentially Protestant in this admission of a merely relative—not an absolute—distinction between scripture and tradition. Theological criticism of the tradition, upon which the Reformers rightly insisted, must necessarily be extended to include theological criticism of the Bible as well. In this insistence, I am following the lead of Luther himself, who pioneered the theological criticism of scripture, even though his pivotal insight in this matter appears to have been forgotten or ignored by most of his heirs. But its importance for mainline Protestantism in our time cannot be gainsaid. For it is only insofar as we can recover Protestantism's original insight that Luther's contemporary heirs will be able to proclaim the gospel and interpret it theologically in such a way that it can be heard once again as good news.

Theology matters. Unfortunately, however, there is more bad theology than good theology. Yet bad theology prevents people from truly understanding the Christian message so as to make a responsible decision about it. While the comprehensive task of theology involves more than biblical exegesis and hermeneutics, how the Bible is properly to be interpreted will

---

12. On this question, see Rolf P. Knierim, *The Task of Old Testament Theology: Substance, Method, and Cases* (Grand Rapids: Eerdmans, 1995).

always remain a central issue for Christian theology. The five major Protestant theologians examined in this volume—Luther, Calvin, Schleiermacher, Barth, and Bultmann—significantly advanced the church's understanding of theology's essential relation to the proper interpretation of the Bible. Together, they constitute a brilliant tradition of bold theological reflection upon scripture that extends from the sixteenth century into the twentieth century. Each of them addressed in a new and fresh way the persistent and vital questions about history, canon, exegesis, hermeneutics, theology, and preaching that must always be asked and answered by the church in every generation. While there are no infallible interpreters of the Bible in Protestantism just as there is no irreformable tradition, those of us who bear responsibility for leading the mainline church in the twenty-first century ignore the enduring contributions of these forebears at our own peril. Protestants have a tradition and we should learn from it, but our task is not to repristinate the past. Rather, through critical and self-critical conversation with our own Protestant heritage, we can hope to make a responsible contribution to a faithful and robust proclamation of the gospel in our own day.

The two interrelated kinds of criticism here defended, historical and theological, are to be placed in the service of a better and deeper understanding of the gospel to which scripture bears witness.[13] Any Protestant church that is unwilling to avail itself of these critical possibilities of understanding to their fullest extent will find itself defenseless when the Bible is usurped by others for purposes that are alien to the religious and moral substance of the biblical tradition. But in that case, the genuine promise of the Reformation heritage has been forfeited. This is surely what the first Protestant would say to us as we face our very difficult challenges today.

---

13. James Barr concurs: "[T]he Bible has to be read critically; just as it has to be critically read in historical regards, so also it has to be critically read in theological respects." *The Bible in the Modern World* (New York: Harper & Row, 1973) 130.

1

Luther's Heritage and Theological Criticism of the Bible

INTRODUCTION

WHEN I WAS THIRTEEN years old, I spent a week at a United Methodist summer camp in the mountains above San Bernardino, California. It is no exaggeration to say that what happened to me during that week profoundly changed my life and set the direction for my later professional vocation as an ordained minister of the church and a teacher of theology. For it was there that I met a young minister who must have seen something in me that suggested to him that I had the makings of a future minister myself. I vividly recall the moment when he asked me if I had ever considered going into the ministry. And I recall just as vividly how I immediately replied, "Oh no, I could never be a minister!" Naturally enough, he wanted to know why I was absolutely certain that I could never become a minister. So, by way of explanation, I confessed to him that I did not believe everything that is found within the covers of the Bible. Since I assumed that a necessary condition of being a minister was believing that whatever the Bible says is true, it was self-evident to me that I could never be one. I fully expected my confession of disbelief to be met with disapproval. But much to my surprise, he was neither shocked nor appalled. He did not lecture me on the need for unquestioning faith as others had done upon learning of my doubt. Instead, he proceeded to ask me some probing questions about the exact nature of my theological difficulties. I could tell from his response as well as the tone of his questioning that he was a very different kind of minister than any I had ever met before. Here was a minister who did not condemn me for my doubt; rather, he treated me respectfully as an intelligent person and took my questions seriously without dismissing them out of hand. This was a new experience for me. Finally, as if to give me an entirely new way to think about the Bible and the question of truth, he made a distinction that I spent the rest of my week at camp trying to understand: "Something isn't true just because it's in the Bible. It's in the Bible because somebody thought it was true."

Although my experiences growing up in the church had been very positive and had instilled in me a deep love of Jesus, by that young age of my life I had already come to realize there was a big discrepancy between how the Bible portrays the creation of the world and what modern science teaches about the origins of things. My father had taken me to the museum of natural history in downtown Los Angeles where I had seen for myself the evidence for the prehistoric existence of dinosaurs of which we read nothing in the book of Genesis. I remember asking my fifth-grade Sunday school teacher when she was teaching us about the creation of the world in the opening chapter of Genesis: "When were the dinosaurs created?" She was quite caught off-guard by my question and candidly admitted that she could not answer it. Back then I did not press my question any further. But by the time I was sent off to church camp, I understood that a choice had to be made between the Bible's account of creation and that given by natural science. Consequently, when asked to consider becoming a minister, I had to reply in all sincerity that this was simply not possible since in the name of truth itself I could not give unqualified assent to everything that the Bible teaches. I also intuitively grasped that if the Bible was wrong in this one matter, it could be wrong in other matters too.

Well-meaning ministers and Sunday school teachers had insisted that Christians must accept the Bible in its entirety without question. We were not free to pick and choose those portions of it that suit us while rejecting the others. The dire warning at the close of the book of Revelation was usually cited as a warrant for this "all or nothing" approach to the teachings of the Bible (Rev 22:18–19). Yet the minister whom I met at summer camp seemed to be saying just the opposite: a responsible engagement with the Bible would evaluate its various statements one by one in order to determine the truth of each individually. After all, when I told him that I didn't believe *everything* in the Bible, he correctly inferred that I did believe *some things* in the Bible! Moreover, by suggesting that the material within the Bible had found its way there because somebody *thought* it was true, he drew my attention to a crucial feature of the Bible that I had never considered in my prior wrestling with it, namely, that the Bible had been written by human beings like me. Even though the proper names of certain persons are also found in the titles of various biblical books (Jeremiah, Isaiah, and Ezekiel or Matthew, Mark, and Luke) the way the Bible was talked about in church had left me with the distinct impression that the claim being made on its behalf was that it had *not* been written by human beings like the rest of us but had been authored by God (or the Holy Spirit). That's undoubtedly what was meant by calling it "the Word of God" and saying it was "inspired." That's also why it was deemed such a serious sin to disbelieve anything within the Bible. Anyone who dared to raise a critical question about the Bible wasn't merely calling into question the views of other human beings but was actually presuming to challenge the authority of God! We were not permitted to disbelieve one part of it since a book inspired by God could not possibly be fallible in any of its parts. But what if the Bible really was a human book? To accept the fully human character of the Bible did not lead of necessity to rejecting it *in toto*. But it did mean that its contents had to be sifted by a thoughtful reader for the truth to be found within it. For me, this was a promising new way of engaging the Bible and taking it seriously that did not require that I abdicate my reason and my conscience.

What that minister at summer camp did for me was of inestimable value. As he had hoped, I ended up going into the ministry. But also, the fact that I am still a Christian at all is to be attributed to his influence. I think it is very likely that I would have ceased to be persuaded of the truth of Christianity altogether had it not been for his insightful words about how I should consider the Bible in relation to the question of truth. He not only encouraged me to continue to think for myself, but he also opened my eyes to see that the question whether something in the Bible is true or not can never be settled by a mere appeal to a doctrine of the Bible's authority.[1]

In retrospect I realize that he had introduced me to the modern historical-critical study of the Bible, although I did not have a name for it at the time. This approach to the Bible seeks to understand its contents by relating them to their historical contexts in the life of ancient Israel or the early church. By the time I was in high school, I knew something about historical-critical methods for studying the Bible since I had gotten into the habit of borrowing theological books from the shelves of our ministers. Once I began to look upon the Bible as a human book that did not demand

---

1. I recently came across this formulation of the same viewpoint in a discussion about the Bible and contemporary theology by an Old Testament scholar: "No one should have to accept certain statements as true simply because they are found in the Bible." Konrad Schmid, "Dogmatik als konsequente Exegese? Überlegungen zur Anschlussfähigkeit der historisch-kritischen Bibelwissenschaft an die systematische Theologie," *Evangelische Theologie* 77 (2017) 327–38 at 332. Translations of German texts are mine unless otherwise indicated.

my obedient submission but, rather, invited me into engaged conversation with its subject matter, I became deeply interested in studying the Bible and learning what it actually had to say as opposed to what was asserted about it by fundamentalists. Although mine was not a fundamentalist church, there were plenty of fundamentalists in my extended family and among my acquaintances. For them, the Bible wasn't truly a human book in any real sense; rather, it was a collection of divine oracles.[2] A fundamentalist cousin could not understand my mother's enthusiasm when the first woman was ordained as a minister in our United Methodist annual conference since to him this act represented nothing but a flagrant defiance of God's explicit command concerning the role of women in the church (1 Cor 14:34–35; 1 Tim 2:11–12). He was also shocked to hear that I did not believe in Mosaic authorship of the Pentateuch since a minister in my church had already introduced me to the Documentary Hypothesis. My most dramatic encounter with fundamentalism, however, occurred during college in a course on evolutionary biology. The professor of the course had been a Christian until he lost his faith while he was studying science in graduate school; once he became convinced of the truth of Darwin's view of the origin of species, he could no longer believe in the truth of the Bible. A former fundamentalist himself, he had now become the target of vocal fundamentalists on our college campus who openly protested against his classes on evolutionary biology. I was a puzzle to him since he had never met a Christian who had no difficulties with what he was teaching. This was because of my encounter with the minister at summer camp less than a decade earlier who had shown me an entirely new way to appreciate the Bible that avoids conflicts with modern forms of knowledge, whether scientific or historical, and that doesn't demand that I reject modern ethical insights such as the full equality of women.

When I began my formal theological studies after college, however, I was surprised to meet many persons who, though professing to accept historical-critical methods of biblical study in principle, still treated the Bible in fact as a supernatural authority requiring our obedient submission, even if in matters pertaining to natural science or history allowances were made for errors. In the 1980s, as I was preparing to become a minister, the moral issue of homosexuality had moved into the center of attention and was stirring up intense controversy in the mainline churches that still continues to this day.[3]

2. See the helpful study of Protestant fundamentalism by George M. Marsden, *Fundamentalism and American Culture*, 3rd ed. (New York: Oxford University Press, 2022).

3. As I write these words, the United Methodist Church is about to split into two denominations as a result of this controversy, which has to do not only with divergent answers to the moral issue posed by homosexuality but also with divergent

To my great bewilderment, I encountered both teachers and fellow students for whom it was axiomatic that our faithfulness as Christians mandated accepting the Bible's statements about homosexuality in spite of the fact that they themselves had already set aside the Bible's statements about women. To them, biblical authority itself was on the line here. Although they were not fundamentalists, their mode of arguing from the Bible as a self-evident authority, regardless of what it said, was of the same logical type that we find in fundamentalism: biblical authority trumps every appeal to reason and human experience.[4] This view of biblical authority was, moreover, asserted to be essential to the historic identity of Protestantism with its elevation of "scripture alone" over tradition and, by implication, any other source such as philosophy that might call the Bible into question.

Experiences like these over the past four decades have made me wonder to what extent mainline Protestantism has attained a theological understanding of the Bible that can actually do justice to its theoretical acknowledgement of the fully historical character of the Bible, or whether in fact our churches have been "limping with two different opinions" (1 Kgs 18:21). I, for one, judge that we have not been fully consistent in this regard. Also, I cannot shake the impression that the anti-intellectual strain permeating our American culture has taken its toll on mainstream Protestantism by its belittling of the importance of a critical theology to undergird our ministry.[5] Few of the seminarians preparing for ordained ministry I have encountered in my capacity as a professor in graduate theological education during the past three decades placed any real value on a rigorous study of theology in its historical and systematic aspects. Those students of a more conservative theological bent were already satisfied that they knew with assurance which doctrines are to be believed by Christians, and they were not about to risk having this sense of assurance shaken by critical interrogation of the bases of their belief; on the other side of the theological spectrum, students of a more liberal theological bent failed to see the relevance of a

---

understandings of biblical authority. Although one can make a distinction between these two aspects of the controversy, one cannot separate them in reality. In recent years, other mainline Protestant denominations have also undergone splits as a result of this interrelated set of questions regarding sexual ethics and biblical authority.

4. In the many heated debates over homosexuality that I recall from those days, I remember some of my fellow students who opposed homosexuality on biblical grounds saying apologetically, "I really wish scripture said something other than what it says in this regard." By way of response, I would usually ask them, "Why do you wish it said something other than what it says unless you really think it *should* say something different?"

5. Richard Hofstadter, *Anti-intellectualism in American Life* (New York: Vintage, 1963).

disciplined examination of doctrinal questions since, to their moralistic way of thinking, it's far more important what a person does than what a person believes. Sadly, I have to come to believe that Protestantism in America now suffers from two forms of anti-intellectualism both of which disregard the necessity of theology as a fully critical inquiry into the meaning and truth of Christian faith: a conservative form with its complacent doctrinal certainties and a liberal form with little doctrinal substance at all. It is no wonder, then, that American Protestantism today is adrift as a result of this serious loss of intellectual content and, following from that, its consequent inability to engage our culture's quest for meaning with both depth of conviction and relevance to contemporary life.[6]

The mainline churches have lost touch with the vital resources of our own Reformation heritage. We have become Protestants in name only, since we no longer probe the theological inheritance that is ours as the heirs of the Reformers by bringing our questions and concerns into conversation with theirs. In this regard, I am reminded of Dietrich Bonhoeffer's characterization of the religious substance in our American churches as a "Protestantism without Reformation."[7] The anti-intellectualism of our culture goes hand in hand with its historical amnesia. But without deep historical understanding of our inheritance from the past, especially of the theological traditions that issued from the Reformation, Protestantism in the United States will remain forever deadlocked between its conservative and liberal forms. In this impasse, conservatives revere a romanticized image of the historical past that does not stand up to critical scrutiny whereas liberals seek to get out from under the tyranny of that past since in their disdain for it they haven't bothered to inquire whether it is more complex than it has been depicted by conservatives and might possibly contain unsuspected resources that could be pressed into service on behalf of their revisionary efforts. As the renowned church historian Jaroslav Pelikan so well put it, "Tradition is the living faith of the dead, traditionalism is the dead faith of the living." He went on to comment, "And, I suppose I should add, it is traditionalism that gives tradition such a bad name."[8] Rightly understood,

---

6. I concur with the judgment of one noted Methodist theologian: "If we want church renewal, we will have to renew thinking in the church. In fact, if there is a renewal of thinking in the church, there will be church renewal. Without it, there won't . . . The church is strong only when it lives by the mature convictions of its members. Mature convictions are shaped in thought." John B. Cobb Jr., *Becoming a Thinking Christian* (Nashville: Abingdon, 1993) 10.

7. Dietrich Bonhoeffer, "Protestantism without Reformation," in *The Bonhoeffer Reader*, ed. Clifford J. Green and Michael P. DeJonge (Minneapolis: Fortress, 2013) 568–91.

8. Jaroslav Pelikan, *The Vindication of Tradition*, The 1983 Jefferson Lecture in the

every living tradition, such as a religious tradition, is constituted by both a conservative pole and a liberal pole; that is, while conserving the old insights, it must prove itself amenable to incorporation of new insights. How to hold both poles together in creative tension so that they are not hardened into rigid opposition to one another is the crucial question if we are to look to our traditions in the hopes of recovering "a usable past" that inspires and orients communal life in the present.[9] In our particular case, understanding the rich and sometimes complex legacy of the Reformation is crucial if Protestants are ever to develop a vital theological interpretation of the Bible that takes with utter seriousness its historical character as a fully human document which still has something to say to us today.

At this point the objection could be raised: Why insist upon study of tradition, even our own Protestant tradition, if it is the Bible alone that is supremely important to us as Protestants? The answer is that our ideas about the Bible and its proper appropriation by the church today do not come from the Bible itself but from the church's postbiblical traditions. As John B. Cobb Jr. explains, "We cannot go to the Bible to learn straightforwardly what kind of authority it has for us. We cannot appeal to the authority of the Bible to inform us just what that authority is."[10] All Christians are heirs to some ecclesial tradition or other that has formed their views of the nature of the Bible and its authority. Cobb clarifies the crucial point: "We cannot separate the authority of the Bible from the authority of the tradition that assigns it authority and determines just what that authority may be and how it functions."[11] For Protestants, our tradition was forged during the Reformation when a new formulation of the meaning of Christian faith was articulated on the basis of an interpretation of the Bible's message that broke with that of medieval Catholicism.

Just a few years ago in 2017, Protestants all over the world commemorated the five-hundredth anniversary of the beginnings of the Reformation in 1517. Yet many Protestants, whether conservative or liberal, would be surprised to learn just how subtle and sophisticated was the view of biblical authority espoused by the first Protestant, Martin Luther. He not only called for a return to the Bible in order that the authentic meaning of Christian faith might be recovered, but he also dared to criticize portions of the Bible that, in his judgment, failed to give adequate expression to the proper

---

Humanities (New Haven: Yale University Press, 1984) 65.

9. I gratefully borrow this felicitous phrase from William J. Bouwsma, *A Usable Past: Essays in European Cultural History* (Berkeley: University of California Press, 1990).

10. Cobb, *Becoming a Thinking Christian*, 57.

11. Cobb, *Becoming a Thinking Christian*, 68.

understanding of this faith. Other Reformers, however, such as John Calvin, who gladly embraced Luther's call to criticize medieval tradition in the light of what the Bible says, were not willing to follow Luther in his freedom to criticize scripture itself. Consequently, there was a conflict between two distinct understandings of the Bible and the kind of authority it possesses already in the sixteenth century among the original Protestant Reformers themselves. As we shall see, this conflict of interpretations subsequently issued in contrasting programs for how to appropriate the Bible theologically in twentieth-century Protestant theology under the conditions of modern historical criticism. A close look at these debates in classical and modern Protestantism can serve to clarify the basic choice that confronts Protestants today as to which of these two strands of our Reformation heritage can be of greatest help to us as we seek to appropriate the Bible theologically in the light of a fully historical-critical understanding of it.

We shall commence this inquiry in reverse order by looking first at the pivotal twentieth-century debate between the two Protestant theologians who did the most to formulate the crucial issues facing us today: Karl Barth and Rudolf Bultmann. We shall then trace the roots of this debate back to the sixteenth century to see how the seeds of their disagreement were sown during the era of the Reformation itself, long before the rise of modern historical criticism. Once we have clarified the basic question before us, we will be in a better position to consider the issues dividing the Protestant churches today and to ask what role the Bible ought to play in them. Our chief aim will be to find a usable past that transcends the dichotomy of conversative and liberal.

THEOLOGICAL EXEGESIS BETWEEN HISTORICISM AND BIBLICISM: BULTMANN'S DEBATE WITH BARTH

A new era in Protestant theology was inaugurated with the publication of Karl Barth's groundbreaking commentary on Paul's Epistle to the Romans (1919, 1922).[12] This historical judgment is surely in keeping with the impact that Barth himself hoped the book would have on his contemporaries. Negatively, he intended it to signal a break with the regnant historical-critical method of biblical exegesis ("historicism") that had characterized liberal Protestant theology in the nineteenth century. Positively, he aspired

---

12. It was in its second edition, from 1922, that Barth's book made its decisive and lasting impact. Karl Barth, *The Epistle to the Romans*, trans. Edwyn C. Hoskyns (London: Oxford University Press, 1933; reprint, 1975).

to recover the sort of "theological exegesis" of scripture exemplified by Luther and Calvin in the sixteenth century. Distinctively twentieth-century Protestant theology thus began with Barth's critique of one approach to biblical exegesis coupled with his call for retrieval of another approach to it. Both critique and retrieval stood in the service of his overriding concern to make the Bible central again to the preaching and theology of his own day, much as it had been to that of the Reformers.

Among Barth's contemporaries enthusiastically endorsing his call for a theological exegesis of scripture was Rudolf Bultmann, who wrote a favorable review of Barth's Romans commentary. Although the two men would later find themselves on opposite sides of the controversy ignited by Bultmann's call for a demythologizing of the New Testament, they were initially allies in challenging the hegemony of historicism in biblical studies. Notwithstanding this early agreement, however, it soon became apparent that there was a serious disagreement between them as to what exactly was entailed in the implementation of their shared aspiration after a theological exegesis of the Bible. The issue turned on the question of the necessity and appropriateness of what in German is called *Sachkritik*, usually translated into English as "content criticism" or "material criticism." *Sachkritik* refers to theological criticism of biblical statements according to the strictly immanent criterion of the Bible's own subject matter (*Sache*) to which the biblical writers were beholden. Even though Barth explicitly acknowledged the legitimacy of *Sachkritik* in principle, he was reluctant to undertake it in fact. Here Bultmann perceived an inconsistency in Barth's practice since Barth had opened the door to *Sachkritik* in his Romans commentary even if he himself refused to walk through it, a point to which Bultmann drew attention in his review. Indeed, the seeds of their later disagreement over the program of demythologizing were sown in this earlier debate over the meaning of *Sachkritik*.

Although the term *Sachkritik* is a modern designation, what it designates is not.[13] As both Barth and Bultmann were well aware, its *locus classicus* is found in Luther's critical handling of certain biblical texts, most famously in his rejection of the canonical standing of the Epistle of James. Not surprisingly, of course, Luther's willingness to criticize the Bible was controversial even among many of his fellow Protestants in the sixteenth century. Calvin, for all his sympathies with Luther's theology, refused to follow Luther in this respect. Like Calvin, Barth sought to read the entire canon of scripture as a unity whereas Bultmann, like Luther, saw himself

---

13. See the excellent article by Robert Morgan, "*Sachkritik* in Reception History," *Journal for the Study of the New Testament* 33 (2010) 175–90.

obligated to subject scripture to criticism on behalf of the gospel to which it bears witness.[14] Since Bultmann was a Lutheran whereas Barth was an heir to the Reformed tradition of Calvin, their debate in the matter of *Sachkritik* can be viewed as a modern reprise of that earlier one between Luther and Calvin, albeit under the conditions of modern historical criticism.

Although Barth was educated in Germany under some of the finest liberal theologians of his day, he ultimately revolted against the liberal tradition of his teachers, thereby initiating two influential movements in twentieth-century theology: *dialectical theology* and *neo-orthodoxy*.[15] Beginning with Schleiermacher, the liberal or "mediating" theology (*Vermittlungstheologie*) of the nineteenth century had aimed at a synthesis of the traditions of the Reformation and the Enlightenment. Its guiding question was: What does it mean to be a Protestant Christian in the light of a modern scientific understanding of nature and a fully historical understanding of religion, including the religion of the Bible?[16] But after World War I had undermined confidence in the basic goodness and rationality of modern civilization, Barth charged that liberal theology's claim to stand in the authentic line of the Reformers was fraudulent on account of its accommodation to modernity. Part and parcel of this indictment was Barth's critique that historical-critical exegesis, which had grown up in the closest connection with liberal theology, is unsuited to deal with the Bible's distinctive subject matter that is supposed to find contemporary expression in preaching. As a corrective, Barth and his early comrades in the dialectical theology movement charted a new path forward for Protestant theology that was neither liberal nor

---

14. For the limited purposes of this essay our discussion is focused solely on the question of theological criticism of the New Testament since from a historical-critical perspective it is not proper to speak of "the gospel" in the Jewish scriptures (Old Testament). *Sachkritik* as here employed thus refers to criticism of the texts of the New Testament in the name of the gospel to which they seek to bear faithful witness. Whether and, if so, how a corresponding *Sachkritik* of the Old Testament could be undertaken apart from the imposition of categories derived from the New Testament is an important question but one that cannot be pursued in this context.

15. Whether *neo-orthodoxy* is the best term with which to characterize Barth's later theology is not a debate I wish to enter. In any case, it should not be thought that Barth simply repristinated Protestant orthodoxy. Against any such misunderstanding it should be noted that Barth's doctrinal revisions of orthodox Protestantism were as far-reaching as those of Schleiermacher.

16. Unlike much contemporary religious liberalism in the United States that shares the anti-intellectualism and ahistorical character of American culture, nineteenth-century German liberal theology was neither anti-intellectual nor ahistorical. Indeed, historical study of the Bible and the postbiblical tradition was its crowning achievement. This difference between a historically deep and a historically shallow theological liberalism makes all the difference in the world!

conservative in the usual senses but, rather, was intended to transcend this antithesis altogether. Aside from recovering certain material themes in the Reformers' theology (e.g., the radical transcendence of God, the depth and pervasiveness of human sin, God's judgment, and the necessity of grace), they also sought to revive the Reformers' way of reading the Bible without, however, repudiating the genuine insights into the historical character of the Bible that had been won by modern historical-critical labor. Herein lay the movement's greatness and also its greatest ambiguity.

Barth began his career as a pastor who endeavored to take seriously the task of the preaching office as this is understood in the Reformed tradition: *ministerium divini verbi*.[17] Accordingly, the pastor is primarily a servant, a minister, called to proclaim God's Word when preaching a sermon upon a biblical text. But Barth's formal theological education had not prepared him to interpret scripture so that it might be heard as the Word of God addressed to his congregation. He could explain what a biblical text *meant* within its original historical context, but he could not say what it *means* on Sunday morning. Barth depicted his plight in these terms:

> I myself know what it means year in year out to mount the steps of the pulpit, conscious of the responsibility to understand and to interpret, and longing to fulfill it; and yet, utterly incapable, because at the University I had never been brought beyond that well-known 'Awe in the presence of History' which means in the end no more than that all hope of engaging in the dignity of understanding and interpretation has been surrendered . . . It was this miserable situation that compelled me as a pastor to undertake a more precise understanding and interpretation of the Bible.[18]

Whereas historical-critical exegesis treats the Bible as a document of the ancient history of religion, Barth's commentary on Romans was offered by way of contrast as an example of what an authentically theological exegesis that takes the Bible seriously as the church's scripture might look like: "The purpose of this book . . . is to direct [readers] to Holy Scripture, to the Epistle of Paul to the Romans, in order that, whether they be delighted or annoyed . . . they may at least be brought face to face with the subject matter of the Scriptures."[19] Whereas the standard historical commentaries set out to understand Paul in his first-century context, Barth's commentary had

---

17. Barth, "Author's Preface to the English Edition," *Epistle to the Romans*, x.
18. Barth, "Preface to the Second Edition," *Epistle to the Romans*, 9.
19. Barth, "Author's Preface to the English Edition," *Epistle to the Romans*, x.

another aim altogether. It sought to understand what Paul would say to the people of the twentieth century.

> Paul, as a child of his age, addressed his contemporaries. It is, however, far more important that . . . he veritably speaks to all men of every age. The differences between then and now, there and here, no doubt require careful investigation and consideration. But the purpose of such investigation can only be to demonstrate that these differences are, in fact, purely trivial. The historical-critical method of Biblical interpretation has its rightful place: it is concerned with the preparation of the intelligence—and this can never be superfluous. But, were I driven to choose between it and the venerable doctrine of Inspiration, I should without hesitation adopt the latter, which has a broader, deeper, more important justification . . . Fortunately, I am not compelled to choose between the two . . . If we rightly understand ourselves, our problems are the problems of Paul.[20]

Two things are of interest here. First, although Barth had to defend himself against the accusation that he was "'an enemy of historical criticism,'" he actually upheld the validity of it. For him, the Bible is not a collection of the very words of God, as Protestant orthodoxy and fundamentalism would have it. Indeed, Barth was an enemy of "biblicism": the belief that the Bible is inerrant and thus authoritative because it is a verbally inspired text. In his view, the Bible is in every respect a human book that is justifiably subject to historical inquiry. For this reason, Barth did not oppose the results of modern historical-critical research into the Bible, much to the chagrin of conservative Protestants.[21] But he did maintain that a *merely* historical

---

20. Barth, "Preface to the First Edition," *Epistle to the Romans*, 5.

21. Barth has been met with hostility by fundamentalists, who reject historical criticism, and with ambivalence by evangelicals, who accept historical criticism only with severe qualifications. Cornelius Van Til, for instance, renders this completely negative verdict on Barth: "The present writer is of the opinion that, for all its verbal similarities to historic Protestantism, Barth's theology is, in effect, a denial of it . . . The choice must therefore be made between Barth and the Reformers." *Christianity and Barthianism* (Grand Rapids: Baker, 1962) vii, 445. For a more appreciative yet still critical assessment, see Mark D. Thompson, "Witness to the Word: On Barth's Doctrine of Scripture," in *Engaging with Barth: Contemporary Evangelical Critiques*, ed. David Gibson and Daniel Strange (New York: T. & T. Clark, 2008) 168–97. As an evangelical Thompson is troubled by those aspects of Barth's doctrine of scripture derived from "the historical and theological criticism of nineteenth-century liberalism" that "survived his revolution" (197). So too Michael S. Horton thinks that Barth has a flawed notion of the orthodox doctrine of inspiration and insists that "a doctrine of Scripture adequate to the Bible's own claims for itself has not yet been offered by Barth or his students." "A Stony Jar: The Legacy of Karl Barth for Evangelical Theology," in *Engaging with Barth*,

approach to the Bible is insufficient since it can deal only with the human religion reflected in the Bible, but not with the God to whom the biblical writers intended to bear witness.[22]

Second, Barth couched his criticism of the reigning liberal historicism in the terms of an argument on behalf of a more *thoroughgoing* historical approach to exegesis, declaring, "The critical historian needs to be more critical."[23]

> I have nothing whatever to say against historical criticism. I recognize it, and once more state quite definitely that it is both necessary and justified. My complaint is that recent commentators confine themselves to an interpretation of the text which seems to me to be no commentary at all, but merely the first step towards a commentary. Recent commentaries contain no more than a reconstruction of the text, a rendering of the Greek words and phrases by their precise equivalents, a number of additional notes in which archaeological and philological material is gathered together, and a more or less plausible arrangement of the material in such a manner that it may be made historically and psychologically intelligible ... *Historians do not wish, and rightly do not wish, to be confined within such narrow limits.*[24]

Accordingly, the truly critical historian wants "to press beyond this preliminary work to an understanding of Paul" that "involves more than a mere repetition ... of what Paul says" because "it involves the reconstruction of what is set out in the Epistle, until the actual meaning of it is disclosed."[25] In this view the historian's task goes beyond a purely positivistic view of it since

---

346–81 at 364.

22. Barth explained, "The Bible is a literary monument of an ancient racial religion and of a Hellenistic cultus religion of the Near East. A human document like any other, it can lay no a priori dogmatic claim to special attention and consideration ... For it is too clear that intelligent and fruitful discussion of the Bible begins when the judgment as to its human, its historical and psychological character has been made and put behind us ... The special content of this human document, the remarkable something with which the writers of these stories and those who stood behind them were concerned, the Biblical object—this is the question that will engage and engross us." "Biblical Questions, Insights, and Vistas," in *The Word of God and the Word of Man*, trans. Douglas Horton (1928; reprint, Gloucester, MA: Smith, 1978) 51–96 at 60–61.

23. Barth, "Preface to the Second Edition," *Epistle to the Romans*, 6.

24. Barth, "Preface to the Second Edition," *Epistle to the Romans*, 6, emphasis added.

25. Barth, "Preface to the Second Edition," *Epistle to the Romans*, 6–7. Eberhard Jüngel nicely clarifies Barth's point: "If the Bible is to have meaning, then what is there must be 'not only ... repeated,' but 'rethought.'" Jüngel, *Karl Barth: A Theological Legacy*, trans. Garrett E. Paul (Philadelphia: Westminster, 1986) 77.

it includes articulating the text's meaning for today.[26] Surprisingly, Barth's examples of this more thoroughgoing historical approach that he wished to commend are taken not from any modern historians at all but, rather, from the Protestant Reformers of the sixteenth century.

> By genuine understanding and interpretation I mean that creative energy which Luther exercised with intuitive certainty in his exegesis; which underlies the systematic interpretation of Calvin . . . How energetically Calvin, having first established what stands in the text, sets himself to re-think the whole material and to wrestle with it, till the walls which separate the sixteenth century from the first become transparent! Paul speaks, and the man of the sixteenth century hears. The conversation between the original record and the reader moves round the subject-matter, until a distinction between yesterday and today becomes impossible.[27]

Apparently, what Barth means is that theological exegesis is not really distinct from historical exegesis; rather, it is an exegesis so penetrating in its grasp of the text's subject matter that the temporal distance between the historical context of the ancient author and the modern reader is thereby bridged.

When we look more closely at what exactly is involved for Barth in "understanding and interpretation" of a text, we learn that in addition to giving a contemporary reformulation of the text's basic point, the exegete must be ready to engage in "criticism" of what the text says in the light of what it means: "Criticism (κρίνειν) applied to historical documents means for me the measuring of words and phrases by the standard of that about which the documents are speaking."[28] This is a perfect statement of *Sachkritik*: testing the words of the text according to the text's subject matter (*Sache*). Such criticism, in turn, presupposes a willingness to face up to "the tension displayed more or less clearly in the ideas written in the text."[29] The text is thus to be interpreted critically according to its own inner norm. Another designation for this procedure is "internal criticism" as distinct

---

26. Barth's statements about the genuine historical task anticipate the idea, now common in hermeneutical discussion, about "the fusion of horizons" (Gadamer) between past and present. Indeed, the hermeneutical character of Barth's view comes to expression when he states, "The understanding of history is an uninterrupted conversation between the wisdom of yesterday and the wisdom of tomorrow." "Preface to the First Edition," *Epistle to the Romans*, 5.

27. Barth, "Preface to the Second Edition," *Epistle to the Romans*, 7.

28. Barth, "Preface to the Second Edition," *Epistle to the Romans*, 8.

29. Barth, "Preface to the Second Edition," *Epistle to the Romans*, 8.

from "external criticism." Whereas an external criticism judges a text by a standard foreign to itself, *Sachritik* is internal: it holds a text accountable to its own internal norm of excellence. So, for example, an external criticism evaluates Paul's letters according to a norm derived from another viewpoint than that to which Paul was beholden (e.g., non-Christian Judaism or Stoicism); an internal criticism, however, tests Paul's writings by the criterion that he explicitly acknowledged: the gospel (Rom 1:1, 16). There is, moreover, nothing specifically theological in this procedure since it can be applied to any serious text in order to test its internal consistency and adequacy in expressing its subject matter (*sachgemäß*).[30]

As Barth explained to a puzzled readership trying to make sense of this new sort of biblical commentary, "For me . . . the question of the true nature of interpretation is the supreme question."[31] And the final goal of the interpretation of any text is to be brought face-to-face with the subject matter itself: *die Sache selbst*.

> The Word ought to be exposed in the words. Intelligent comment means that I am driven on till I stand with nothing before me but the enigma of the matter; till the document seems hardly to exist as a document; till I have almost forgotten that I am not its author; till I know the author so well that I allow him to speak in my name and am even able to speak in his name myself.[32]

Barth's commentary, in which Paul's subject matter was rethought and translated anew into the language of the twentieth century, was the "*fait accompli* that has called forth the hermeneutical reflection of our times."[33] Its promise lay in its proposal of a conception for theological exegesis of scripture that bridges the gap between yesterday and today (thus moving decisively beyond historicism) without, however, denying the genuine insights into the historical character of the Bible that had been attained by modern scholarship (thus resisting any relapse into biblicism).

---

30. Barth, "Preface to the Second Edition," *Epistle to the Romans*, 12. Barth did not understand himself to be proposing a "special" theological hermeneutic for the exegesis of biblical texts but, rather, as reflecting upon what is involved in the exegesis of every humanly significant text, including "the study of Lao-Tse and Goethe" (12). Hence, the Bible is to be interpreted as any other book, which means according to its subject matter (*Sache*).

31. Barth, "Preface to the Second Edition," *Epistle to the Romans*, 9.

32. Barth, "Preface to the Second Edition," *Epistle to the Romans*, 8.

33. James M. Robinson, "Hermeneutic since Barth," in *Language, Hermeneutic, and History: Theology after Barth and Bultmann* (Eugene, OR: Cascade Books, 2008) 69–146 at 87.

Bultmann found himself in substantial agreement with the program for theological exegesis laid out by Barth, apparently somewhat to Barth's surprise since Bultmann was not only a consummate practitioner of historical-critical method in the study of the New Testament but also an heir to the "history-of-religions school" that represented the epitome of historicism.[34] Like Barth, Bultmann believed it was necessary to push beyond historicism's method of using biblical texts as sources to reconstruct early Christianity as a phenomenon of ancient history in order that the way might be cleared for the New Testament to address the reader (or hearer) with its claims. Whereas the method of the modern historian requires that the exegete adopt a posture of critical distance and objectivity toward the text so as not to fall victim to anachronism, the text itself seeks to engage the interpreter's subjectivity since its subject matter concerns the question of how human beings are to understand their own existence. Historicism operates "with the presupposition . . . that it is possible to interpret the text without, at the same time, interpreting its subject matter."[35] But this is false because "every word we utter about history is necessarily a word about ourselves."[36] Since we are historical beings, our study of history is necessarily self-involving (*tua res agitur*): "historical interpretation is also self-interpretation."[37] For this reason, "there is no neutral exegesis" since "the interpretation of the text always goes hand in hand with the exegete's interpretation of himself."[38] So Bultmann draws this contrast between historicism and a theological exegesis: "Historical exegesis asks 'What is said?' We ask: 'What is meant?'"[39]

Notwithstanding his praise for Barth and endorsement of Barth's intention, Bultmann was not uncritical of Barth—or, more precisely, of what he perceived to be inconsistencies on Barth's part. In his review of the second edition of Barth's *Romans*, Bultmann prefaced his objection to Barth's exegetical practice with this dual affirmation of the common ground that united them:

---

34. Barth, "Preface to the Third Edition," *Epistle to the Romans*, 16.

35. Rudolf Bultmann, "The Problem of a Theological Exegesis of the New Testament," in *Beginnings of Dialectic Theology*, ed. James M. Robinson, trans. Keith R. Crim and Louis De Grazia (Richmond, VA: John Knox, 1968) 236–56 at 238.

36. Bultmann, "Problem of a Theological Exegesis of the New Testament," 242.

37. Bultmann, "Problem of a Theological Exegesis of the New Testament," 238, 245.

38. Bultmann, "Problem of a Theological Exegesis of the New Testament," 242.

39. Bultmann, "Problem of a Theological Exegesis of the New Testament," 239. This kind of exegesis focused on the subject matter (*Sachexegese*) "comes to what is meant only through what is said, and yet measures what is said by what is meant" (*Sachkritik*). Bultmann, "Problem of a Theological Exegesis of the New Testament," 241.

> As it is self-evident for him that the philological historical explanation of the text is a necessary side of exegesis, it is self-evident to me that a text can be explained only when one has an inner relationship to the matter with which the text deals.[40]

Nonetheless, Bultmann reproached Barth for doing exegetical violence to Paul's Letter to the Romans. Barth's justifiable insistence that interpretation has to measure the words in the text by its subject matter "cannot, if one is in earnest, occur without criticism." The requisite criticism is not attempted "from a standpoint taken outside the text and its subject matter," which Bultmann in full agreement with Barth rejected; rather, "it is the consistent carrying out of the basic principle," enunciated by Barth, "of understanding the text on the basis of the subject matter."[41]

> One must measure by the subject matter to what extent in all the words and sentences of the text the subject matter has really found adequate expression, for what else can be meant by "measuring"? In Barth, however, I find nothing of such measuring and of the radical criticism based on it. It is impossible to assume that everywhere in the Letter to the Romans the subject matter has found adequate expression, unless one intends to establish a modern dogma of inspiration, and something like this seems to stand behind Barth's exegesis—much to the detriment of the clarity of the subject matter itself.[42]

Bultmann saw his reproach of Barth to be a strictly internal criticism: holding Barth to his own avowed principles of exegesis and interpretation!

---

40. Bultmann, "Karl Barth's *Epistle to the Romans* in its Second Edition," in Robinson, ed., *Beginnings of Dialectic Theology*, 100–120 at 118. Robinson clarifies that for Barth—as now also for Bultmann—"the view of the subject to object basic to the critical historical method, to the effect that the subjective element is to be eliminated so as to attain the highest possible objectivity, has been relativized by the basic recognition of the hermeneutical relevance of the subject . . . The question with regard to the subject is not simply whether he can eliminate his subjectivity as a source of prejudice, but whether he 'understands himself aright,' i.e., whether he is grappling with what is 'serious,' or, as we might say today, whether he is asking the right question, whether his concern is with the ultimate. If that be the case, his subjectivity provides an access to the subject matter of the text that is indispensable as a heuristic medium of interpretation, if it is really that subject matter, serious both then and now, that he is seeking to understand. One's subjectivity does not simply introduce distortions; it insures that the phenomena with which the text was grappling—if it is a serious text—are not overlooked or distorted into curiosities." "Hermeneutic since Barth," 88.

41. Bultmann, "Barth's *Epistle to the Romans*," in *Beginnings of Dialectic Theology*, 119.

42. Bultmann, "Barth's *Epistle to the Romans*," in *Beginnings of Dialectic Theology*, 119.

Because "the subject matter [the gospel] is greater than the word which interprets it [Paul's Letter to the Romans]," Bultmann declared that "no man—not even Paul—can always speak only from the subject matter itself."[43] In Paul, "there are other spirits speaking besides the *pneuma Christou* [spirit of Christ]"; for this reason, "criticism can never be radical enough." Indeed, "such criticism can only serve to clarify the subject matter."

> When I discover in my exegesis of Romans tensions and contradictions, heights and depths, when I endeavor to show where Paul is dependent on Jewish theology or on popular Christianity, on Hellenistic Enlightenment or Hellenistic sacramental beliefs, then I am practicing not only philological historical criticism . . . but I am . . . showing where and how the subject matter is expressed, in order to grasp the subject matter, which is greater even than Paul . . . Such criticism therefore is—it follows from Barth's own basic premise of "measuring by the subject matter"—inseparable from exegesis and real history. *Only in such criticism can the historical work attain its final goal, in which it meets systematic theology which has traveled on another road.*[44]

It is only *Sachkritik*, in other words, that makes historical exegesis of the text truly theological.

Barth, however, strongly objected to Bultmann's criticism that he failed to go far enough:

> Bultmann complains that I am too conservative . . . Bultmann further goes on to hint that there lurks behind my whole method of exegesis a 'modern form of the dogma of Inspiration' . . . I have never attempted to conceal the fact that my manner of interpretation has certain affinities with the old doctrine of Verbal Inspiration.[45]

But did Barth and Bultmann mean the same thing here by "inspiration"? Barth's original comment that he would unhesitatingly adopt the doctrine of inspiration over historicism were he forced to choose between them clearly meant no more than that Paul, though a figure of the distant past, could still speak to us today.[46] But Bultmann suspected that Barth tacitly assumed the doctrine of a verbally inspired text in the manner of biblicism on account of

---

43. Bultmann, "Barth's *Epistle to the Romans*," in *Beginnings of Dialectic Theology*, 120.

44. Bultmann, "Barth's *Epistle to the Romans*," in *Beginnings of Dialectic Theology*, 120, emphasis added.

45. Barth, "Preface to the Third Edition," *Epistle to the Romans*, 16, 18.

46. Barth, "Preface to the First Edition," *Epistle to the Romans*, 5.

his unwillingness to engage in the *Sachkritik* he himself had originally called for, since only on the basis of this doctrine can one proceed as though the *Sache* ("the spirit of Christ") always comes to adequate expression in Paul's words. Curiously, Barth replied by denying that there are any words of Paul's "which are not words of 'those other spirits'" whether Jewish or Hellenistic.

> Is it really legitimate to extract a certain number of passages and claim that there the veritable Spirit of Christ has spoken? Or, to put it another way, can the Spirit of Christ be thought of as standing in the Epistle side by side with 'other' spirits and in competition with them? It seems impossible to set the Spirit of Christ—the veritable subject-matter of the Epistle—over against other spirits, in such a manner as to deal out praise to some passages, and to deprecate others where Paul is not controlled by his true subject-matter.[47]

Barth then laid down an "either-or" (his phrase) for the exegete: "The question is whether or no he is to place himself in a relation to his author of utter loyalty." The commentator must always assume that "when he fails to understand, the blame is his and not Paul's."[48]

Barth's reply to Bultmann is puzzling: while some of his statements seem to retract what he had earlier said about the necessity of *Sachkritik*, other statements of his seem to reaffirm what he had once said.[49] To be sure,

---

47. Barth, "Preface to the Third Edition," *Epistle to the Romans*, 16–17. Gary Dorrien has unfortunately confused the issue between them with this utterly misleading characterization: "Is the Spirit of Christ the sole subject of the scriptural witness, or are the Bible's other spirits also part of the defining subject matter of scripture? Barth's early refusal to link the Spirit of Christ and the Bible's other sociohistorical spirits reappeared in all of his later debates with Bultmann. In various ways he persistently denied that the Bible's other spirits deserved to be linked by a compromising 'and' to the Spirit of Christ." *The Barthian Revolt in Modern Theology: Theology without Weapons* (Louisville: Westminster John Knox, 2000) 104. For Bultmann, "the Spirit of Christ" *is* the sole subject matter of the scriptural witness, which is precisely why Paul has to be criticized when *he*, not Bultmann, is led astray by other spirits!

48. Barth, "Preface to the Third Edition," *Epistle to the Romans*, 17.

49. On the one hand, Barth insisted, "The problem is whether the whole must not be understood in relation to the true subject-matter which is—The Spirit of Christ . . . Even so, the extent to which the commentator will be able to disclose the Spirit of Christ in his reading of Paul will not be everywhere the same. But he will know that the responsibility rests on his shoulders: and he will not let himself be bewildered by the voices of those other spirits, which so often render inaudible the dominant tones of the Spirit of Christ . . . Nor will he rest content until paradoxically he has seen the whole in the fragments . . . so that all the other spirits are seen in some way or other to serve the Spirit of Christ." "Preface to the Third Edition," *Epistle to the Romans*, 17. On the other hand, he conceded, "Is there any way of penetrating the heart of a document—of any document!—except on the assumption that its spirit will speak to our spirit through the

Bultmann readily agreed that the exegete should always strive for loyalty to the author without, however, granting that such loyalty ought to preclude criticism when the author goes astray: "faithfulness to the author may be demonstrated by sometimes having to correct the material into which we are led by him."⁵⁰ But he could not agree at all with Barth's assertion that the spirit of Christ nowhere speaks plainly in the text.

> [Y]our statement that it is only other spirits that come to *words* in Romans seems to me to lead to the ridiculous conclusion that one can either expound every word that is spoken or written as testimony to the πνεῦμα Χρ. [spirit of Christ] or one can expound none at all.⁵¹

Yet Barth maintained that he was "completely unable to understand Bultmann's demand": "He asks me to think and write WITH Paul . . . and then suddenly . . . to turn around and write 'critically' ABOUT him and against him."⁵² But there is no contradiction here, as Barth implied, for what could it possibly mean to think *with* Paul if one may never be allowed to think *against* Paul?⁵³

---

actual written words? *This does not exclude a criticism of the letter by the spirit, which is, indeed, unavoidable.* No human word, no word of Paul, is absolute Truth. In this I agree with Bultmann." "Preface to the Third Edition," *Epistle to the Romans*, 18–19, emphasis added. Although it certainly seems to me that Barth is speaking out of both sides of his mouth here, Hartwig Thyen rushes to his defense against Bultmann without, however, shedding any light on the issue that might clear up these apparently contradictory statements. "Rudolf Bultmann, Karl Barth, und das Problem der 'Sachkritik,'" in *Rudolf Bultmanns Werk und Wirkung*, ed. Bernd Jaspert (Darmstadt: Wissenschaftliche Buchgesellschaft, 1984) 44–52. Like me, Hans Weder is puzzled by Barth: "It remains unclear how this critique of the letter by the spirit [acknowledged as legitimate by Barth] can occur except as a critique of the Pauline word by the spirit of Christ and wherein exactly this critique would differentiate itself from the *Sachkritik* of Bultmann." "Die Externität der Mitte: Überlegungen zum hermeneutischen Problem des Kriteriums der Sachkritik am Neuen Testament," in *Jesus Christus als die Mitte der Schrift: Studien zur Hermeneutik des Evangeliums*, ed. Christof Landmesser et al., Beihefte zur Zeitschrift für die neutestamentliche Wissenschaft 86 (Berlin: de Gruyter, 1997) 291–320 at 306.

50. Letter of Bultmann to Barth (Dec. 31, 1922) in *Karl Barth—Rudolf Bultmann: Letters 1922–1966*, ed. Bernd Jaspert, trans. Geoffrey W. Bromiley (Grand Rapids: Eerdmans, 1981) 4.

51. Letter of Bultmann to Barth (Dec. 31, 1922) in Jaspert, ed., *Letters*, 5, emphasis original.

52. Barth, "Preface to the Third Edition," *Epistle to the Romans*, 18.

53. Barth's objection to "Bultmann's demand" implies that to think with Paul means to subject oneself to him. But that is not real thinking. No one who engages in genuine dialogue exhibits this kind of "utter loyalty" to an interlocutor. The only loyalty that can ever be required is loyalty to the common subject matter under discussion. Indeed, in every mutual examination of a serious topic, argument—in the sense of questioning and

The same issue between them resurfaced in Bultmann's review of another early book by Barth, *The Resurrection of the Dead* (1924, first ed.), which is a commentary on 1 Corinthians. While Bultmann once again praised Barth for his profound grasp of Paul's fundamental purpose in the letter ("he has rightly seen the decisive point") as well as for bringing discussion of it "out of the area of explanation in terms of its historical context into the sphere of material discussion of its content," Bultmann judged that "the presentation of his exegetical insights lacks a certain clarity and intellectual precision."[54] Since Barth's commentary, which aims at a theological exegesis of Paul's letter, does not oppose "historical-philological interpretation," Bultmann urged "a more exact exegesis which starts out from the determination of the meaning of the text in its own period" in order "to attain a still sharper conceptual comprehension of the result."[55] The result will be "material criticism," but one "which stems from the text itself" instead of an arbitrary exegesis that explains away difficult passages in the text.[56] Bultmann was cognizant of the risk involved in *Sachkritik*, and he therefore insisted that "the exegesis must be developed on the basis of the most exact knowledge of the contemporary background and by means of careful and penetrating analysis of the content."[57] Yet Barth, though brilliantly elucidating the theological content of what Paul *means*, at times refused to acknowledge what Paul actually *says* and how what he says contradicts what he means. So, for example, Barth claimed that when Paul speaks of "the resurrection of the dead," this is really a paraphrase for "God." Bultmann agreed. But Barth then denied that Paul also tries "to make the resurrection of Christ credible as an objective historical fact," which for Bultmann is an instance where "Paul is betrayed by his apologetic into contradicting

---

even criticism of the interlocutor's ideas—is bound to occur, yet such argument hardly constitutes a betrayal of one's dialogue partner. In this regard see the thoughtful essay by David Tracy, "Argument, Dialogue, and the Soul in Plato," in *Witness and Existence: Essays in Honor of Schubert M. Ogden* (Chicago: University of Chicago Press, 1989) 91–105. Tracy insists, "Arguments are a necessary moment in any properly dialectical conversation" (96). "Dialectical" here refers to conversation in search of the truth, as in Plato's dialogues. On the somewhat different meaning of "dialectic" in "dialectical theology," see Bultmann, "The Question of 'Dialectic' Theology: A Discussion with Erik Peterson," in *Beginnings of Dialectic Theology*, 257–74.

54. Bultmann, "Karl Barth, *The Resurrection of the Dead*," in *Faith and Understanding*, ed. with an introd. by Robert W. Funk, trans. Louise Pettibone Smith, Fortress Texts in Modern Theology (Philadelphia: Fortress, 1987) 66–94 at 69.

55. Bultmann, "Barth, *The Resurrection of the Dead*," 72.

56. Bultmann, "Barth, *The Resurrection of the Dead*," 72.

57. Bultmann, "Barth, *The Resurrection of the Dead*," 93.

himself."⁵⁸ Consequently, while endorsing many of Barth's insights into what Paul means, Bultmann distanced himself from Barth's unwillingness to criticize Paul's statements on the basis of his subject matter:

> I regret Barth's failure to recognize that this meaning can be ascribed to Paul only on the basis of a critical study of the content. Barth himself involuntarily employs such criticism in his own ingenious paraphrases. But I do not think this kind of criticism, this analysis, is so easy to practice. However much I admire Barth's sure grasp of the central ideas of the text, I cannot proceed by his method . . . In my judgment there is need of much more rigorous exegetical work and of closer analysis of the text if assured results are to be attained.⁵⁹

It is nonetheless clear from these appreciative albeit critical reviews that Bultmann sought to put historical-critical scholarship into service of the kind of theological exegesis advocated by Barth: "Barth has shown a new direction. The work is not finished, but we stand at a new beginning."⁶⁰

What, then, are we to make of this early disagreement between these two representatives of dialectical theology? Although they were united in their aim to recover a theological exegesis of the Bible that moved from interpretation of the biblical text to interpretation of the text's subject matter (*Sache*), their united front proved to be fragile as soon as Bultmann tried to hold Barth accountable to his own explicit statement that exegesis of the text's subject matter (*Sachexegese*) demands criticism of the text on the basis of its subject matter (*Sachkritik*). Since Barth refused to follow Bultmann in his willingness to think *against* Paul as a necessary requirement of thinking *with* Paul (even though it was Barth himself who first annunciated the demand for such willingness), in his perplexity Bultmann was led to remark, "In this question I cannot at root see any difference between your exegetical approach and mine, great though the difference may be in exegetical practice."⁶¹ In this connection two observations are pertinent.

The first thing to note is that in spite of their agreement that a recovery of theological exegesis oriented toward scripture's subject matter required moving beyond historicism without relapsing into biblicism, Barth and

---

58. Bultmann, "Barth, *The Resurrection of the Dead*," 83.
59. Bultmann, "Barth, *The Resurrection of the Dead*," 86.
60. Bultmann, "Barth, *The Resurrection of the Dead*," 93.
61. Letter of Bultmann to Barth (Dec. 31, 1922), in Jaspert, ed., *Letters*, 4. Jüngel comments, "Barth's exchange with Bultmann was critical, but it also embraced a far-reaching consensus." Jüngel, *Karl Barth: A Theological Legacy*, 80.

Bultmann occupied very different positions on the continuum between these two extremes. Bultmann never wavered in his commitment to the historical-critical enterprise of interpreting the New Testament in its ancient religious and philosophical context. While he held that a *merely* historical approach was insufficient, he never denied that it was absolutely necessary. For him, a responsible theological exegesis such as Barth called for could only be undertaken on the basis of the results obtained by historical criticism. Even after the movement of dialectical theology was disbanded, Bultmann not only continued to think along the lines laid down in response to the initial impulse he had received from the early Barth, but he also went on to elaborate a hermeneutically sophisticated program for theological exegesis making full use of historical-critical scholarship. In retrospect, Bultmann gave this explanation of his relation to both dialectical theology and the liberal legacy of historical criticism:

> It seemed to me that in this new theological movement it was rightly recognized, as over against the "liberal" theology out of which I had come, that the Christian faith is not a phenomenon of the history of religion . . . and that therefore theology does not need to look upon it as a phenomenon of religious or cultural history. It seemed to me that, as over against such a view, the new theology had correctly seen that Christian faith is the answer to the word of the transcendent God that encounters man and that theology has to deal with this word and the man who has been encountered by it. This judgment, however, has never led me to a simple condemnation of "liberal" theology; on the contrary, I have endeavored throughout my entire life to carry further the tradition of historical-critical research as it was practiced by the "liberal" theology and to make our more recent theological knowledge fruitful for it.[62]

---

62. Bultmann, "Autobiographical Reflections," in *Existence and Faith: Shorter Writings of Rudolf Bultmann*, trans. Schubert M. Ogden, Living Age Books (New York: Meridian, 1960) 283–88 at 287–88. One cannot overstate the importance of the early Barth for Bultmann's theological development. In 1956 he listed Barth's *Romans* as one of the six most important books that had a "decisive significance" for his work as a theologian and exegete. Konrad Hammann, *Rudolf Bultmann: A Biography*, trans. Philip E. Devenish (Salem, OR: Polebridge, 2013) 466. Indeed, he always maintained that he continued faithfully down the path pioneered by the early Barth long after Barth himself had turned away from it: "The decisive impulse for me was what you once described in the preface to the second edition of your *Romans* . . . I do not intend to reverse the revolution achieved by you some thirty years ago but to solidify the new path methodologically." Letter of Bultmann to Barth (November 11–15, 1952) in Jaspert, ed., *Letters*, 101.

With Barth, however, things were different. His enthusiasm for historical criticism was never more than lukewarm.[63] Already in 1926, before the dissolution of their alliance, Barth's feelings about Bultmann had begun to sour. That year Bultmann's book appeared in which he presented his reconstruction of the message of Jesus based on his form-critical identification of the earliest layer of the synoptic tradition.[64] Barth did not hide his dismay:

> I absolutely cannot comprehend how or by what right one comes to carving precisely this Jesus out of the New Testament and setting Him up. I had expected that the radical criticism of Bultmann . . . would bring it about that New Testament science would henceforth look away from *all* other pictures of Jesus than the completely concrete one of the New Testament writers . . . My disappointment in Bultmann's book consisted in the fact that I saw it proceeding in the old way, with an uncontrolled mixture of the usual historical criticism and the new material criticism [*Sachkritik*]; in the way according to which the New Testament is read as historical source rather than as witness.[65]

After his break with his erstwhile colleagues in the movement of dialectical theology including Bultmann, Barth distanced himself from his earlier position expressed in his *Romans* and embarked upon the writing of his *Church Dogmatics*, in which he formulated his mature theology. In his later work, he never ceased to affirm the partial validity of historical-critical exegesis even though he tended to ignore it whenever it did not suit his theological purposes. Indeed, it is quite difficult to pin down with precision Barth's relation to historical criticism.[66] Still, it is fair to say that he felt far more

---

63. Walter Lindemann comments, "The doubtless sincerely meant explanations of Barth that 'theological' exegesis should in no wise displace historical-critical method stand in contradiction to the extensive abdication of precisely this method in his own exegetical works. It was understandable, therefore, when representatives of the historical-critical method simply concluded that there was a disparagement, if not utter rejection of historical criticism in Barth. To be sure, the negative results of radical criticism, such as was practiced by form criticism, suited Barth's purpose since thereby the historical ground was taken out from underneath the tacit dogmatic-religious categories of the liberal exegetes, but he appeared to have attributed hardly any positive function to historical criticism at all." *Karl Barth und die kritische Schriftauslegung*, Theologische Forschung (Hamburg: Reich, 1973) 82.

64. Bultmann, *Jesus and the Word*, trans. Louise Pettibone Smith and Erminie Huntress Lantero (New York: Scribner, 1962).

65. Letter of Barth to Paul Althaus (May 30, 1928), cited by Bruce L. McCormack, *Karl Barth's Critically Realistic Dialectical Theology: Its Genesis and Development, 1909–1936* (Oxford: Clarendon, 1995) 394.

66. Mary Kathleen Cunningham summarizes the results of her study of Barth's exegetical practice: "In spite of his theoretical claim that he does not intend to annul the

sympathy for biblicism than for historicism, as his repeated admissions of his affinity for the doctrine of inspiration bear out, in spite of his denial that the Bible is a verbally inerrant text. Curiously in his statements *about* the Bible, Barth sounds rather like Bultmann; but in his actual use *of* the Bible, he is very different from him.[67]

The second thing to note is that the confessional difference between them increasingly came to the fore. In a letter to Barth from 1927, Bultmann wondered if the old Lutheran-Calvinist anthesis was a factor at play in their difficulties with reaching mutual understanding, and he expressed the hope that they could avoid a reprise of that opposition since the common ground uniting them was so much more important.[68] In his reply, Barth acknowledged the difference that the confessional divide was bound to make: "In some way, the old controversies between the Lutherans and the Reformed, which were never settled, do cause us difficulties on both sides and will perhaps come to a head in a great explosion."[69] In his detailed study of Barth's theological development, Bruce McCormack places great weight upon this confessional antithesis as a decisive factor contributing to Barth's eventual break with Bultmann.

> Seen in general terms, Barth's concern with . . Bultmann was very much bound up with his growing realization that his own Reformed starting-point had to bring him into conflict with Lutheranism. This was not a petty struggle over institutional identity; the issues were substantive. At first, both sides would have liked to believe that what united them was of greater importance than confessional differences. But eventually it became

---

results of biblical scholarship in the last centuries, in practice Barth's treatment of the Bible . . . has the effect of severely limiting the value of this kind of scholarship for his exegesis of Scripture . . . Comparing Barth's exegesis with that of representative biblical scholars has thus revealed Barth's tendency to deal with critical scholarship in an ad hoc fashion and to find the results of this kind of interpretation helpful only insofar as they serve to illumine and do not challenge his fundamental Christological focus." *What Is Theological Exegesis? Interpretation and Use of Scripture in Barth's Doctrine of Election* (Valley Forge, PA: Trinity, 1995) 75.

67. Barth wrote, "Scripture is holy and the Word of God because by the Holy Spirit it became and will become to the Church a witness to divine revelation." Karl Barth, *The Doctrine of the Word of God*, vol. I/2 of *Church Dogmatics*, trans. G. T. Thompson and Harold Knight (Edinburgh: T. & T. Clark, 1956) 457. Bultmann said, "Theology, therefore, is always exegesis inasmuch as it has access to revelation only through the witness of Scripture and seeks to grasp by exegesis what Scripture, understood as witness, says." "Question of 'Dialectic' Theology," 273.

68. Letter of Bultmann to Barth (April 21, 1927) in Jaspert, ed., *Letters*, 32.

69. Letter of Barth to Bultmann (April 28, 1927), in Jaspert, ed., *Letters*, 32.

clear that these differences did exist and that they were having a considerable impact on how major issues were construed.[70]

In this regard, McCormack notes that already in Barth's 1922 lectures on Calvin one can observe the emergence of "a carefully circumscribed affirmation of the Reformed Scripture-principle."

> Barth's critical attitude toward biblical history had been considerably supplemented by a positive appreciation of the authority of the biblical text. This was indeed a new element in his thinking.[71]

A year later (1923) Barth identified "the scriptural principle" as the hallmark of a Reformed theology: "the whole Scriptures, and not a part of them."[72] This ringing affirmation of the entire biblical canon certainly appears to be in keeping with Barth's reluctance to engage in *Sachkritik*.

The "great explosion" prophesied by Barth finally occurred decades later in the debate over Bultmann's demythologizing program. In the meantime, Bultmann had found his second great inspiration—after Barth's *Romans*—in the existentialist philosophy of his colleague Martin Heidegger.[73] Although the term *Sachkritik* was not employed this time around, the same issue was at stake as before. Bultmann maintained that demythologizing, while occasioned by the modern scientific worldview, is actually demanded by the New Testament itself. And since the question to which the New Testament addresses itself is the strictly existential question as to how human beings are to understand themselves authentically, existentialism provides an adequate conceptuality in which to translate the message of the New Testament in nonmythological terms. Indeed, Bultmann saw a precedent for this hermeneutical procedure in Paul and Luther:

> Indeed, de-mythologizing is a task parallel to that performed by Paul and Luther in their doctrine of justification by faith alone

---

70. McCormack, *Karl Barth's Critically Realistic Dialectical Theology*, 392.

71. McCormack, *Karl Barth's Critically Realistic Dialectical Theology*, 305.

72. Barth, "The Doctrinal Task of the Reformed Churches," in *Word of God and the Word of Man*, 218–71 at 240–41.

73. Bultmann reflected upon his encounter with Heidegger and the consequent rift with Barth: "existential philosophy, which I came to know through my discussion with Martin Heidegger, has become of decisive significance for me. I found in it the conceptuality in which it is possible to speak adequately of human existence and therefore also of the existence of the believer. However, in my efforts to make philosophy fruitful for theology, I have more and more come into opposition to Karl Barth. Nevertheless, I remain grateful to him for the decisive things I have learned from him." "Autobiographical Reflections," 288.

without works of the law. More precisely, de-mythologizing is the radical application of the doctrine of justification by faith to the sphere of knowledge and thought. Like the doctrine of justification, de-mythologizing destroys every longing for security. There is no difference between security based on good works and security built on objectifying knowledge.[74]

Once again, Barth registered his protest against Bultmann's critical hermeneutical procedure in the name of loyalty to the text of the New Testament.[75] Yet Barth also knew that Bultmann's program for theology, however radical it may be, "is inconceivable apart from his Lutheran background." Hence, Barth readily conceded that "Bultmann is simply a Lutheran—*sui generis*, of course."[76] With this concession, Barth acknowledged Bultmann as a modern-day heir to Luther even as Bultmann's example only served to confirm Barth in his long-standing reservations about Lutheranism that he harbored as a Reformed theologian.[77] It is to his credit, therefore, that when conservatives in the Lutheran Church in Germany wanted to put Bultmann

---

74. Bultmann, *Jesus Christ and Mythology* (New York: Scribner, 1958) 84.

75. "I cannot say I recognize in this translation [i.e., from ancient mythology into the modern terminology of existentialism] the basic pattern of the New Testament message." Barth, "Rudolf Bultmann—an Attempt to Understand Him," in *Kerygma and Myth: A Theological Debate*, vol. 2, ed. Hans-Werner Bartsch, trans. Reginald H. Fuller (London: SPCK, 1962) 83–132 at 91.

76. Barth, "Rudolf Bultmann—an Attempt to Understand Him," 92.

77. Barth believed that much of the anthropological and subjectivist orientation of modern theology that he criticized could be traced back to Luther's influence. He saw these same tendencies revived in Bultmann's work. Notice how Barth characterized the divergent ways the Lutherans and the Reformed articulate their shared conviction that "God and faith" belong together: Luther "asked the question . . . *how* the human is saved" whereas the Reformed asked "*who* saves the human." For Barth, this means that Luther is focused on the human subject of faith whereas the Reformed are focused on the divine object of faith. Barth, *Theology of the Reformed Confessions*, trans. Darrell L. Guder and Judith J. Guder, Columbia Series in Reformed Theology (Louisville: Westminster John Knox, 2002) 81. This may well be an accurate statement of a *difference in emphasis*, though surely *not in content*. The theologies of Luther and Bultmann, though methodologically or formally anthropological in their orientation, are not anthropocentric or subjectivist in a material or substantive sense because for both theologians *faith in God* is the answer to the human being's existential predicament. As Bultmann explained, "[S]ince revelation is the eternal event, judging or forgiving man, the object of theology is nothing other than the conceptual presentation of *man's existence as determined by God*." "The Question of 'Dialectic' Theology," 273–74, emphasis added. H. Richard Niebuhr seeks to do justice to the legitimate concerns of Barth and Bultmann when he insists, "Theology must attend to the God of faith if it is to understand faith no less than it must attend to faith in God if it would understand God"; *Radical Monotheism and Western Culture with Supplementary Essays*, foreword by James M. Gustafson, Library of Theological Ethics (Louisville: Westminster John Knox, 1993), 12.

on trial for heresy, Barth advised them against this course of action with these words of caution: "those who throw stones at Bultmann should be careful lest they accidentally hit Luther."[78]

THE GOSPEL AND THE CANON OF SCRIPTURE: LUTHER'S *SACHKRITIK* AND CALVIN'S DISSENT

Modern scholars distinguish between the "formal principle" and the "material principle" of the Reformation.[79] The formal principle refers to the authority on which the Reformers based their theology. The material principle refers to their theological understanding of the content of this authority. So, if we asked them, "What is the authoritative source and norm of your theology?" they would have replied, "scripture alone" (*sola scriptura*). If we then asked them, "What do you believe scripture teaches?" they would have replied, "faith alone" (*sola fide*). In both cases, the little word "alone" (Latin: *sola*) was a denial of a Roman Catholic "and." Their formal principle denied the authority of the Roman Catholic tradition: instead of "scripture *and* tradition," the Reformers insisted upon the sole authority of the Bible as the source and norm of Christian doctrine. Their material principle denied the soteriological doctrine of Catholic theology that justification presupposes sanctification (i.e., perfection in love of God and neighbor); instead of "faith *and* works of love," the Reformers insisted upon the sole sufficiency of faith for our justification. Crucial here is that the word "faith" was redefined by the Reformers to signify "trust" whereas the Catholics typically defined it as intellectual "assent" or "belief"; so too the Reformers redefined "grace" to mean "mercy" or "forgiveness" whereas the Catholics defined it as a "supernatural power" or a "spiritual medicine" that sanctifies the soul, thereby making it acceptable to God (*gratia gratum faciens*). Accordingly, Catholic grace is communicated through the sacraments (the means of grace) while Protestant grace is communicated through preaching the gospel, which is the good news of the message of God's forgiveness.[80] Preaching thus evokes

---

78. Barth, "Rudolf Bultmann—an Attempt to Understand Him," 90. Barth wrote to Bishop Theophil Wurm: "[N]o controversy should be initiated between the church and the theology of Rudolf Bultmann . . . I even conjecture that the existence of a 'heretic' like Bultmann, who is so superior to most of his accusers in knowledge, seriousness, and depth, might be indirectly salutary to the church." Letter of May 29, 1947, in Jaspert, ed., *Letters*, 145.

79. The distinction goes back to Albrecht Ritschl, "Über die beiden Prinzipien des Protestantismus," in *Gesammelte Aufsätze* (Freiburg: Mohr Siebeck, 1893) 1:234–47.

80. Indeed, one could say (though the Reformers never do) that the sermon is the real Protestant sacrament since preaching is the "means of grace" by which God's mercy

and sustains our trust that God has forgiven us through Christ. This trust or confidence (faith) in the truth of God's promise of forgiveness (the gospel) suffices as our sole proper response to God's mercy (grace). This, in short, is the heart of Luther's reformation of doctrine, which Calvin also fully affirmed when he became a Protestant.

In classical Protestant theology, the term "Word of God" has two distinct albeit related meanings. It refers both to the gospel that is proclaimed and the scripture on which all authentic proclamation of the gospel is based. In the vocabulary of the Reformers, *gospel* does not designate primarily the narratives of Matthew, Mark, Luke, and John; rather, it means the message of salvation and its proclamation in speech. This is how the apostle Paul used the Greek word *euangelion*: it is both the act and the content of preaching. Consequently, the Reformers looked upon the act of preaching itself as the Word of God, provided of course that the content of the sermon is genuinely evangelical.[81] Before the texts we now know as the New Testament were written, the gospel was proclaimed orally.[82] Still, the Reformers also spoke of the written words of the Bible as the Word of God. This double reference of the term "Word of God" is the source of the systematic ambiguity in their theologies that necessitated the modern scholarly distinction between the material and the formal principles of the Reformation. The question is: What is the relationship between the Word of God as gospel and the Word of God as scripture?

---

is mediated to sinners.

81. *Evangelical* is used here in its original etymological sense as pertaining to the gospel, not in its modern sense as referring to a conservative movement within Protestantism. Gerhard Ebeling explains the point with this comment on Luther's theology: "The Word of Scripture . . . is the Word of God when it is a word proclaimed in the present, a *viva vox evangelii*—naturally in the form of interpretation based on the word of Scripture, and yet in such a way that this word confronts us not as something written but as an oral word, that is, one uttered here and now . . . In this way the point is driven home that the proclaiming of the Word of God belongs to the very essence of this Word, and therefore that interpretation also belongs to this essence (because of the Word's necessary foundation in the testimony of the Scripture)." *The Problem of Historicity in the Church and Its Proclamation*, trans. Grover Foley (Philadelphia: Fortress, 1967) 14–15.

82. Jaroslav Pelikan explains, "The designation of the word of God in the gospel as an 'oral word' . . . was a persistent theme. When he referred to the word of God in the gospel, Luther explained, he was 'not speaking about the written gospel, but about the vocal one.' . . . Christ himself had not written but preached, and had not commanded his disciples to write but to preach, so that 'the gospel might be brought out of dead Scripture and pens into the living voice and mouth.'" *Reformation of Church and Dogma (1300–1700)*, vol. 4 of *The Christian Tradition: A History of the Development of Doctrine* (Chicago: University of Chicago Press, 1984) 180.

The Reformers inherited from their medieval forebears in the Christian tradition the belief that the scriptures are divinely inspired. In the articulation of their distinctive formal principle of scripture alone, they were not affirming anything new about the Bible. Rather, they were denying divine inspiration to the postbiblical tradition of the church ("popes and councils can err").[83] In pitting scripture against tradition, they were attempting to liberate the Bible from the tradition so that the message of scripture (gospel) could be heard on its own terms apart from the distorting filter of subsequent tradition: *scriptura sui ipsius interpres* ("scripture is its own interpreter"). Thereby they insisted that the church must validate its doctrine according to the biblical norm. But there was more to this juxtaposition of scripture and tradition than first meets the eye since the Reformers actually redefined what they meant by "scripture."

First, they rejected the Latin Vulgate translation that was authoritative for Catholicism; in its place they availed themselves of the humanistic study of ancient languages in order to read the Bible in Hebrew and Greek.[84] This daring move uncovered discrepancies between the original text of scripture

---

83. "The distinctive element in this affirmation is really what it denies rather than what it affirms. What marks Luther off from [his theological opponents] is not that he asserts the authority of the Bible but that he denies the authority of church and pope." B. A. Gerrish, "The Word of God and the Words of Scripture: Luther and Calvin on Biblical Authority," in *The Old Protestantism and the New: Essays on the Reformation Heritage* (Chicago: University of Chicago Press, 1982) 51–68 at 54.

84. The Renaissance gave rise to humanism, the study of ancient languages and history, which, when applied to the Bible, was perceived as a severe threat by scholastic theologians: "When humanists began to apply their skills to sacred texts, theologians closed ranks to defend their territory from encroachment." The Reformers shared with the humanists two objectives: "the quest for an unadulterated biblical text and a historically correct interpretation." Erika Rummel, *Humanist-Scholastic Debate in the Renaissance and Reformation*, Harvard Historical Studies 120 (Cambridge: Harvard University Press, 1998) 6, 10. Rummel, 10, cites the slogan coined by Bernd Moeller: "Ohne Humanismus keine Reformation" ("Without humanism, no Reformation"). In 1506 Reuchlin published his *Rudiments of the Hebrew Language*, and in 1516, a year before Luther posted the Ninety-Five Theses, Erasmus published his Greek text of the New Testament. Heiko A. Oberman explains their significance: "[C]onservative theologians . . . stubbornly adhered to the Vulgate . . . [and] succeeded in having the great German Hebraist Johannes Ruechlin condemned in Rome . . . Now they were endeavoring to silence Erasmus." "Luther . . . was unquestionably one of the theologians who could appreciate what humanist scholarship had achieved: without knowledge of the ancient languages there could be no reliable exegesis of the Scriptures! When Erasmus published his edition of the Greek New Testament in 1516, Wittenberg hailed the work as revolutionary . . . In contrast to Erasmus, Luther even numbered among the first—of the humanists of his time, among the few—who used Ruechlin's works to study Hebrew. Thus, Luther recognized that the mastery of ancient languages was a necessary tool in accomplishing a clear textual interpretation of the Bible." *Luther: Man between God and the Devil*, trans. Eileen Walliser-Schwarzbart (New York: Doubleday, 1989) 214.

and the Vulgate upon which the Catholic Church based its doctrinal claims. Accordingly, the Reformers posited deep discontinuity between scripture and the medieval tradition.[85] This critical posture toward the postbiblical tradition, however, created a problem for the Reformers, who were consequently at a loss as to how they could justify their acceptance of the authority of the New Testament canon given their denial of the inspiration of the church's tradition that had canonized these writings.[86] Second, the Reformers demoted the Apocrypha from its canonical status by embracing the Masoretic text and canon of the Jews as their own Old Testament. As a result, the Bible recognized by Protestants was much smaller in scope than the Bible acknowledged by their Catholic opponents. Finally, the Reformers rejected every allegorical or spiritualizing hermeneutic in favor of an exegesis based upon the literal-historical sense of the text. Clearly the Protestant appeal to the Bible alone was radical, indeed!

Since the Reformers set out to test critically the postbiblical tradition according to the norm of scripture, they initially presumed to have the entire Bible on their side in the polemic against Catholicism and its doctrine of justification. After all, in order for the Reformers to implement their program consistently, there had to be complete overlap between the formal principle of scripture alone and the material principle of faith alone. Yet, notwithstanding their far-reaching redefinition of what they meant by scripture, there was one text in the New Testament that appeared to support the Catholic position on justification against Luther and the Protestants. Notoriously, the Epistle of James seems to contradict Paul—or at least Luther's interpretation of Paul. James states categorically, "a person is justified by works and not by faith alone" (Jas 2:24). Compare this with Paul, who declares just as categorically, "a person is justified by faith apart from works" (Rom 3:28). Luther offered to give up his doctor's cap to anyone who could bring James into harmony with Paul. It is a testimony to Luther's honesty that he admitted he could not reconcile these two passages of scripture with one another. Consequently, Luther's verdict on James was bold and daring: James "does violence to Scripture, and so contradicts Paul and all Scripture . . . I therefore refuse him a place among the writers of the true canon of my

---

85. Euan Cameron comments on the Reformers' "cavalier defiance" of the church's postbiblical tradition: "the older generation had interpreted Scripture through a tradition, rather than contradicting tradition *and* the Church in the name of Scripture." *The European Reformation* (Oxford: Clarendon, 1991) 187, emphasis original.

86. "Nowhere did the Reformation view of authority seem to its critics to be more vulnerable than on the canon of Scripture." Pelikan, *Reformation of Church and Dogma*, 266.

Bible."[87] Besides drastically reducing the extent of the Old Testament canon, Luther also clearly exercised criticism of the received New Testament canon by denying the apostolic authorship of James.[88] Here, however, he did not mean exactly what the tradition had meant by "apostolic," namely, that an author of a New Testament text was either one of Jesus' original apostles (e.g., Matthew, Peter, etc.) or a disciple of an apostle (e.g., Mark, traditionally believed to be Peter's disciple). Luther actually redefined the concept of "apostolicity." Instead of mere historical proximity to Jesus, it now meant correct preaching of the gospel:

> The true touchstone for testing every book [in the Bible] is to discover whether it emphasizes the prominence of Christ or not . . . What does not teach Christ is not apostolic, not even if taught by Peter or Paul. On the other hand, what does preach Christ is apostolic, even if Judas, Annas, Pilate, or Herod does it.[89]

Luther thus found in scripture, specifically in Paul's letters, the theological norm by which to measure scripture or, as it is often described, "a canon within the canon"—and that entailed criticizing scripture when it fails to "teach Christ."[90] In so doing he pioneered *Sachkritik*.

---

87. Martin Luther, "Preface to the Epistles of St. James and St. Jude," in *Martin Luther: Selections from His Writings*, ed. John Dillenberger (Garden City, NY: Doubleday, 1961) 35–37 at 36.

88. In addition to his criticism of James, Luther also raised critical questions about Hebrews, Jude, and Revelation. "One of the most striking features of Luther's German New Testament is the remarkable freedom with which he judges the relative worth of the various books. In the list of New Testament books which immediately follows his prefatory 'Instruction' four of the books appear unnumbered, and are set apart from the others by a blank space: Hebrews, James, Jude, and the Apocalypse. This is precisely the way in which Luther marks off the canonical from the apocryphal books of the Old Testament. The individual prefaces to the four downgraded books afford an explanation and justification for this severe judgment, perhaps the best illustration of Luther's 'critical methods' . . . To some extent it can be shown that his critical judgments were suggested to him by the Humanists; in the Annotations to his Greek New Testament Erasmus expressed opinions very similar to Luther's on these four problem-books. And yet even where Luther is apparently leaning most heavily on Erasmus we can detect, at the same time, his genuine independence. In the last analysis, *Luther's downgrading certain books of the New Testament must be taken as evidence of his theological convictions*, not merely of his confidence in scholarly criticism." B. A. Gerrish, *Grace and Reason: A Study in the Theology of Luther* (1962; reprint, Chicago: University of Chicago Press, 1979) 146–47, emphasis added.

89. Luther, "Preface to the Epistles of St. James and St. Jude," 35–36. When Luther says "teach Christ" or "preach Christ," he means "justification by faith alone." For Luther, the real meaning of christology can only be explicated in soteriological terms.

90. The word "canon" means "norm." The word also designates the list of books

Although Calvin saw himself as a loyal follower of Luther, whom he called "the pathfinder" in recognition of his role in initiating the Reformation, Calvin was not uncritical of Luther and in particular took issue with his exegesis of James.[91] Calvin believed that James does not actually disagree with Paul but, rather, combats a distorted version of Paul's theology. There is certainly something to be said on behalf of this view.[92] Clearly, James takes aim at people who boast of having faith and even appeal to their faith as a pretext for doing nothing to help their neighbors in need. But, as Calvin pointed out, the notion of faith criticized by James is not the robust notion of faith found in Paul's letters. Luther too noted that James talks only of "a commonplace faith in God."[93] The Reformers called it "demons' faith," that is, a mere intellectual assent to the proposition that one God exists: "You believe that God is one; good for you! Even the demons believe that—and shudder" (Jas 2:19, my translation). For Calvin as for Luther, faith in the genuinely Pauline sense is inherently active in doing good works for the neighbor's benefit ("faith working through love," Gal 5:6). Indeed, the situation described by James ("faith by itself, if it has no works, is dead," Jas 2:17) was inconceivable to them given Paul's notion of faith. Yet precisely for that reason, Calvin did not agree with Luther that James stands in contradiction to Paul since James is fighting against a counterfeit of Paul's actual position and thus vindicates Paul: "Obviously, if this faith contains nothing but a belief that there is a God, it is not strange if it does not justify."[94] In this Calvin claimed to have succeeded where Luther confessed failure, namely, in reconciling James with Paul. Still, Luther would not have been satisfied; although he admitted "it would be possible to 'save' the epistle by a gloss," he thought any such gloss would purchase its harmonization of James and Paul at the price of the plain sense of what James says since, in direct opposition

---

found in the Bible which for that reason are called canonical. Hence, a canon within the canon refers to the theological norm by which the biblical books are judged to be adequate or not in their role as witnesses to the gospel (the real norm). This implies that the Bible itself is a "normed norm" (*norma normata*), whereas the gospel is the unnormed norm (*norma normans sed non normata*).

91. Gerrish, "The Pathfinder: Calvin's Image of Martin Luther," in *The Old Protestantism and the New*, 27–48 at 39.

92. For a good overview of the issue in modern biblical scholarship, see the excursus on "Faith and Works in Paul and James" in Martin Dibelius, *James: A Commentary on the Epistle of James*, trans. Michael A. Williams, Hermeneia (Philadelphia: Fortress, 1975) 174–80.

93. Luther, "Preface to the Epistles of St. James and St. Jude," 35.

94. John Calvin, *Institutes of the Christian Religion* (1559), 2 vols. ed. John T. McNeill, trans. Ford Lewis Battles, Library of Christian Classics (Philadelphia: Westminster, 1960) 3.17.11 (1:815).

to Paul, he declares that justification is by works and not by faith alone.[95] And Calvin tacitly agreed when he conceded that, in order to reconcile them, one has to posit that James uses the word "justify" differently than Paul does: "If you would make James agree with the rest of Scripture . . . you must understand the word 'justify' in another sense than Paul takes it."[96] But here Calvin's exegesis is strained in the extreme.

The exegetical debate since the sixteenth century has moved back and forth between the poles represented by Luther and Calvin. Be that as it may, in the contrasting answers of Luther and Calvin to the question about James we see illustrated the basic divergence between two Protestant attitudes toward the Bible. For Calvin, it was unthinkable that there could ever be a contradiction within the Bible since all of scripture is inspired by God. Hence, the exegete has to strive to find an explanation (a gloss) of any text that initially gives the impression of being out of harmony with the rest of the Bible in order to show that it really is not. This does not mean that Calvin failed to distinguish between scripture as the Word of God and the gospel as the Word of God. He did distinguish between them. Whereas we are to rely for assurance of salvation solely upon the gospel since this is God's promise of forgiveness, Calvin insisted that we are also to obey every word of God in the Bible, whatever its content may be:

> Faith is certain that God is true in all things whether he command or forbid, whether he promise or threaten; and it also obediently receives his commandments, observes his prohibitions, heeds his threats. Nevertheless, faith properly begins with the promise, rests in it, and ends in it.[97]

Thus, while Calvin distinguished between all of God's words in scripture and God's promise in the gospel, he could never admit a conflict between them. By contrast, Luther did not hesitate to criticize scripture when he believed that a choice had to be made between it and the gospel.[98]

The amazing freedom with which Luther criticized the canon of scripture would no doubt come as a surprise to conservative Protestants today, for whom any criticism of the Bible is unthinkable and blasphemous, just as some of Luther's ardent supporters in the sixteenth century, such as Calvin,

---

95. Luther, "Preface to the Epistles of St. James and St. Jude," 35.

96. Calvin, *Institutes*, 3.17.12 (1:816).

97. Calvin, *Institutes*, 3.2.29 (1:575).

98. "For other Protestants the Bible was central, but for Luther it was subordinate to the truth of the basic doctrine he found in it." Donald J. Wilcox, *In Search of God and Self: Renaissance and Reformation Thought* (1975; reprint, Prospect Heights, IL: Waveland, 1987) 303.

also had difficulty with it. But, in truth, the first Protestant not only subjected the postbiblical tradition of the church to criticism in the name of the Bible but also subjected the Bible itself to criticism in the name of the gospel! Luther's boldness in this regard was unprecedented for a medieval theologian. But it also raises the question what exactly he meant by "scripture alone."

Roland Bainton, in his study "The Bible in the Reformation," made this observation:

> But if the Scripture were the authority, what then was the scripture? That question might seem long ago to have been settled because the canon, both of the Old Testament and of the New, had been fixed since the days of the early Church. But if, as the reformers said, the Gospel was prior to the canon and only those books should be received which proclaimed the Gospel, might not the canon be re-examined? ... Luther behaved as if he were minded to open a controversy on the canon not only of the Old Testament but also of the New.[99]

Jaroslav Pelikan correctly stated that "[t]he theology of Martin Luther was a theology of the word of God." Yet Pelikan posed the question: "Was this word of God identical with the Bible?"

> He could deal with various books of both the Old and New Testament, above all the Epistle of James, in a fashion that was difficult to harmonize with a high doctrine of biblical inspiration and inerrancy. Above all, Luther could sometimes dwell upon the centrality and authority of the gospel with an almost obsessive intensity, testing liturgical practice, ethical precept, and even theological dogma by this criterion rather than by the norm of conforming to the literal meaning of the biblical text.[100]

Another scholar of the Reformation, Heinrich Bornkamm, well summarized Luther's view:

> The Bible is therefore not in and of itself Holy Scripture ... Unquestionably there is much in the Bible that is not determined by Christ ... [W]hat the Holy Scripture is becomes apparent only from the vantage point of the gospel.[101]

---

99. Roland Bainton, "The Bible in the Reformation," in *The Cambridge History of the Bible*, vol. 3: *The West from the Reformation to the Present Day* (Cambridge: Cambridge University Press, 1963) 1–37 at 6.

100. Pelikan, *Reformation of Church and Dogma*, 183, 181.

101. Heinrich Bornkamm, *The Heart of Reformation Faith: The Fundamental Axioms of Evangelical Belief*, trans. John W. Doberstein (New York: Harper & Row, 1965)

Finally, Heiko Oberman had this to say about Luther's approach toward scripture:

> The exclusive authority of the Holy Scriptures was not part of his Reformation discovery—a fact that gave rise to tensions in the sixteenth century and has caused misunderstanding to the present day . . . His quest did not concern the authority of the Bible, which was self-evident to him; he wanted to know how this authority could be properly expressed, how the Word of God could be ascertained among the wealth of scriptural testimony.[102]

These comments from four impressive scholars—and many others could just as well have been cited—shall suffice to make the point that Luther was no biblicist: "The Bible for him was not strictly identical with the Word of God."[103] For Luther, the Bible was important only to the extent that it sets forth Christ: the gospel of justification by faith alone. Indeed, scripture can and should be criticized to the extent that it does not do this. In Luther's view, therefore, the formal principle of scripture alone is clearly subordinated to the material principle of faith alone.

Things were quite different in the Reformed camp. There the designation "reformed" gave expression not only to the shared Protestant self-consciousness of opposition to Catholicism (i.e., reformed according to the Word of God, unlike Rome, which does not submit itself to God's Word), but also to the sense of being distinct from the Lutherans (i.e., *more* reformed according to the Word of God than they are!). But in this case, "the Word of God" meant the entire canon of scripture: "Reformed teaching, therefore, put at the head of its agenda (and at the head of many of its doctrinal statements) the task of carrying 'reform in accordance with the word of God' to its necessary consequences, with a consistency and a rigor that went considerably beyond Luther."[104] This is also how Barth characterized the two main Protestant confessions:

> Scripture did not play quite the same part in Reformed Protestantism as in Lutheran. Its dignity here was one of principle

---

40–41.

102. Oberman, *Luther: Man between God and the Devil*, 223.

103. Bainton, *Here I Stand: A Life of Martin Luther* (New York: Abingdon, 1950) 331.

104. Pelikan, *Reformation of Church and Dogma*, 183. "Unlike other Reformation confessions, the [Lutheran] Augsburg Confession did not open with a statement of the authority and inspiration of Scripture, nor with a list of the canonical books of the Old and New Testaments" (182).

as it never was in Lutheranism, no matter how highly the latter regarded it. Introducing reformation now meant establishing the Word of God in the Bible as the norm of faith and life.[105]

Speaking of Zwingli and Calvin, Barth commented:

> It is really a *formal* principle that is grasped here . . . If only the Bible is heard again, then the necessary consequences will follow . . . [T]his is the *new thing* that Zwingli and Calvin learned neither from *Erasmus* nor *Luther* . . . They were not so bound to the one particular theme that Luther had discovered in the Bible. To be sure, they *also* put it at the heart of their proclamation. But one will always find that it was developed in Luther more profoundly and more powerfully. Thus, they were freer to let the Bible speak in its fulness, the entire Bible, freer to avoid reducing the Word of God to the doctrine of the forgiveness of sins. They let the Bible simply *speak* for itself as the form that best handles the question of its content *itself*.[106]

Barth noted that the Lutheran church has been called "the church of the material principle, the doctrine of justification," whereas the Reformed church, by contrast, has been called "the church of the formal principle of the Reformation, the principle of Scripture."[107] He further admitted that among the Reformed "lesser prominence [was] given to the content [of scripture], which was the starting point for Luther," since the Reformed "began by establishing biblical authority."[108] Not surprisingly, then, the Reformed theologians could not bring themselves to endorse Luther's *Sachkritik*. Since Luther not only disparaged James as "an epistle of straw" but also faulted the book of Revelation for its obscurity ("'a revelation . . . should be revealing'"[109]), one sixteenth-century Reformed statement took him to task for presuming to criticize God's Word in scripture:

> In all of the books of the New Testament there is no hard knot to confuse us, nor do we hold that there might be some *useless straw* in them or that they mix up *one thing in another in a disorderly way*. And if the *human spirit cannot make its sense of the Revelation* or other books, then we pay no regard to its

---

105. Barth, *The Theology of John Calvin*, trans. Geoffrey W. Bromiley (Grand Rapids: Eerdmans, 1995) 386.

106. Barth, *Theology of the Reformed Confessions*, 43–44, emphasis original.

107. Barth, *Theology of the Reformed Confessions*, 39.

108. Barth, *Theology of John Calvin*, 386–87.

109. Bainton, *Here I Stand*, 331.

problem. For we know well that we humans should be guided by the Scripture, not the Scripture by us.[110]

This Reformed criticism of Luther, cited by Barth with apparent approval, clearly expresses a very different attitude toward the Bible than that held by the German Reformer. Barth further elaborated upon the significance of this major difference between the Lutheran and the Reformed confessions in order to make it unambiguously clear what is at stake here for Protestantism:

> It becomes understandable in this context why a number of Reformed confessional documents take such an unusual interest in the concept of the biblical *canon*. This was an interest that Lutheranism could not have had because . . . it did not place such emphasis upon the isolated normativity of the Bible. For the Reformed, it is precisely the Bible's isolated normativity that is important.[111]

With that final sentence Barth hit the nail on the head! He then threw down the gauntlet:

> [T]he Scripture principle is the only article of faith that has persisted up to today in the doctrinal statements of all Reformed churches . . . Whether we will then . . . read the Bible 'as if the living words of God were heard'—that is the fateful question

---

110. "The Zurich Confession" (1545), cited by Barth, *Theology of the Reformed Confessions*, 50. There is, however, at least one Reformed confession from the sixteenth century that affirms Luther's *Sachkritik* in principle, even while disagreeing with Luther's exegesis in fact. "The Second Helvetic [Swiss] Confession" (1566), written by Heinrich Bullinger, Zwingli's successor in Zurich, had this to say on the controverted question of James and Paul: "Wherefore, in this matter we are not speaking of a fictitious, empty, lazy, and dead faith, but of a living, quickening faith. It is and is called a living faith because it apprehends Christ who is life and makes alive, and shows that it is alive by living works. And so James does not contradict anything in this doctrine of ours [*sola fide*]. For he speaks of an empty, dead faith of which some boasted but who did not have Christ living in them by faith (James 2:14ff.). James said that works justify, yet without contradicting the apostle [Paul] (*otherwise he would have to be rejected*)." *The Constitution of the Presbyterian Church (U.S.A.), Part I: The Book of Confessions* (Louisville: The Office of the General Assembly, 1996) 5:111, emphasis added. This is a remarkable statement. On the one hand, Bullinger agrees with Calvin's exegesis of James as a matter of fact; against Luther, James does not contradict Paul. On the other hand, Bullinger agrees with Luther's willingness to criticize scripture on behalf of the gospel as a matter of principle (just in case Calvin is wrong and Luther is right about James!). Notwithstanding his affirmation of Protestantism's formal principle ("We believe and confess the canonical Scriptures . . . to be the true Word of God," *The Book of Confessions*, 5:001), Bullinger upholds the legitimacy of *Sachkritik*. Here, clearly, the formal principle of *sola scriptura* is subordinated to the material principle of *sola fide*.

111. Barth, *Theology of the Reformed Confessions*, 49.

whose answer will decide the future of Reformed (and not only Reformed) Protestantism.[112]

While we must agree with Barth that this is the fateful question that will decide the future of Protestantism, there is reason to disagree with him as to how this question should be answered.

PROTESTANTISM AND THE BIBLE: THE LUTHERAN ROAD LESS TRAVELED

Barth was surely right to see in Bultmann a modern-day heir of Luther, just as their debate in the matter of *Sachkritik* was a modern reprise of that earlier one between Luther and Calvin. Our examination of these debates is instructive not only in making the historical point that from its inception Protestantism has harbored within itself two contrasting models of biblical authority, but also in clarifying the fundamental choice between them that has to be made by Protestants today, who, as they have recently commemorated the five-hundredth anniversary of the Reformation, must decide what the genuine legacy of the Reformation is in this matter. What is surprising and even ironic—since it is Luther who gave birth to Protestantism—is how little influence Luther's model of biblical authority has had in the history of Protestantism. Hence, the question is whether there are any compelling reasons that should lead Protestants today to choose the Lutheran model over its Reformed counterpart. I think there are two: historical and ethical.

The first problem for the Reformed "scripture principle" is that it is difficult to see how it can be salvaged in the light of what modern historical-critical study of the Bible has taught us. Harry Y. Gamble succinctly summarizes the problematic implications for the normative status of the New Testament (NT) canon that have arisen from critical investigation into the history of the canon itself as well as from exegesis of the documents within the canon.

> [T]he limits of the canon cannot any longer be defended on the basis of the explicit warrants adduced on its behalf by the ancient church. Historical criticism has shown that the ancient church was most often mistaken in its claims that the canonical writings were written by apostles, while the history of the canon makes it doubtful that theoretical criteria (apostolicity, catholicity, etc.) were effective reasons for its canonization. For all these

---

112. Barth, *Theology of the Reformed Confessions*, 64, referring to Calvin, *Institutes*, 1.7.1 (1:74–75).

reasons, the traditional boundaries of the NT canon have been deprived of clear and self-evident validity.[113]

> The concept of the canon and its normative function has been called into question even more by the exegesis of the NT texts than by the history of the canon. It has been the extraordinary result of modern historical study that among the canonical texts there is a wide range of theological orientations which are not only diverse but to some extent also incompatible and mutually contradictory . . . By throwing into sharp relief the extent of theological diversity within the canon, historical-critical exegesis has made it impossible to sustain the formal and legal understanding of the canon, widespread in Protestantism and Catholicism alike, according to which the canon is a doctrinal unity possessing equal authority in all its parts, with theological inconsistencies being ruled out in principle. In practical terms, this means that a theological claim cannot now be vindicated by the simple shibboleth, "The NT says . . ." not because the NT does not say it, but because it says much else besides and not with straightforward consistency. Taken as a whole, therefore, the canon cannot constitute a sharply effective theological norm.[114]

Unless one is committed, for whatever reason, to the belief that the text of scripture is verbally inspired by God—which is precisely where Barth departed from Calvin—the canon *per se* loses its absolute authority.[115] By humanizing the Bible, historical criticism has abolished the sharp distinction between it and the rest of Christian tradition. It is thus no longer plausible to pit scripture as a collection of divine words against a merely human tradition of interpretation.[116]

---

113. Harry Y. Gamble, *The New Testament Canon: Its Making and Meaning*, Guides to Biblical Scholarship (Philadelphia: Fortress, 1985) 83.

114. Gamble, *New Testament Canon*, 85–86.

115. Barth spoke of "the fallibility of all the human words of the Bible, of their historical and scientific inaccuracies, their theological contradictions, [and] the uncertainty of their tradition." *Doctrine of the Word of God*, I/2, 531. He even pointed out that "its capacity for error extends to its religious or theological content" (509). Although Barth emphatically rejected a doctrine of biblical inerrancy, Thompson takes note of the fact that Barth also "refused to identify actual errors in the Bible." "Witness to the Word," 194. Gordon H. Clark, an orthodox Calvinist, asks of Barth, "Can Biblical authority survive the abandonment of verbal inspiration?" By "biblical authority" Clark means "the scriptural principle." He candidly admits to being confused by all that Barth denies and affirms about the Bible: "Barth's theory of inspiration is unquestionably a mystery." *Karl Barth's Theological Method* (Philadelphia: P & R, 1963) 185, 214.

116. Cobb correctly explains, "The Bible is part of the tradition. On this point,

Whereas historical criticism has posed a severe challenge to the Reformed scripture principle, Luther's alternative is remarkably able to meet this challenge. His redefinition of "apostolic" and his recognition of theological diversity within the Bible seem uncannily "modern" by comparison with biblicism. Oberman deems that, while the Reformation's formal principle has now lost all intellectual credibility, Luther himself would not have been troubled by this loss in the least.

> He started from a different and, in fact, contradictory principle, which was to be ignored in the Protestant longing for a "paper pope": "God and the scriptures are two different things, as different as Creator and creature." This historically innovative principle forms the basis of . . . a new and crucial point of departure for present-day theology. It is this principle that distinguishes Luther from the biblicism of both his own and later eras.[117]

As far as the canon is concerned, Gerhard Ebeling, a Lutheran theologian, has this to say:

> [T]he Protestant Church possesses complete freedom to revise the canon. This thought can only shock the person who has forgotten that it was not the eighteenth or nineteenth century but Luther who brought this question to the fore . . . The freedom which he thus proclaimed toward the early Catholic canon belongs to the essence of the Reformation understanding of the Scriptures . . . *The content of Scripture does not receive its authority from the fact that it stands in Scripture; on the contrary, Scripture receives its authority from its content.*[118]

Gamble asks the crucial question that has to be posed to adherents of the scripture principle:

> How is it possible, once the theological diversity of the canon is admitted, to give equal authority to all the canonical documents? *Either historical results will not be taken seriously, or a perspective will be found outside the canon which determines how scripture is to be interpreted, in which case the authority of the canon will be given up anyway* . . . Each view is in its own way an

---

Catholics have spoken more wisely than have Protestants . . . The Bible can only have the sort of authority that a tradition can have." *Becoming a Thinking Christian*, 68.

117. Oberman, *Luther: Man between God and the Devil*, 221, citing Luther, *De servo arbitrio*, in the Weimar edition of *Luthers Werke* (Weimar: Böhlau, 1883–) 18.606, 11–12.

118. Ebeling, *Problem of Historicity in the Church*, 63–65, emphasis added.

admission that the formal canon does not and cannot serve as an effective theological norm.[119]

It is not surprising, therefore, that Barth, in order to maintain the scripture principle of Calvin, had to minimize the significance of historical criticism for theological exegesis.[120] That is no less true of his followers today, who accept it grudgingly and only with severe qualifications.[121]

Not all modern Reformed theologians rush to defend the scripture principle, however. Some of them esteem Luther a far better guide in this regard than Calvin.[122] Edward Dowey, who penned the most important book on Calvin during the last century, rendered this verdict:

---

119. Gamble, *New Testament Canon*, 87, emphasis added.

120. Gamble's observation that in the effort to salvage the scriptural principle "historical results will not be taken seriously" is demonstrated by Barth's disregard of historical criticism when it does not suit his theological purposes. Nowhere is this more apparent than in his Christianizing exegesis of the Old Testament, a point noted by Bultmann in a letter to Barth (November 11-15, 1952), in Jaspert, ed., *Letters*, 97. On this issue see Capetz, "The Old Testament as a Witness to Jesus Christ: Historical Criticism and Theological Exegesis of the Bible according to Karl Barth," *Journal of Religion* 90 (2010) 475–506, also published as "Karl Barth on the Old Testament as Christian Scripture," Chapter 4 in this volume (pages 139-71, below).

121. In the effort to diminish the importance of historical criticism for a theological exegesis of the Bible, one disciple of Barth, Hans W. Frei, has tried to argue—unsuccessfully, in my view—that what the Reformers meant by the literal sense of the text is not what modern historical criticism means by it. *The Eclipse of Biblical Narrative: A Study in Eighteenth and Nineteenth Century Hermeneutics* (New Haven: Yale University Press, 1974). The truth about the relation between Reformation hermeneutics and modern historical criticism is far better captured by Ebeling's classic essay "The Significance of the Critical Historical Method for Church and Theology in Proclamation," in *Word and Faith*, trans. James W. Leitch (Philadelphia: Fortress, 1963) 17–61. Oddly, another disciple of Barth, Brevard S. Childs, agrees with Frei, but goes beyond him and moves explicitly in the direction of Catholicism in order to defend his "canonical" approach to biblical studies. For Childs, not only must one accept the authority of the ancient church that decided the New Testament canon, but also one must say that the literal sense is not the historical sense disclosed by modern criticism; rather, it is the meaning ascribed to the biblical text by the church's confessional tradition. Ironically for someone who claimed to be a Calvinist, Childs repeats the arguments of Luther's opponent John Eck and the Decree of Trent without being aware of it. Childs is thus able to salvage the scripture principle only by ceasing to be a genuine Protestant. See his article, "The *Sensus Literalis* of Scripture: An Ancient and Modern Problem," in *Beiträge zur alttestamentlichen Theologie: Festschrift für Walther Zimmerli zum 70. Geburtstag*, ed. Herbert Donner et al. (Göttingen: Vandenhoeck & Ruprecht, 1977) 80–93. See Eck, *Enchiridion of Commonplaces against Luther and Other Enemies of the Church*, trans. Ford Lewis Battles, Twin Brooks Series (Grand Rapids: Baker, 1979) 13; and "The Canons and Decrees of the Council of Trent," in *Creeds of the Churches*, ed. John H. Leith, 3rd ed. (Louisville: Westminster John Knox, 1982) 400–439 at 403–4.

122. Friedrich Schleiermacher, who was ever conscious of his allegiance to the

> Calvin had in his hand, as it were, the very instrument by which Luther had already freed himself of slavish adherence to the Bible and tortuous exegesis: the principle of "Christ, the Lord of Scripture"—but he did not wield it . . . We must conclude, in fact, that two "interpretations" exist side by side in Calvin's theology concerning the object of the knowledge of faith, because he never fully integrated and related systematically the faithful man's acceptance of the authority of the Bible *en bloc* with faith as directed exclusively toward Christ.[123]

If in the usage of the Reformers two distinct meanings of the phrase "Word of God" can be discerned, one referring to the Bible as an inspired compendium of God's words and the other referring to the gospel, then historical criticism has highlighted the importance of the latter meaning for modern Protestants precisely to the extent that the former meaning has lost all credibility. In truth, no aspect of the Reformers' program stands in greater need of a complete overhaul than their formal principle of "scripture alone." To reiterate: although this traditional approach to biblical authority is no longer tenable, Luther's alternative clearly is. Brian Gerrish, who calls himself "an honest Calvinist," concurs in judging that Luther's approach has the distinct advantage of being "hospitable to a modern understanding of the Bible."

> For one possible response to the theological problems raised by biblical criticism . . . is to recover Luther's understanding of the Bible as a witness to the revelation in Christ and to discard the medieval remnants that still cling to this thinking . . . It has required all the impact of modern scientific, literary, and historical criticism to drive Protestantism back to its original insight.[124]

Indeed, just as Luther pressed the entire arsenal of humanistic learning into the service of the Reformation, so too historical criticism can be deployed on behalf of Protestant theology today.

Reformed tradition, said, "The authority of Holy Scripture cannot be the foundation of faith in Christ; rather must the latter be presupposed before a peculiar authority can be granted to Holy Scripture." *The Christian Faith*, trans. H. R. Mackintosh and J. S. Stewart (Philadelphia: Fortress, 1976) 591 (§128).

123. Edward A. Dowey Jr., *The Knowledge of God in Calvin's Theology*, 3rd expanded ed. (1952; reprint, Grand Rapids: Eerdmans, 1994) 160–62.

124. Gerrish, "Word of God and the Words of Scripture," in *The Old Protestantism and the New*, 65. For his self-appellation, see Gerrish "The Secret Religion of Germany: Christian Piety and the Pantheism Controversy," in *Continuing the Reformation: Essays on Modern Religious Thought* (Chicago: University of Chicago Press, 1993) 109–26 at 126.

Bultmann's signal achievement has been to show both *that* and *how* it is possible to appropriate the insights into biblical religion and literature gained by modern historical research on behalf of Protestant theology's effort to provide a responsible statement of the gospel for our time. In the "Epilogue" to his *Theology of the New Testament*, he penned this classic account of the necessarily reciprocal relationship that exists between the historical and the theological tasks:

> Since the New Testament is a document of history, specifically of the history of religion, the interpretation of it requires the labor of historical investigation. The method of this kind of inquiry has been worked out from the time of the Enlightenment onward and has been made fruitful for the investigation of primitive Christianity and the interpretation of the New Testament. Now such labor may be guided by either one of two interests, that of reconstruction or that of interpretation—that is, reconstruction of past history or interpretation of the New Testament Writings. Neither exists, of course, without the other, and they stand constantly in a reciprocal relation to each other. But the question is: which of the two stands in the service of the other? Either the writings of the New Testament can be interrogated as the "sources" which the historian interprets in order to reconstruct a picture of primitive Christianity as a phenomenon of the historical past, or the reconstruction stands in the service of the interpretation of the New Testament writings under the presupposition that they have something to say to the present. The latter interest is the one for which historical labor is put to service in the presentation here offered.[125]

Whereas the New Testament scholar *qua* historian uses the texts as sources for reconstructing early Christianity as a part of ancient religious history, the same scholar *qua* theologian interprets the texts with reference to the *Sache* with which they have to do. Bultmann was thus able to make good on the early Barth's programmatic call for a theological exegesis that does not shortchange the indispensable lessons of historical-critical research—in a way Barth himself was never able to pull off—precisely because, as a Lutheran, Bultmann was working with Luther's view of the relation between scripture and the gospel.[126] Specifically, this entails *Sachkritik*.[127]

---

125. Bultmann, *Theology of the New Testament*, 2 vols., trans. Kendrick Grobel (New York: Scribner, 1951, 1955) 2:251.

126. Eduard Lohse, "Rudolf Bultmann als Lutherischer Theologe," *Luther: Zeitschrift der Luther-Gesellschaft* 45 (1974) 49–54.

127. "The dogmatic-axiomatic assertion of the authority of the biblical canon allows

Luther criticized the Epistle of James insofar as it contradicts Paul's theology; but Luther went further than this by indicating that he would even be willing to criticize Paul himself if Paul had said something that was not "apostolic" in the sense of that which "teaches Christ." This is the criticism that Bultmann called for in his debates with Barth. For Bultmann as for Luther, *Sachkritik* is not only the right but also the duty of a Protestant theologian. Accordingly, he insisted that "theological propositions—even those of the New Testament—can never be the object of faith" since "faith can be nothing else but the response to the kerygma" (the gospel), that is, "God's word addressing man as a questioning and promising word, a condemning and forgiving word."[128]

> And that is just where the problem lurks! For both the kerygma and faith's self-understanding always appear in the texts, so far as they are expressed in words and sentences, already interpreted in some particular way—i.e., in theological thoughts.[129]
>
> Therefore, it is not possible simply and sharply to distinguish kerygmatic statements in the New Testament from theological ones, nor to derive from the New Testament a self-understanding not formulated in theological statements. Nevertheless, he who sets forth a New Testament theology must have this distinction constantly in mind and must interpret the theological thoughts as the unfolding of the self-understanding awakened by the kerygma.[130]

Hence, the theological thoughts of the New Testament "can only be the explication of the understanding which is inherent in faith itself" and "may be only relatively appropriate, some more so, others less so." We have to reckon, therefore, with the possibility that in some of these texts faith's own self-understanding "may not be clearly developed, that it may be hindered—bound perhaps by a pre-faith understanding of God, the world, and man, and by

---

Barth's reserve toward a theological *Sachkritik* within the canon to appear as consistent. But if we have to do with human witnesses, as Barth knows we do when dealing with the biblical texts, then the exegete must assume that as human witnesses they bear witness to the theological 'center' more or less adequately (*sachgemäß*). One cannot, as Barth does, approach all interpretations of the Christian faith in the history of theology with the legitimate suspicion that perhaps alien elements (*sachfremde Elemente*) have entered into the witness of the texts on the one hand, while exempting all interpretations within the biblical canon from this criticism on the other hand." Lindemann, *Karl Barth und die kritische Schriftauslegung*, 90.

128. Bultmann, *Theology of the New Testament*, 2:240.
129. Bultmann, *Theology of the New Testament*, 2:239.
130. Bultmann, *Theology of the New Testament*, 2:240.

a corresponding terminology." Accordingly, the demand arises for "content criticism (*Sachkritik*) such as Luther, for example, exercised towards the Epistle of James and the Revelation of John."[131] The clear implication of Bultmann's argument is that the New Testament is the primary source of Christian theology but not its primary norm. This primary norm is prior to the New Testament canon and thus cannot be identified with it. Hence, the canon is a *norma normata* ("normed norm") but is not itself the *norma normans sed non normata* ("the norm that norms but is not normed") since this can only ever be the *kerygma* or gospel, i.e., that which each text within the New Testament seeks to interpret and by which it is to be judged.[132]

The second problem for the scripture principle is ethical. The application of this principle has had and continues to have morally reprehensible consequences. Appeal to the Bible has been used to justify the enslavement of Africans, the subordination of women to men in marriage as well as women's exclusion from ordained ministry, and the categorical moral condemnation of homosexuality. The Enlightenment not only put the twin challenges of natural science and historical criticism on the modern theological agenda, but also posed an ethical challenge to unjust social and economic arrangements that claim divine sanction for themselves. Just as the theological propositions of the New Testament can never be the object of faith, neither can its ethical propositions be the object of faith. Just as the former need to be demythologized, so too must the latter be "deideologized." What the Bible says about the state, slavery, or gender and sexuality requires a critical ethical-political hermeneutical method that is the necessary complement to existentialist interpretation.[133] This has been the major contribution of

---

131. Bultmann, *Theology of the New Testament*, 2:238.

132. Schubert M. Ogden makes the point well: "Because not even the New Testament is the canon of the church, which is rather the apostolic witness to Jesus Christ that is historically prior to the New Testament, the authority of scripture for determining the appropriateness of theological assertions is but a derived or secondary authority. Consequently, merely to establish that an assertion is derived from scripture or warranted by it is not sufficient to authorize the assertion as theologically appropriate. It is further necessary to establish that the scriptural source or warrant for the assertion is itself authorized by the original witness of the apostles, which is the sole primary authority for determining the appropriateness of theological assertions." "The Authority of Scripture for Theology," in *On Theology* (San Francisco: Harper & Row, 1986) 45–68 at 62.

133. Bultmann explained, "To de-mythologize is to deny that the message of Scripture and of the Church is bound to an ancient worldview which is obsolete." *Jesus Christ and Mythology*, 36. Dorothee Soelle was the first to call for a "deideologizing" of scripture to complement its demythologizing by Bultmann. *Political Theology*, trans. with an introd. by John Shelley (Philadelphia: Fortress, 1974). Ogden also sees the need for this: "[I]t is precisely Bultmann's procedure of existentialist interpretation that not

liberation theologies after Bultmann, yet there is every reason to think it would have met with his approval.

> It is self-evident . . . that the New Testament's thoughts about the state and society are incomplete because the possibilities and problems of forms of the state and society which history has introduced in the meantime could not be present to the minds of the New Testament authors. It is likewise clear that the world of modern science and technology imposes upon believing comprehension new tasks which could not yet occur to the minds of the New Testament period. Therefore the theological thoughts of the New Testament can be normative only insofar as they lead the believer to develop out of his faith an understanding of God, the world, and man in his own concrete situation.[134]

Both theologically *and* ethically, therefore, the New Testament can legitimately be criticized.[135]

Unfortunately, however, recognition of the legitimacy of such criticism has not usually been characteristic of Protestantism. Not only has historical criticism had to fight for its right, but theological criticism (including ethical criticism) has been met by still greater resistance, even by those who purport to accept historical criticism. Since, however, the moral stakes in retention of the scriptural principle are so high, let us consider the most recent example of it.

In the still ongoing controversy over homosexuality that has convulsed the Protestant churches, Richard B. Hays has been at the forefront of the opposition to revision of the church's traditional proscription of homosexual relations in any form. Why? For him, it all boils down to biblical authority. The church, Hays insists, is to be a "[s]cripture-shaped community."[136] Ac-

---

only requires, but also allows for, such further development." "Women and the Canon: Some Thoughts on the Significance of Rudolf Bultmann for Theology Today," in *Doing Theology Today* (1996; reprint, Eugene, OR: Wipf & Stock, 2006) 230–44 at 244. Ogden clarifies that "a deideologizing of the gospel . . . involves so reinterpreting the gospel's meaning as to disengage it from all interpretations whereby in one way or another it has been made to sanction existing injustice and oppression." "The Concept of a Theology of Liberation: Must Christian Theology Today Be So Conceived?" in *On Theology*, 134–50 at 137.

134. Bultmann, *Theology of the New Testament*, 2:238.

135. Whereas ethics is here distinguished from theology in the narrow sense, ethics can and should also be understood as constituting one aspect of the larger task of theology in the broad sense. Hence, *Sachkritik* is appropriate when applied to the New Testament's ethical statements as well.

136. Richard B. Hays, *The Moral Vision of the New Testament: Community, Cross, New Creation; A Contemporary Introduction to New Testament Ethics* (San Francisco:

cordingly, the church's fidelity to God or Christ is to be measured by its obedience to what the Bible says. Consequently, exegesis replaces ethical argument, since for Hays Christian ethics is "fundamentally a hermeneutical enterprise":

> [I]t must begin and end in the interpretation and application of Scripture for the life of the community of faith. Such a pronouncement will prove controversial in some circles, but it represents the classic confessional position of catholic Christianity, as sharpened in its Reformation traditions.[137]

Hays refuses to give "a formal apologetic argument in defense of the authority of Scripture" on the grounds that "the most powerful argument for the truth of Scripture is a community of people who exemplify the love and power of God that they have come to know through the New Testament."[138] But his refusal disguises the fact that Hays has conflated the affirmation of biblical authority with his own understanding of it, so that any who dissent are in effect rendered *extra ecclesiam* since, after all, it is non-Christians to whom apologetic arguments are directed. To be sure, he does mention "some who would identify themselves as Christian theologians" but

> for whom the Bible is seen as a source of oppression and moral blindness, particularly with regard to issues of sexual ethics; for such interpreters, the most crucial question about the teaching of the New Testament is how we can get critical leverage against it . . . *Such forthright repudiation of biblical authority by self-identified Christian thinkers is a historical phenomenon that is both relatively recent and unlikely to exercise any lasting influence within the church.*[139]

Notice how Hays equates criticism of the New Testament with a "forthright repudiation of biblical authority" itself. I presume that both Luther and Bultmann would fall under this verdict.

Not surprisingly, Hays takes the Bible's statements about morality to be absolute and as overriding any considerations that might call into question the adequacy of its ethical teachings:

> [T]he canonical scriptures constitute the *norma normans* of the church's life, whereas every other source of moral guidance (whether church tradition, philosophical reasoning, scientific

HarperSanFrancisco, 1996) 10.
    137. Hays, *Moral Vision of the New Testament*, 10.
    138. Hays, *Moral Vision of the New Testament*, 10.
    139. Hays, *Moral Vision of the New Testament*, 11n29, emphasis added.

investigation, or claims about contemporary religious experience) must be understood as *norma normata*.¹⁴⁰

For Hays, therefore, it is axiomatic that what the Bible says about homosexuality is normative for Christians today: "the Bible's perspective is privileged, not ours."¹⁴¹ He declares:

> To take the New Testament as authoritative . . . is to accept this portrayal [of homosexuality in Romans 1] as "revealed reality," an authoritative disclosure of the truth about the human condition. Understood in this way, the text requires a normative evaluation of homosexual practice as a distortion of God's order for creation.¹⁴²

Hays then goes on to ask, "Do we grant the normative force of Paul's analysis?"¹⁴³ But surely, we can ask Hays by way of reply: Which is it? Is this God speaking or a first-century Hellenistic Jew? "Revealed reality" or "Paul's analysis"? Are they the same thing? Nonetheless, given his axiom that Paul here speaks for God in this matter, Hays has ruled out the possibility of authentic ethical debate in the churches on the question of the morality of homosexuality that might lead us to answer his rhetorical question by saying, "No, we do not accept Paul's analysis as normative."

By taking what Paul says in Rom 1:18–32 as "revealed reality," Hays inverts the actual sense of the text. Paul himself does not defend his own

---

140. Hays, *Moral Vision of the New Testament*, 10.

141. Hays, *Moral Vision of the New Testament*, 296. Hays has lavish praise for Barth's use of scripture in ethics (225–39). Georgia Harkness, who had a heated exchange with Barth over the equality of women in the church at the 1948 meeting of the World Council of Churches, did not think Barth's use of scripture in this matter was responsible. Her report of their exchange is found in Rosemary Skinner Keller, *Georgia Harkness: For Such a Time as This* (Nashville: Abingdon, 1992) 251. I once asked a Barthian theologian who teaches at a Presbyterian seminary why he believed that homosexuality is immoral. He answered, "Because the Presbyterian Church is constitutionally committed to a high view of biblical authority." I asked in reply, "Is the Presbyterian Church committed to a high view of the truth? What if the Bible does not teach the truth about the lives of gay people?" He had no further comment. For my analysis of the Presbyterian controversy that subsequently led to a split in that denomination, see Paul E. Capetz, "Defending the Reformed Tradition? Problematic Aspects of the Appeal to Biblical and Confessional Authority in the Present Theological Crisis Confronting the Presbyterian Church (U.S.A.)," *Journal of Presbyterian History* 79 (2001) 23–39.

142. Hays, *Moral Vision of the New Testament*, 396. Apparently, Hays assumes that "revelation" means the supernatural communication of information. But Bultmann has marshalled some important arguments against the assumption that this is the true meaning of revelation in the New Testament. See his essay "The Concept of Revelation in the New Testament," in *Existence and Faith*, 58–91.

143. Hays, *Moral Vision of the New Testament*, 397.

"analysis" in this manner; instead, he presumes that his case can be defended solely on the basis of reason and experience, thus inviting his readers to give or to withhold their assent to his argument on these terms alone. Paul even employs the categories of Stoic philosophers to set forth two points: first, nature itself teaches the existence of one deity who is creator of all so that the Gentiles have no need of Israel's scriptures to know this truth (natural theology); second, homosexuality is immoral because it is "against nature" (natural-law ethics). On his own grounds, then, the truth of Paul's two claims can only be validated philosophically.[144] But the two claims do not stand or fall together. Paul may be right about the first yet wrong about the second, or vice versa. So, if we disagree with Paul's indictment of homosexuality, it is not because we reject "revealed reality," but, rather, because we fail to be convinced rationally and experientially by "Paul's analysis," i.e., his first-century Jewish-Hellenistic interpretation of nature as to its moral implications.[145]

From the perspective of those who take the historical and thus fully human character of the Bible to heart, equating Paul's analysis with revealed reality is tantamount to idolatry: worshiping a god of paper and ink made by human hands! Ironically, Hays illustrates by his own example the invidious moral consequences that follow upon misplaced religious devotion, which is the very point Paul is most concerned to make in Rom 1. The consequences for his fellow humans who are homosexual are disastrous since Hays's appeal to the Bible only serves to perpetuate their inequality and lack of full participation in the church.[146] The fact that Hays sincerely believes Paul's interpretation is based on supernatural revelation does not change a thing: his failure consists in refusing to defend his view of biblical authority against the alternative Lutheran model (which he never mentions), even

---

144. For an incisive philosophical analysis and criticism of the major arguments against homosexuality, see Pim Pronk, *Against Nature? Types of Moral Argumentation Regarding Homosexuality*, translated by John Vriend, foreword by Hendrik Hart (Grand Rapids: Eerdmans, 1993).

145. James D. Smart correctly apprehends the crucial insight underlying the demand for *Sachkritik*: "Biblical authors had their own self-understanding which was only in part determined by the revelation of God to which they witnessed ... So also Paul, as an inhabitant of the Hellenistic age, united in himself a self-understanding that belonged to his age with a self-understanding that was the fruit of his hearing of the gospel, the latter alone having power in it to break out of that age into a new one." *The Divided Mind of Modern Theology: Karl Barth and Rudolf Bultmann, 1908–1933* (Philadelphia: Westminster, 1967) 181.

146. At the present time, there are thirty countries around the world that recognize the legal and moral right of same-sex couples to marry. For modern civilization, this is as significant, ethically speaking, as the abolition of slavery and recognition of the right of women to vote.

though acceptance of Hays's view of homosexuality requires prior acceptance of his unsubstantiated view of biblical authority.[147] If homosexuality is intrinsically immoral, then let Hays argue the case philosophically as Paul presumed to do, without making an authoritarian appeal to an ancient text artificially exempted from ideological criticism.[148] Hence, from the perspective of the Lutheran model that Hays implicitly rejects, we have to say that his is not a responsible Protestant use of the Bible today.

This blunt assessment needs to be made without equivocation since Hays is no fringe figure on the far right of the theological spectrum. He has been a professor at both Yale and Duke Divinity Schools and is an ordained minister in the United Methodist Church. Yet the difference between Hays and a fundamentalist is merely a difference in degree, not a difference in kind. No matter how much he may avail himself of the tools of modern historical criticism, he uncritically assumes that a premodern view of scripture as a revealed text is constitutive of Protestantism without offering a compelling argument why other Protestants should take his view seriously. Furthermore, when he claims that the best argument on behalf of biblical authority is simply the love exemplified by Christians who live according to its precepts, I can only ask why it is that gay people have for the most part rejected Christianity on the grounds that it is intrinsically oppressive and hateful since they have been turned away by their own churches. Or what about the southern white slaveholders who defended their divine right to own slaves? Did they exhibit the love of God that is supposed to issue from Hays's view of biblical authority?[149] In a time when Protestantism

---

147. Sadly, too much Christian theology consists of rationalization of positions that cannot be defended when subjected to critical scrutiny according to strictly public criteria of argument.

148. Ogden rightly explains, "In the nature of the case, no authority, properly so-called, can be a sufficient authorization for the truth of the assertions derived from it or warranted by it. Unless the assertions made by the authority are themselves already authorized as true by some method other than an appeal to authority, no assertion derived from them or warranted by them can by that fact alone be an authorized assertion. This is not to deny, of course, that an assertion authorized by appeal to authority may very well be true. The point is simply that, if it is so, the fact that it is authorized by authority is not itself sufficient to make it so." "Authority of Scripture for Theology," in *On Theology*, 47.

149. See J. Albert Harrill, *Slaves in the New Testament: Literary, Social, and Moral Dimensions* (Minneapolis: Fortress, 2006), whose examination of the use of the Bible before and during the Civil War shows that Christians who defended slavery as divinely sanctioned had the strongest exegetical argument on their side whereas the abolitionists, by contrast, had an uphill battle when trying to argue their case by appealing to the Bible. See my review of Harrill's book in *Bulletin for the Institute of Reformed Theology* 7.1 (2007) 10–11.

finds itself in steady decline, we have to judge Hays's view of biblical authority—and, consequently, of homosexuality—as just another example of what Bultmann called a "false stumbling block" that prevents intellectually and morally serious people from hearing the gospel and thereby being confronted with the true stumbling block of Christian faith.[150] By means of his appeal to authority, Hays forecloses the possibility of ethics, understood as a rational inquiry, as being out of bounds for faithful Christians. Contrary to what Hays says, questions concerning the justice of slavery or the equality of women or moral sexual conduct are not exegetical (or "hermeneutical") questions. They are ethical questions, which can only be decided by the full critical use of human reason.[151]

Hays misleadingly frames the issue as the question whether or not we are willing to acknowledge the authority of the Bible. But the real issue is not whether the Bible has authority for Christians but, rather, wherein its authority properly consists.[152] For Bultmann, a theological exegesis has to be an existentialist interpretation of the Bible because "theological interpretation of the biblical writings is a way of understanding and explicating their meaning that is oriented by the same existential question to which they themselves intend to give answer."[153] This entails, however, that scripture's authority "is limited solely to its decisive authority in answering this existential question" of authentic human self-understanding and "does not extend to the various assumptions naturally made by those to whom we owe

---

150. "De-mythologizing . . . will eliminate a false stumbling block and bring into sharp focus the real stumbling block, the word of the cross." Bultmann, *Jesus Christ and Mythology*, 36.

151. On the opening page of his book, Harrill cites these words of John Henry Hopkins (1792–1868), who was an Episcopal bishop: "If it were a matter to be determined by personal sympathies, tastes, or feelings, I should be as ready as any man to condemn the institution of slavery, for all my prejudices of education, habit, and social position stand entirely opposed to it. But as a Christian . . . I am compelled to submit my weak and erring intellect to the authority of the Almighty. For then only can I be safe in my conclusions, when I know that they are in accordance with the will of Him, before whose tribunal I must render a strict account in the last great day." This bishop tacitly confessed that he knew slavery was wrong, but his misguided loyalty to the Bible prevented him from following what his reason and conscience told him.

152. Daniel Day Williams correctly said of Bultmann that "he has acutely shown that the issue today cannot be formulated simply as to whether or not the Bible is the supreme authority for Christian faith." *What Present-Day Theologians are Thinking*, rev. ed. (New York: Harper & Row, 1959) 65.

153. Ogden, "Theology and Biblical Interpretation," in *Doing Theology Today*, 36–51 at 48.

it when they formulated the preaching of the apostles or explicated the self-understanding arising from the apostolic preaching."[154] Ogden explains:

> But a still more important implication of Bultmann's view is that even the consequences that are drawn in the canon for belief and action depend for their authority entirely upon the self-understanding of faith. To the extent that they are indeed necessarily implied by the existential understanding of faith evoked by the New Testament proclamation, they too are normative for witness and theology. But insofar as they are due simply to assumptions made in the situations in and for which this self-understanding was explicated, they no longer have any binding authority.[155]

Clearly, then, the New Testament's assumptions about slavery, gender, or sexuality are not binding on contemporary Christians, and to insist that they are is to mistake what it is about scripture that *is* authoritative, for this confuses the good news of the gospel with the various mixed messages within the Bible, thereby placing a false stumbling block in the way of faith in the gospel itself.

Barth confessed that if he were forced to choose between historical criticism and the doctrine of inspiration, he would adopt the latter. I, however, would choose the former, since the historical-critical method takes the biblical texts seriously as fully human documents of antiquity and thus views them as fallible and subject to criticism. This is no way precludes a theological exegesis of them, as Bultmann has demonstrated. But it is only when we are in earnest about their historical and human character that the typically Protestant form of idolatry is forever precluded: biblicism.[156] Nothing, in my judgment, has done more harm to the cause of Protestant ministry and theology in the modern world than this identification of the words of the Bible with the words of God. Whereas Hays calls for a "scripture-shaped church," I call instead for a "gospel-shaped church." In my view, a scripture-shaped

---

154. Ogden, "Women and the Canon," in *Doing Theology Today*, 230–44 at 241.

155. Ogden, "Women and the Canon," in *Doing Theology Today*, 241–42.

156. Surprisingly, it is no longer only antimodernist theologians on the Right who reject historical criticism, since nowadays even some postmodernist theologians on the Left are denying its value for a theological exegesis. For an analysis of this novel circumstance, see Paul E. Capetz, "Theology and the Historical-Critical Study of the Bible," *Harvard Theological Review* 104 (2011) 459–88, published under the same title as Chapter 2 in this volume (pages 70-104). In the light of Luther's (and Calvin's) full embrace of humanistic scholarship, I do not see how those Protestants today who call for a theological exegesis that dispenses with the necessity of historical criticism—which, after all, is a continuation of the humanist legacy—can do so apart from severing their ties to the heritage of the Reformation's biblical scholarship.

church is precisely the problem, to which a gospel-shaped church is the antidote, for nothing less is at stake here than the integrity of the gospel or, as Paul puts it, "the truth of the gospel" (Gal 2:5). Accordingly, a gospel-shaped church understands that the gospel is the sole Word of God to which scripture bears witness and so does not view *Sachkritik* as a "forthright repudiation of biblical authority" (Hays). Rather, it is emboldened by the precedent of the first Protestant, who dared to say, "If our adversaries cite Scripture against Christ, I will cite Christ against Scripture."[157] Sadly, however, most Protestants who revere Luther's memory do not follow his example. Amid all the recent fanfare of celebrations around the globe commemorating the five-hundredth anniversary of the birth of Protestantism, we should not fail to note the irony and, indeed, to lament the tragedy that "the ways in which the Reformers were children of their time have triumphed over the ways in which they were pioneers in the use of the Bible."[158]

A USABLE PAST

The minister at summer camp whose insightful words made it possible for me not to reject the Bible entirely when confronted with the challenges posed by modern knowledge was an heir of Luther's heritage. If he hadn't shown me how to distinguish the authentic message of Christian faith from the Bible that bears witness to it, I am certain that I would not be a Christian today. Like many others, I would have found it necessary to liberate myself from a religious tradition that too often pits fidelity to the Bible against the results of natural and social science, honest historical research, and modern ethical reflection. Fortunately, however, that minister showed me another way to consider the Bible that does not exempt it from critical questioning. He thereby enabled me to hear the gospel that calls for my existential decision and commitment.

Luther's heritage is not the property of Lutherans alone. It belongs to all Protestants, who, by whatever route, trace their lineage back to his reformation. Not only is it the foundation of Calvin's Reformed tradition, but it also gave decisive impetus to the Methodist movement of John Wesley. Notwithstanding their modifications of what they inherited from Luther, both Calvin and Wesley held fast to the basic understanding of the gospel that Luther first articulated as a result of his intense wrestling with the texts

---

157. Bainton, "Bible in the Reformation," 20–21, citing Luther on Gal 3:14 in *Luthers Werke*, 40, 1, 458, lines 8–9.

158. Paul L. Lehmann, "The Reformers' Use of the Bible," *Theology Today* 3 (1946) 328–44 at 342.

of the New Testament. Calvin characterized Luther's doctrine of justification as the "main hinge" on which Christian religion turns.[159] And Wesley's "Aldersgate experience," when he felt his heart "strangely warmed," was occasioned by hearing Luther's "Preface" to Paul's Epistle to the Romans being read aloud: "I felt I did trust in Christ, Christ alone for salvation; and an assurance was given me that he had taken away *my* sins, even *mine*, and saved *me* from the law of sin and death."[160] This is the message of good news that Luther sought to recover for his contemporaries by clearing away the debris of medieval tradition that had been overlaid on top of the New Testament. Yet this is precisely the message I would have missed had it not been for the minister at summer camp who introduced me, albeit implicitly, to Luther's way of thinking about the relation of the Bible to the gospel.

John Cobb has posed the question: "Can Christ become good news again?"[161] In the light of our specific focus here, Cobb's question can be reformulated: How is it possible for people in our culture today to hear the Christian message to which the New Testament bears witness as a saving and healing message so long as it continues to be associated with an intellectually and morally problematic doctrine of biblical authority? The controversy in the churches over homosexuality is merely the most recent occasion for asking this question, but it is not the main theological reason for posing it. Albeit in another form, the question is as old as the Reformation itself. The five-hundredth anniversary of the Reformation is an opportunity for Protestants to take stock of ourselves as heirs of Luther. But if it is true, as I believe, that the anti-intellectual strain of American culture coupled with its historical amnesia have conspired to create a "Protestantism without Reformation," as Bonhoeffer so tellingly characterized it, how can we ever lead our churches in a responsible manner that brings our contemporary questions and concerns into serious dialogue with Luther, who first forged our distinctive Protestant tradition?

Not too long ago, I heard a self-styled "progressive" United Methodist minister who favors a change in her denomination's policy toward gay people dismiss the first Protestant as having no relevance to the church in our time: "Luther was a fundamentalist," she asserted with dogmatic self-assurance as if to wipe her hands clean of his legacy once and for all. Not

---

159. Calvin, *Institutes*, 3.11.1 (1:726).

160. John Wesley, "The Aldersgate Experience," in *John Wesley*, ed. Albert C. Outler (New York: Oxford University Press, 1964) 51–69 at 66, emphasis original.

161. John B. Cobb Jr., *Can Christ Become Good News Again?* (St. Louis: Chalice, 1991). In the spirit of Cobb's question, Paul Tillich likened the church to "a treasure chest which is often closed, which we must open again and again." *The Irrelevance and Relevance of the Christian Message*, ed. Durwood Foster (Cleveland: Pilgrim, 1996) 62.

only is her comment anachronistic since there were no fundamentalists in the late Middle Ages, but it is shockingly ignorant. How can anyone possibly liken Luther to a fundamentalist? And yet, sadly, over the course of almost thirty years as a professor in graduate theological education, I have often heard comments like this from students and ministers to the left of center on the theological spectrum who had no use for the historical study of the Christian tradition at all. This is as much a form of ahistorical anti-intellectualism as anything to be found on the theological right.[162] If we recall that Hays is also a United Methodist minister, though on the opposite side of the conflict concerning sexual ethics, a troubling picture begins to emerge. With a rhetorical sleight of hand, he couched his appeal to biblical authority as though he had the entire classical Christian tradition solidly behind him yet without even a mention of Luther's alternative way of thinking about biblical authority. Luther is no minor figure in the classical Christian tradition! When I think that Hays is a minister in the same denomination as that minister on the left who disdainfully dismissed Luther out of hand as a fundamentalist, I can only lament the low level to which theological discussion has sunk among mainline Protestants in this country. If this is how the lines are being drawn today, can the church ever move forward out of such an impasse? Is it any wonder that the United Methodist Church is about to split in two? I return to Pelikan's astute observation that "it is traditionalism that gives tradition such a bad name."[163] Whereas those on the right revere a romanticized image of the church's past that does not stand up to critical scrutiny ("traditionalism"), those on the left who seek to free themselves from the tyranny of that past by rejecting tradition altogether do not even bother to inquire whether it is more complex than it has been depicted by traditionalists and thus might harbor unsuspected resources that could be pressed into service on behalf of their revisionary concerns.[164]

162. I recall one student in particular who passionately objected that the seminary where I taught even offered a course on Luther's theology given his mean-spirited statements about the Jews and his controversial stance during the Peasants' War. It goes without saying that Luther's own statements and positions are as subject to the demand for *Sachkritik* as are those of anyone else in the Christian tradition.

163. Pelikan, *Vindication of Tradition*, 65. Tillich made the same point: "Tradition is good. Traditionalism is bad. The traditionalist attitude toward the tradition stops one from asking for the living meaning of its elements. They are taken for granted and not questioned any longer. But only if the tradition is transformed again and again can it be saved as a living reality. A deadly consequence of traditionalism is the avoidance of serious issues." *The Irrelevance and Relevance of the Christian Message*, 17–18. Tillich is right: traditionalism avoids serious issues.

164. In another context, I have argued that Luther's views on marriage and celibacy are also of great relevance to the current controversy in the churches regarding sexuality. See Paul E. Capetz, "Reformation Views on Celibacy: An Analogy for Gay

Without a doubt, the present essay would be dismissed as "liberal" by those on the right and rejected as "conservative" by those on the left. Herein lies the chief obstacle to the vitality of the mainline Protestant churches today. If we are to hope for a vibrant future, we will need to recover a usable past that transcends this dichotomy. Every theology worth its salt has to be *both* conservative *and* liberal in some significant sense if it aspires to assist the church in moving forward through the controversies of the present day. That is, it must simultaneously preserve the old insights and incorporate new insights. As the Lutheran theologian Paul Tillich put it, "there must always be two things in church life: the duality of tradition and reformation."[165] Calvin himself gave expression to exactly this understanding of the theological task when he said of himself and his comrades in the Reformation, "Our constant endeavor, day and night, is *not just* to transmit the tradition faithfully, *but also* to put it in the form we think will prove best."[166] A faithful handing on of the inherited Christian tradition involves the willingness to revise it.

My aspiration here has been to identify a usable past that is able to transcend this false dichotomy of traditionalists on the right and despisers of tradition on the left by recovering what I believe is the authentic Protestant tradition concerning the Bible and the gospel. If we fail in this endeavor, our churches will become increasingly unable to proclaim the gospel with both existential power and intellectual conviction. Hence, with Luther, I too must say, "Here I stand."

Protestants Today," in *Embrace of Eros: Bodies, Desires, and Sexuality in Christianity*, ed. Margaret D. Kamitsuka (Minneapolis: Fortress, 2010) 115–31, 318–21.

165. Tillich, *Irrelevance and Relevance of the Christian Message*, 49.

166. Calvin, *Defensio contra Pighium*, in *Calvini opera* (Braunschweig: Schwetschke, 1863–1900) 6:250, cited and translated by B. A. Gerrish, "Continuity and Change: Friedrich Schleiermacher on the Task of Theology," in *Tradition and the Modern World: Reformed Theology in the Nineteenth Century*, The Andrew C. Zenos Memorial Lectures 1977 (Chicago: University of Chicago Press, 1978) 13–48 at 13, emphasis added.

2

Theology and the Historical-Critical Study of the Bible[1]

ONE SALIENT CHARACTERISTIC OF our current situation is the emergence of a growing consensus among theologians and biblical scholars alike that the time has come to "dethrone" historical criticism as the reigning paradigm of scriptural exegesis for the sake of recovering a theological interpretation of the Bible on behalf of the church.[2] To illustrate this new development, I have chosen to focus on the arguments of three prominent biblical scholars, each of whom has made a sustained case about the negative effects of historical criticism upon theological exegesis: They are Brevard S. Childs, Christopher R. Seitz, and Dale B. Martin. All three scholars have close ties to Yale and, not surprisingly, they bear a sort of family resemblance to one another inasmuch as their work partakes of theological themes and concerns that have been prominent at that school in recent decades. Notwithstanding their antagonistic posture toward historical criticism, all three are gifted practitioners of the very method whose dominance they seek to overturn. Since I am not a biblical scholar, I must enter into discussion with them as a theologian who is equally concerned about the relations between biblical studies and theology. At the outset, however, it is necessary to clarify that my own theological orientation prevents me from embracing their call to depose historical criticism. Their initial premise that historical criticism is

1. This essay was first delivered as a lecture to the Hebrew Bible Graduate Research Workshop of the Department of Near Eastern Languages and Civilizations at Harvard University on December 7, 2009.

2. Dale B. Martin, *Pedagogy of the Bible: An Analysis and Proposal* (Louisville: Westminster John Knox, 2008) 3.

somehow inimical to a theological treatment of the Bible strikes me as false and misleading, given that I am a liberal Protestant for whom historical-critical interpretation of both the biblical and the postbiblical tradition is constitutive of theology's proper task. Contrary to the impression given by their explicit formulations, it appears that the real target of their polemics is not historical scholarship per se but, rather, the normative uses to which it is put in theologies informed by it.

Since historical criticism has been so closely tied to liberal Protestantism, a critique of the former has usually been accompanied by a critique of the latter, and this is true today as well. For two centuries theologically conservative scholars have assaulted the liberal approach to both theology and the Bible. What is unprecedented about the contemporary scene is that it is now also under siege by those on the theological left. Most often these radical, nonliberal theologians base their critiques of liberal theology on explicitly postmodernist arguments. As a result, the critique of the left is more distinctly philosophical, calling into question the modernist assumptions—which postmodern scholars believe to be outdated—behind liberal theology and its ally, historical criticism. Ironically, those who oppose liberal Protestantism on conservative theological grounds are more than happy to avail themselves of the rhetoric, if not the actual substance, of these same postmodern theories. Consequently, this novel circumstance demands that whoever would seek to defend a liberal Protestant theology today must be prepared to do battle on two fronts.[3] To the extent that the

---

3. It would perhaps be more accurate to describe my position as "revisionist" (utilizing the typology of David Tracy) so as to acknowledge that it involves a self-critical retrieval of the nineteenth-century tradition and not a simple repristination of it: "[T]he revisionist theologian is committed to continuing the critical task of the classical liberals and modernists in a genuinely post-liberal situation . . . The revisionist Christian theologian joins his secular colleague in refusing to allow the fact of his own existential disenchantment with the reifying and oppressive results of Enlightenment disenchantment to become the occasion for a return to mystification, Christian or otherwise. Rather he believes that only a radical continuation of critical theory, symbolic reinterpretation, and responsible social and personal *praxis* can provide the hope for a fundamental revision of both the modern and the traditional Christian self-understandings." Tracy, *Blessed Rage for Order: The New Pluralism in Theology* (New York: Seabury, 1975) 32–33. Keeping Tracy's helpful clarification in mind, I nonetheless designate my own position as liberal for the purpose of locating it squarely in the lineage of Schleiermacher through Troeltsch as well as of those twentieth-century neo-orthodox theologians (Bultmann, Tillich, and the Niebuhrs) who maintained significant continuity with their nineteenth-century predecessors. Peter C. Hodgson calls for "*a revisionary, postmodern liberal theology* as opposed to a postliberal, countermodern theology" and adds, "I happen to believe that the term 'liberal' is wonderfully appropriate." Hodgson, "Liberal Theology and Transformative Pedagogy," in *The Future of Liberal Theology*, ed. Mark D. Chapman (Burlington, VT: Ashgate, 2002) 99–128 at 100, emphasis original.

common denominator uniting both the right and the left is their rejection of modernity and of liberal Protestantism for having hitched its wagon to "the Enlightenment project"[4]—as it is disdainfully called—I confess to being more at home on the modern than on the postmodern side of that nebulous boundary that is the site of the current debates. Although the constraints of a single essay do not permit me to argue fully for a liberal Protestant theology—including its insistence upon the necessity of historical criticism—I do argue from this position as I take up the discrete challenges posed by these three scholars.

My discussion will proceed in three stages: First, I attempt to present the viewpoints of these three scholars as they themselves understand them; second, I engage in a critical analysis of their arguments; and, third, I conclude with a brief word in defense of an understanding of theology for which historical-critical study is essential.

WHAT IS SO BAD ABOUT HISTORICAL CRITICISM?

Childs spent his brilliant career attempting to chart a new course for biblical studies after the collapse of the "Biblical Theology Movement" in the 1960s—a course that would redeem that movement's aspiration to bridge the gap between academic scholarship and the church's preaching. In his diagnosis of the movement's demise, Childs pinpointed "the conviction that revelation was mediated through history" as the main source of the trouble.[5] In opposition to this focus on the events lying behind the biblical text, Childs proposed a return to the canon as "the proper context for interpreting the

---

4. Jon D. Levenson, *The Hebrew Bible, the Old Testament, and Historical Criticism: Jews and Christians in Biblical Studies* (Louisville: Westminster John Knox, 1993) 118. Levenson argues a similar case against liberal Protestantism and historical criticism from an Orthodox Jewish perspective. It was my original intention to include a discussion of Levenson's arguments, but upon further reflection I judged that they merit a more thorough response than can be given here on account of his justified criticisms of anti-Judaism in modern Protestant biblical scholarship. I hope at some point to take up the important issues he raises.

5. Brevard S. Childs, *Biblical Theology in Crisis* (Philadelphia: Westminster, 1970) 39. One of the movement's leading figures, G. Ernest Wright, insisted upon "history as the arena of God's activity" and thus defined biblical theology as "first and foremost a theology of recital" of those historical events (e.g., the exodus) wherein faith confesses to discern "the redemptive handiwork of God." Wright, *God Who Acts: Biblical Theology as Recital*, Studies in Biblical Theology 1/8 (London: SCM, 1952) 38. For Wright, as for his teacher William Foxwell Albright, the study of archaeology was crucial in authenticating the historicity of the events to which the Bible bears witness.

Bible theologically."[6] Childs criticized the Biblical Theology Movement for "its failure to take the Biblical text seriously in its canonical form."[7] Like his mentor Karl Barth, Childs aspired to retrieve the kind of theological exegesis exemplified by Luther and Calvin without, however, rejecting the valid insights and discoveries of historical criticism.[8] But unlike other biblical theologians, Childs did not want to base a theological exegesis directly upon the results of historical study. In his view, this endeavor is misguided and explains why "[t]he field of biblical studies for the last two hundred years has been strewn with countless attempts to recover serious theological exegesis which have not succeeded."[9] Historical criticism, by disregarding scripture's canonical context and focusing upon ever smaller units of study, has had "corrosive effects" upon theological exegesis.[10]

Childs sought to reverse the legacy of Semler, who called for an investigation of the canon unfettered by doctrinal constraints.[11] Semler "set out to destroy the dogmatic, apologetic concept of the canon"[12] and "succeeded in seriously damaging the central pillar on which Protestant orthodoxy ... had sought to construct its house."[13] For Semler, the formation of the canon was a purely historical affair that should not predetermine how modern exegetes interpret the literature found within it. Semler was thus intent on liberating biblical interpretation from the church's creedal and confessional traditions, and in this respect he saw himself as a faithful follower of Luther. For Childs, by contrast, the canon is an eminently theological issue: "at stake in recovering a truly theological understanding of Scripture" is the demand that biblical scholars "put aside the long-standing prejudice of the Enlightenment, whose goal was to free the study of the Bible from the so-called

---

6. Childs, *Biblical Theology in Crisis*, 97.

7. Childs, *Biblical Theology in Crisis*, 102.

8. Childs judged that "Barth remained invulnerable to the weaknesses that beset the Biblical Theology Movement." *Biblical Theology in Crisis*, 110.

9. Childs, "Toward Recovering Theological Exegesis," *Pro Ecclesia* 4 (1997) 16–26 at 18.

10. Childs, "Toward Recovering Theological Exegesis," 18.

11. Johann Salomo Semler, *Abhandlung von freier Untersuchung des Canons*, 4 vols. (Halle: Hemmerde, 1771–1776). A modernized, critical edition of Semler's programmatic essay introducing this multivolume work was prepared by Heinz Scheible and appeared in the series Texte zur Kirchen- und Theologiegeschichte 5 (Gütersloh: Gütersloher/Mohn, 1967).

12. Childs, *The New Testament as Canon: An Introduction* (Philadelphia: Fortress, 1984) 6.

13. Childs, *Introduction to the Old Testament as Scripture* (Philadelphia: Fortress, 1979) 35.

heavy hand of dogma."[14] This disagreement between Semler and Childs about the canon's status reflects a profound difference of opinion as to the meaning of the Reformation heritage in the modern world.

Following Barth, Childs charged that "Protestant liberalism transformed the theocentric focus of Scripture into anthropology."[15] Interpreters now treated the Bible as a human document and no longer as a divinely revealed or inspired text; as such, it was to be studied with the same methods used to interpret any other document from the history of religion. Yet the price to be paid for anchoring the Bible so firmly in antiquity was the loss of relevant meaning in it for today. For this reason, Childs insisted, "Our modern critical understanding of the task of exegesis . . . needs major overhauling."[16] His proposal that the canon serve as the sole proper context for theological exegesis is intended not only "as a rejection of the method that would imprison the Bible within a context of the historical past" but also as a restoration of the doctrine of inspiration: "the claim for the inspiration of Scripture is the claim for the uniqueness of the canonical context of the church through which the Holy Spirit works."[17]

Since the death of Childs, his program continues to be developed by Seitz, who also sets clear limits to the role of historical criticism in relation to theological exegesis. He grants at least this much: "Historical work at the formal, literary level is indispensable, or we will introduce anachronisms and false questions the text never wished to entertain." But then he draws a firm line not to be crossed: "In my view, historical criticism plays no positive theological role whatsoever. Its only proper role is negative . . . It shows how the Bible is not like other books."[18] Seitz questions the presumption of "neutrality" or "objectivity" on the part of modern historians: "It has never been entirely clear what it might mean to talk about the Bible neutrally."[19] Although this sounds like a postmodern critique of a positivist ideal of pure objectivity in exegesis, Seitz quickly dispels this impression by adding that there can be no "objective or neutral reader" of the Bible because the "literature's own claims to privileged speech forbid it."[20] Whereas scholars

---

14. Childs, "Toward Recovering Theological Exegesis," 16.

15. Childs, "Toward Recovering Theological Exegesis," 17.

16. Childs, "Toward Recovering Theological Exegesis," 25.

17. Childs, *Biblical Theology in Crisis*, 99–100, 104. Childs also faulted the Biblical Theology Movement for "its total failure to come to grips with the inspiration of Scripture." *Biblical Theology in Crisis*, 103.

18. Christopher R. Seitz, *Word without End: The Old Testament as Abiding Theological Witness* (Waco, TX: Baylor University Press, 2004) 14, 97.

19. Seitz, *Word without End*, 63.

20. Seitz, *Word without End*, 73.

such as Gerhard von Rad sought to delineate how the biblical writers posed and answered their own theological questions, "we should reverse the order of concern." "Instead of asking how Israel thought about itself and God," we should be asking another question altogether: "How does the God we confess raised Jesus from the dead think about Israel and the world?" Seitz states categorically, "The Old Testament does not present itself as Israel's reflection on God ... The Old Testament presents itself from the very beginning from the perspective of God."[21]

In Seitz's diagnosis, the fundamental problem afflicting biblical theology today is "not the failure of theologians/dogmaticians to talk to biblical scholars, and the reverse. This is but a symptom of a form of specialization whose more damaging strain persists at the level of biblical studies itself, namely, the relative isolation of Old Testament from New Testament interpretation."[22] As an antidote, Seitz "calls for a reattachment of the Old Testament to the New Testament ... and a return to older forms of typological reading, now taken up, post historical criticism."[23] This means that Christians should not hesitate to "read the Old Testament christologically."[24] For Seitz, at stake is not only the integrity of the Christian Bible as comprising both an Old and a New Testament but also the complementarity existing between scripture and tradition. Prior to modernity, the church had always interpreted scripture according to the orthodox "rule of faith" (*regula fidei*).[25] This by no means implies that an alien set of categories had been imposed upon scripture from without since, as Seitz tells us, the church's doctrine as formulated in its creeds is essentially nothing but exegesis of the Bible.[26] Not only is the Old Testament to be interpreted in light of the New and vice versa, but also scripture and tradition are not to be torn asunder after the fashion of ancient heretics and modern historical critics.

Martin is concerned about how the Bible is being taught in theological education and sets out to provide a "critical assessment of the value

21. Seitz, *Word without End*, 8.

22. Seitz, *Word without End*, 104.

23. Seitz, *Word without End*, 8. Here Seitz joins forces with George A. Lindbeck, "The Story-Shaped Church: Critical Exegesis and Theological Interpretation," in *Scriptural Authority and Narrative Interpretation*, ed. Garrett Green (Philadelphia: Fortress, 1987) 161–78.

24. Seitz, *Word without End*, 21.

25. Seitz, *Word without End*, 17.

26. Seitz, *Word without End*, 9. Seitz attributes this notion of doctrine-as-exegesis to David S. Yeago, "The New Testament and Nicene Dogma: A Contribution to the Recovery of Theological Exegesis," *Pro Ecclesia* 3 (1994) 152–64. Childs also makes reference to this article in highly laudatory terms. "Toward Recovering Theological Exegesis," 16.

of historical criticism *from the inside*," as he puts it. His overarching aim is to put an end to "the captivity of Scripture to modernity and historical criticism."[27] Nonetheless, he explains that he is not advocating that we jettison the historical approach altogether but rather "that we dethrone it as the only or foundational method taught, and that we supplement it with other methods, approaches, and theories."[28]

> As a historical critic, I am insisting that we must put aside the modern hegemony of historical criticism; that historical criticism cannot provide the Christian meaning of the text; that we do ourselves, our churches, and our students a disservice by allowing historical criticism the domination it currently enjoys in theological education.[29]

Martin believes that students preparing for the ministry "are not being taught how to think critically . . . about what it is they are doing, and should do, when they interpret texts."[30] By this, he means the lack of explicit training in interpretation theory, recognizing that "learning about theory of interpretation is not the same as learning to interpret," the latter of which goes on all the time in theological education as elsewhere.[31]

Martin is the most philosophically oriented of these three scholars, and he takes his cues from postmodern theorists who contest the assumption underlying historical criticism that "there is 'meaning' inherent in the text needing merely proper excavation to be brought to light."[32] He is convinced that emphasizing "the difference between exegesis and eisegesis currently does more harm than good," since it "reinforces a notion about texts and meaning that is false in itself," namely, that "texts simply have meaning as a property within themselves" or that "texts may constrain interpretations of themselves."[33] For instance, he wants readers to become aware of the metaphors they use to talk about the process of textual interpretation. One such metaphor, rejected by Martin, "treats the text as if it were another human agent who speaks."[34] This metaphor implies passivity on the part of the interpreter, since what is required of us is that we "listen as carefully

---

27. Martin, *Pedagogy of the Bible*, ix, 98, emphasis original.
28. Martin, *Pedagogy of the Bible*, 3.
29. Martin, *Pedagogy of the Bible*, 109.
30. Martin, *Pedagogy of the Bible*, 18.
31. Martin, *Pedagogy of the Bible*, 18.
32. Martin, *Pedagogy of the Bible*, 7–8.
33. Martin, *Pedagogy of the Bible*, 29–30.
34. Martin, *Pedagogy of the Bible*, 29–30.

and objectively as possible, and try to avoid distorting the utterance."[35] But this metaphor is highly misleading for the simple reason that "texts are not agents who speak. No text has ever spoken."[36] We are the agents in the act of interpretation, exercising agency whenever we persuade someone else to adopt our reading of a text. Hence, Martin likes to say, "Texts don't mean; people mean with texts."[37] The ethical impulse in Martin's proposal comes to expression when he insists that "[h]uman beings must take responsibility for their interpretations."[38]

Martin correctly observes that a text "means different things when approached from different perspectives."[39] So there is no reason in principle to deny the existence of multiple "legitimate readings" of texts "alongside the historical critical reading."[40] Specifically, Martin wishes to rehabilitate premodern ways of reading the Bible. When students learn only historical-critical methods, they come to their courses in church history or theology and wonder why premodern exegetes were so stupid or weird.[41] In defense of premodern exegesis, Martin asks, "Have Christians throughout the centuries been wrong to read Ps 22 as speaking about the crucifixion of Christ?"[42] Though Martin rejects the idea that the meaning of a text is what its author intended, he points out that for premodern Christians authorial intention referred not primarily to the text's human author but to its divine author.

> A medieval theologian would say that even if the human author of the psalm did not foresee the fulfillment of his words in the crucifixion, that need not prohibit us from taking the psalm as a prophecy of the crucifixion. The medieval theologian may well point out . . . that, theologically speaking, the author of Scripture is ultimately not that ancient human author, but God. And God surely intended the text to contain more meaning than the limited original human author could have imagined.[43]

---

35. Martin, *Pedagogy of the Bible*, 29–30.
36. Martin, *Pedagogy of the Bible*, 29–30.
37. Martin, *Pedagogy of the Bible*, 31.
38. Martin, *Pedagogy of the Bible*, 38.
39. Martin, *Pedagogy of the Bible*, 12.
40. Martin, *Pedagogy of the Bible*, 33.
41. Martin, *Pedagogy of the Bible*, 16; this was an observation made by one of the professors interviewed by Martin in preparation for the writing of his book.
42. Martin, *Pedagogy of the Bible*, 39.
43. Martin, *Pedagogy of the Bible*, 39.

Martin says that his goal is "not to argue for divine intention as providing the meaning of the scriptural text"[44] but only to point out that long before the emergence of modern critical methods Christians have been making sense of the Bible in multiple ways and, therefore, it is wrong to insist upon historical criticism as a condition of correct exegesis. Martin thus affirms that "premodern scriptural interpretation was anything but arbitrary . . . and that it is something from which we 'postmodern' Christians may learn quite a lot."[45] Like Childs, Martin agrees with Hans W. Frei, who argued that it has been a mistake for modern scholars to equate the literal sense (*sensus literalis*) of the Bible with its historical sense.[46]

> For premodern theologians, the literal sense of Scripture referred to the divine intention, not merely the human intention . . . And of course, since historical criticism can say nothing about God's intentions for the meaning of Scripture, historical criticism is not necessary from a theological point of view for the Christian reading of the Bible.[47]

Moreover, those Christians who insist upon the necessity of historical criticism are guilty of "reading" premodern Christians out of the church: "To insist that historical criticism is necessary for the Christian reading of Scripture is to say that no Christian before the modern period read Scripture Christianly."[48] Martin then goes on to pose this challenge to any who might wish to argue contrariwise:

> If Christians today insist that historical criticism is necessary for interpreting Scripture, they should provide just such a compelling theological rationale for that claim. In my opinion, no such compelling theological argument has been forthcoming, and I doubt one is possible.[49]

---

44. Martin, *Pedagogy of the Bible*, 40.

45. Martin, *Pedagogy of the Bible*, 47.

46. Martin, *Pedagogy of the Bible*, 116n1; the reference is to Hans W. Frei, *The Eclipse of Biblical Narrative: A Study in Eighteenth and Nineteenth Century Hermeneutics* (New Haven: Yale University Press, 1974). Childs invokes Frei's work as "demolishing the familiar thesis that the Reformers and the nineteenth-century critics shared a similar view regarding the literal sense of the text." Childs, "The *Sensus Literalis* of Scripture: An Ancient and Modern Problem," in *Beiträge zur alttestamentlichen Theologie: Festschrift für Walther Zimmerli zum 70. Geburtstag*, ed. Herbert Donner et al. (Göttingen: Vandenhoeck & Ruprecht, 1977) 80–93 at 88; see also Seitz, *Word without End*, 97–98.

47. Martin, *Pedagogy of the Bible*, 43.

48. Martin, *Pedagogy of the Bible*, 43.

49. Martin, *Pedagogy of the Bible*, 44.

The "main problem" today is "a lack of ability to think theologically—that is, the ability to put together a theological argument, case, or rationale."[50] And since this ability is essential if we are to make "appropriate Christian use of Scripture," its lack must be remedied.[51]

HISTORY AND THEOLOGY, OR: WHAT IS A THEOLOGICAL EXEGESIS?

These three scholars are united in their belief that historical criticism has had a deleterious effect upon the church's ability to reflect theologically upon its scriptures. For this reason, they call for a theological exegesis or biblical theology that makes only minimal use of historical criticism (Childs and Seitz) or possibly even none at all (Martin). Since they are opposed to a theological treatment of the Bible for which the historical interpretation of biblical religion and its development is constitutive, it behooves us to ask some questions about their understandings of historical criticism as well as to introduce certain conceptual distinctions into the discussion so as to clarify what they are really saying and not saying.

Seitz is right to insist that the problem today is not the lack of conversation between biblical scholars and theologians, but that is where my agreement with him ends. Whereas he pleads for reuniting Old and New Testaments in a single biblical theology by means of typology, I seek clarity on the relation between history and theology. Childs objected to the view famously put forward by Krister Stendahl that "the descriptive task of Biblical theology should be radically separated from the constructive task of the theologian."[52] With Childs, I agree that biblical theology should not be limited to the descriptive, historical task since "[t]here is little hope of the Biblical and theological disciplines interacting in a beneficial way unless Biblical scholars are working constructively in theology."[53] Childs, Seitz, and Martin are not only historians but also theologians, and appropriately so. Therefore, the issue is not that of relating two separate disciplines within a common curriculum but of properly distinguishing between two logically distinct types of questions and asking about their possible relations, regardless of whether such questions are posed by biblical scholars or theologians.

50. Martin, *Pedagogy of the Bible*, 28.
51. Martin, *Pedagogy of the Bible*, 28.
52. Childs, *Biblical Theology in Crisis*, 79; see Krister Stendahl, "Biblical Theology, Contemporary," in *The Interpreter's Dictionary of the Bible*, 4 vols., ed. George Arthur Buttrick (Nashville: Abingdon, 1962) 1:418–32.
53. Childs, *Biblical Theology in Crisis*, 93.

I understand a historical question about a biblical text to be descriptive and explanatory in nature: What is being said and why? This includes asking whether events actually occurred in the way reported by the text. By contrast, a theological question is hermeneutical and normative in nature: How is the claim made by the text to be understood, and is it true? This includes asking about its possible contemporary application. It is easy to suspect that this logical distinction between types of questions has been illicitly collapsed by these three scholars in their broadsides against historical criticism. Before any substantive conversation about the value of historical criticism can proceed, they owe it to their readers to clarify how they understand these questions and their relations to one another.

Let us begin with the issue of a strictly historical interpretation of the Bible. I do not think anyone is actually denying that there is a "historical sense" (*sensus historicus*) of the biblical text and that historical-critical method is our best available means of discerning it—although I would like to be reassured of this. Nevertheless, all three scholars charge historical critics with a lack of self-criticism regarding their presuppositions. Is this a criticism of historical critics as historians or as theologians? Martin comes close to questioning the possibility of historical knowledge altogether when he decries the failure of historical criticism to secure consensus as to what the historical sense of the text is. Perhaps he is merely pointing out that we can never attain final certainty about the past because our evidence is often incomplete, and that is why equally reputable scholars arrive at different conclusions given the sparse evidence at our disposal. Alternatively, maybe he is saying that historical knowledge deals in matters of probability, and thus our best historical judgments will always be subject to revision. If this is all Martin is saying, there can be no objection and, indeed, these same points were made long ago by Ernst Troeltsch.[54] Or is Martin making a stronger claim that historians are deceived in pursuing historical knowledge by means of this method? In one passage he writes, "[M]ost interpreters assume (if they do not claim outright) that the proper method for ascertaining 'what the text *meant*' is historical criticism."[55] Is it not? If not, why not? And

---

54. Ernst Troeltsch clarified that "in the realm of history there are only judgments of probability." "Historical and Dogmatic Method in Theology," in *Religion in History*, trans. James Luther Adams and Walter F. Bense (Minneapolis: Fortress, 1991) 11–32 at 13.

55. Dale B. Martin, *Sex and the Single Savior* (Louisville: Westminster John Knox, 2006) 126, emphasis original. Martin says, "The great bogeyman of historiography . . . is anachronism" (*Pedagogy of the Bible*, 7). Shouldn't historians worry about anachronism? Elsewhere, Martin qualifies this taunt by admitting that even he tries to avoid anachronism when operating as a historical critic (*Sex and the Single Savior*, 162). Then if this is so, why mock the effort of conscientious historians to spot their own culturally

what better method is there for ascertaining the answer to historical questions? Would Martin say to Helmut Koester that his attempt to reconstruct the early history of Christianity by strict and conscientious application of historical-critical method is based upon a misguided premise? If so, then Martin should explain to Koester what methods he should have employed when writing his *Introduction to the New Testament*.[56]

But this does not appear to be Martin's driving concern since his remarks to this effect always appear in the context of polemics with other biblical scholars who move directly from the historical meaning to its contemporary application. This becomes clear in his argument with Richard B. Hays over the use of scripture in the current debate on the morality of homosexuality. Martin points to "the centrality [Hays] ascribes to historical criticism in his method," while noting that "Hays wants to derive our ethics from a rather passive 'listening' to the text."[57] Martin correctly identifies that for Hays whatever the Bible says about homosexuality as this can be ascertained through historical criticism is assumed to be binding on Christians today. Martin not only doubts that Hays has accurately understood the historical sense of the relevant texts but also suspects that Hays has allowed his own heterosexist bias to affect what he finds in the texts.[58] While fully sharing Martin's insistence upon the need for ideology critique in biblical studies, I still have to ask if his is really a critique of historical-critical method as our best means for understanding the past or merely a critique of the ideological blinders with which certain historical critics

conditioned biases when studying the past by calling concern for anachronism a "bogeyman"? Martin goes on to deny that "the historical-critical method is objective or non-biased" and that it can "provide a reliable foundation even for knowledge of the past." As with other postmodernists, Martin's use of terms such as "objective" and "foundation" is so heavily freighted with negative connotations that it is difficult to know precisely what is being said. Does Martin assume that the only conceivable alternative to the position he represents is a naïve defense of pure objectivity in historical interpretation coupled with absolute certainty regarding our epistemological foundations? I agree with Richard J. Bernstein that such a dichotomy is "misleading." *Beyond Objectivism and Relativism: Science, Hermeneutics, and Praxis* (Philadelphia: University of Pennsylvania Press, 1983) 19. Bernstein points out the irony that the obsessive polemic against "objectivism" and "foundationalism" is "parasitic" upon the very Cartesianism it seeks to overcome. Though desiring to be fair to Martin, I find it difficult to distinguish rhetoric from substance in his writings.

56. Helmut Koester, *Introduction to the New Testament*, 2 vols., 2nd ed. (New York: de Gruyter, 2000). Wayne A. Meeks has said, "Koester has brilliantly demonstrated here that the historical-critical approach has been neither superseded nor completed." Review of Helmut Koester, *Einführung in das Neue Testament*, *Journal of Biblical Literature* 101 (1982) 445–48 at 447.

57. Martin, *Sex and the Single Savior*, 30.

58. Martin, *Sex and the Single Savior*, 60–61.

operate. If Martin is only pointing out that no method—whether historical or scientific—can preclude its ideological misuse, then I fully agree with him. But this is not the same as saying that there is something amiss with historical-critical method per se. Is it not, rather, the case that the problem with Hays's approach stems from his prior theological commitment to a notion of biblical authority that stands in significant tension with, if not outright contradiction to, a consistently historical interpretation of the Bible as a human document subject to all the possibilities of ideological distortion we detect in other ancient texts?[59] But if this is so, then the crucial issue to be debated is the nature of theology and ethics as normative inquiries (their sources, norms, and methods), not any modernist assumptions Hays brings to the task of exegesis.[60] Strictly philosophical considerations about what it means to interpret a text would not be sufficient to dissuade Hays from his normative conclusions about the morality of homosexuality drawn directly from what he takes, rightly or wrongly, to be the historical sense of the Bible.

For the sake of clarity, therefore, Martin should explain whether his critique of historical criticism is restricted to normative uses of the Bible that axiomatically assume the historical sense to be binding on today's church, or if it is also directed at disciplined attempts to understand the historical sense of any ancient religious text, whether it be Paul's Letter to

---

59. Richard B. Hays clearly states his guiding premise regarding biblical authority when discussing Paul's statements in Romans 1: "To take the New Testament as authoritative . . . is to accept this portrayal [of homosexuality] as 'revealed reality,' an authoritative disclosure of the truth about the human condition. Understood in this way, the text requires a normative evaluation of homosexual practice as a distortion of God's order for creation." Hays then goes on to ask, "Do we grant the normative force of Paul's analysis?" Given his axiomatic assumption that Paul speaks for God in this matter, Hays has thus ruled out the possibility of authentic ethical debate on the morality of same-sex relations that might lead us to answer his question with a "No"! *The Moral Vision of the New Testament: Community, Cross, New Creation; A Contemporary Introduction to New Testament Ethics* (San Francisco: HarperSanFrancisco, 1996) 396–97.

60. Martin concludes, "Hays is in the end very much a modernist . . . Hays's approach fully assumes not only the validity but even the necessity of historical-critical methods." *Sex and the Single Savior*, 30. This statement is only half true: Hays is a modernist insofar as he affirms the indispensability of historical-critical method in biblical exegesis, but he is definitely not a modernist insofar as his use of historical criticism is a purely technical one that refuses to draw out the full implications of a consistently historical interpretation of religion—including the Bible as a human product of the history of religion. Troeltsch clearly understood the difference between a genuine historicism and a half-hearted use of historical method that in the end takes refuge in a supernatural premise that "claims an authority that is dogmatic rather than historical, intrinsic rather than based on comparison, immutable rather than sharing the conditions of historical existence . . . The miraculous is truly decisive." Troeltsch, "Historical and Dogmatic Method in Theology," 22.

the Romans or the Mithras Liturgy.⁶¹ To be sure, calls for historians to be self-critical are always timely. Historiography, like every other humanistic discipline, operates with presuppositions that are philosophical in nature. The best historians are the ones who not only apply their craft according to the proper methods but also can step back from their historical work to reflect upon its assumptions for the sake of a better historical scholarship. Positivistic historians who fancy they operate without bringing their subjectivity to bear on matters of historical interpretation are clearly deluded, since there is no pure objectivity in work of this kind.⁶² But Martin is not the first to point this out. In my judgment, no one has done a better job of clarifying what is involved here than Rudolf Bultmann did in his essay "Is Exegesis without Presuppositions Possible?"⁶³ So the issue is not whether historians work with philosophical presuppositions but whether they are working with the right ones. How do we know which presuppositions are the right ones? That is where hermeneutics—or theory of interpretation—comes into play. It is one of the merits of Martin's scholarship that he takes this point seriously, even if I cannot follow him in much of what he says.

When Seitz talks about the inevitable presuppositions of exegesis, the way he frames the question implies that the only valid presuppositions are those of orthodox Christian faith: "[L]et there be no delusion about the *willful* decisions of all interpreters and the prior commitments they bring to the reading process."⁶⁴ The statement would not cause alarm were it not for the characterization of interpretive decisions as "willful." This is reminiscent of the language used by the church fathers to disparage heretics! Would it be unfair to interpret Seitz in this light? Recall that his reason why there can be no neutral reader is not that of Bultmann for whom all readers, simply by

---

61. On the historical and theological significance of the Mithras Liturgy, see Hans Dieter Betz, *Gottesbegegnung und Menschwerdung: Zur religionsgeschichtlichen und theologischen Bedeutung der Mithrasliturgie*, Hans-Lietzmann-Vorlesungen 6 (Berlin: de Gruyter, 2001). Betz does not collapse the distinction between historical interpretation and theological assessment.

62. Peter Machinist correctly explains that "historians, try as they might, can never really remove themselves from the history they record. The past is never simply 'out there'; it is always the past as perceived, as encountered, by someone. This does not mean, however, that there are no boundaries or standards that govern our investigation of the past, for the past is also not merely the (re)creation of its recorder; it is an external reality, which demands attention and care in the way it is perceived, even if the process of perception cannot remain neutral." "The Voice of the Historian in the Ancient Near Eastern and Mediterranean World," *Interpretation* 57 (2003) 117–37 at 117–18.

63. Rudolf Bultmann, "Is Exegesis without Presuppositions Possible?" in *New Testament and Mythology and Other Basic Writings*, ed. and trans. Schubert M. Ogden (Philadelphia: Fortress, 1984) 145–53.

64. Seitz, *Word without End*, 81, emphasis added.

virtue of their humanity, have to ask and answer the existential questions of what it means to be human and to be so authentically. Seitz tells us that the reader stands before a text claiming for itself to be "privileged speech" since it speaks not from a human standpoint but "from the perspective of God."[65] If this is indeed the case, then there can be only two responses: obedience or disobedience. After reading this passage, I began to appreciate better Martin's polemic against "the myth of textual agency."[66] Seitz has hypostasized the biblical text so that it is an agent who speaks with the authority of God. But if this is the only adequate presupposition with which to approach the text for what it truly is, why do nontheological biblical scholars fail to recognize it? Recall as well that for Seitz the legitimate role of historical criticism lies in showing "how the Bible is not like other books."[67] Yet historical criticism has shown precisely the opposite by identifying the many parallels to other Near Eastern and Hellenistic religions and their literatures found within the Bible. Hence, one can ask whether Seitz even grants that a historian can truly understand the Bible apart from Seitz's own theological commitments.

Of these three scholars, Childs is the least ambiguous when it comes to the legitimacy of a purely historical reading of the text on the basis of historical-critical method. Not only does Childs affirm that "historical criticism is an indispensable teacher," but he also admits:

> It is still possible for someone who does not share the theological concerns of the canonical literature to describe the theological struggle of a biblical text in bearing witness to a theological reality of the Christian faith, the testimony to which transcends . . . the dimensions of historically verifiable accounts. Still it is rare to find penetrating theological exegesis of the New Testament by one who shares little or nothing of the faith reflected by the literature.[68]

Moreover, with respect to the notion of "authorial intention" against which Martin contends, Seitz observes, "Childs never abandoned one matter close to the heart of historical-critical inquiry: the intentionality of the text, the notion that this is a deliberately crafted narrative."[69] Seitz calls this "an enlarged and sophisticated notion of authorial intention" that understands

---

65. Seitz, *Word without End*, 73, 8. Seitz never tells us where the Bible makes this claim for itself.

66. Martin, *Sex and the Single Savior*, 1–16.

67. Seitz, *Word without End*, 97.

68. Childs, *The New Testament as Canon*, 45, 39.

69. Seitz, *Word without End*, 80.

"the proper legacy of historical-critical method" to consist in a concern "for intentionality in biblical texts, not so much in precanonical but rather in final scriptural form."[70] Presumably, what is meant here is a human, not a divine, intention: Those editors who gave the scriptures their final canonical form intended the texts to be read in one way rather than another. For Childs, historical criticism is not only indispensable but also fully sufficient for the task of delineating these editorial intentions as reflected in the shaping of the canon.

After Childs has given us an exhaustively naturalistic historical account of how Israel and the church shaped the final form of their scriptures, it comes as something of a surprise when we are then told that a doctrine of inspiration is necessary as a condition of theological exegesis. It might reasonably have been inferred that one could agree with Childs that the canon, for whatever reason, should serve as the context for a theological exegesis apart from invoking a doctrine of inspiration. Even if he does not exactly equate them in theory, in practice Childs insists upon both a canonical reading of the scriptures and an affirmation of their divine inspiration. Their close connection becomes clear when we are told that apart from commitment to his canonical approach we can never hope to recover the literal or plain sense of the text as understood by Luther and Calvin.[71] Why not? The answer hinges on "the issue of referentiality" or "the Bible's function as a medium of revelation."[72] For one brief shining moment the Reformers held together both the *sensus historicus* and the *sensus literalis* because, while rejecting allegorical exegesis in the name of grammatical-historical exegesis, they affirmed that the true referent of the text is the self-revelation of God. Modern historical criticism, by divorcing the sense of the text from its divine referent, delivers only the historical sense without the literal sense and thus has broken the line of continuity with the Reformation.

While much that Childs says about the canonical shaping of the scriptures and premodern exegesis may be on target in a purely descriptive sense, there is a logical sleight of hand going on when he moves from these observations of a historical nature to his prescriptive theological claims. As a historical critic Childs has had to surrender the doctrine of orthodox Protestantism that, in the words of one of its modern exponents, "looks upon the Bible as an oracular book," authored by God in such a manner

---

70. Seitz, *Word without End*, 80, 82.

71. Childs writes, "In terms of classic Christian theology, there can be no genuine *sensus literalis* apart from a commitment to the canon." "The *Sensus Literalis* of Scripture," 93.

72. Childs, "Critical Reflections on James Barr's Understanding of the Literal and the Allegorical," *Journal for the Study of the Old Testament* 15.46 (1990) 3–9 at 4.

that "every one of its affirmations of whatever kind is to be esteemed as the utterance of God, of infallible truth and authority."[73] Childs is explicit that he makes no claims for the Bible's inerrancy when it comes to historical or scientific matters. Moreover, he fully admits that the historical factors determining the biblical canon were purely human and thus fallible: "In no sense is a claim to the infallibility of the canonical process being defended."[74]

> The New Testament canon did not fall from heaven, nor is any view of its formation adequate which does not assign the historical early church the active and dominant role in its formation.[75]

Childs even allows for the legitimacy of *Sachkritik* (i.e., a theological criticism of biblical statements on the basis of what is taken to be scripture's subject matter or *Sache*), although he never gives us an example of when this might be appropriate.[76] Given all these concessions, with what right does Childs accuse historical critics of turning from theocentrism to anthropocentrism on account of their belief that the biblical text is "no longer considered to be a direct channel of divine revelation, but rather and foremost a product of human culture whose author reflected his own historically conditioned perspectives"?[77] All he is saying is that modern historical critics do not work with the premise that the biblical text is divinely inspired. But Childs provides no reasons or arguments why anyone, especially those trained in historical criticism of the Bible, should adopt this premise.

Childs knows that modern theology is replete with attempts to formulate a doctrine of revelation that is logically independent of the doctrine

---

73. Benjamin Breckenridge Warfield, *The Inspiration and Authority of the Bible*, ed. Samuel G. Craig (1927; reprint, London: Marshall, Morgan & Scott, 1951) 106, 112.

74. Childs, *Introduction to the Old Testament*, 665.

75. Childs, *The New Testament as Canon*, 44.

76. Childs, *Biblical Theology of the Old and New Testaments: Theological Reflection on the Christian Bible* (Minneapolis: Fortress, 1992) 721. Childs criticizes Luther's exegesis for harboring "an arbitrary and individualistic tendency" that "led in the direction of setting up a 'canon within the canon'" (*Introduction to the Old Testament*, 44). Yet if even Luther, whose critique of James is the *locus classicus* of *Sachkritik*, does not provide us with a good example of what a theological criticism of scripture might look like, who does? "Preface to the Epistles of St. James and St. Jude," in *Martin Luther: Selections from His Writings*, ed. John Dillenberger (Garden City, NY: Anchor, 1961) 35–37. Like Childs, Seitz is equally concerned to insure that *Sachkritik* is never wielded in such a way as to result in the conclusion that "the church does not stand under the authority of God's Word written (the Bible) so much as under the authority of the Word of God, Jesus Christ." He remarks that this distinction "bears a superficial resemblance to the *Sachkritik* logic of Martin Luther as applied to the whole of scripture," but without explaining why it is superficial. *Word without End*, 95–96.

77. Childs, "Critical Reflections," 4.

of the Bible's inspiration. Even though H. Richard Niebuhr, for example, sought to redefine revelation strictly within the limits of Troeltsch's historicism, no one can deny that Niebuhr's material understanding of biblical and Christian faith is one of the most radically theocentric in the entire history of theology.[78] But this is unacceptable to Childs: "In terms of classic Christian theology, any appeal to a doctrine of revelation apart from inspiration must be resisted."[79] Why? Childs himself formulates the difficult question he anticipates any intelligent reader is bound to ask in light of his admissions regarding the purely historical and hence fallible character of the canonical process: "How can one place any significance on the canon when, from a critical point of view, the criteria used in its compilation are no longer accepted as valid?"[80] Good question! But then, instead of answering the question, Childs avoids it by asserting:

> The fact that the church confessed its faith in the divine origin of its Scripture in a thoroughly time-conditioned fashion can be readily acknowledged. But the theological issue at stake is the rightness of the claim for divine authority to which the church responded in setting apart certain writings as Scripture.[81]

The appropriate premise is to believe that "the text of Scripture, when infused by the Spirit *with the full ontic reality of God*, resonates with a fresh voice . . . which transcends its original historical origins."[82] But we do not need a doctrine of inspiration to account for the obvious fact that the Bible has continued to speak to people down through the ages and still does so today. Childs thus wanted to have it both ways: Though a radical historical critic, he nevertheless aspired to be a good *sola scriptura* Calvinist. These two commitments, however, pulled him in opposing directions. Hence, his program is as internally unstable as that of Barth, whom he follows.[83] When Childs praises Barth for insisting that "the living, unfettered voice of God in Scripture cannot be held captive to the norms of human rationality," I have

---

78. H. Richard Niebuhr, *The Meaning of Revelation* (New York: Macmillan, 1941).
79. Childs, "The *Sensus Literalis* of Scripture," 92.
80. Childs, *Biblical Theology in Crisis*, 104.
81. Childs, *Biblical Theology in Crisis*, 105.
82. Childs, "Toward Recovering Theological Exegesis," 25, emphasis added.
83. For my critical analysis of Barth, see Paul E. Capetz, "The Old Testament as a Witness to Jesus Christ: Historical Criticism and Theological Exegesis of the Bible according to Karl Barth," *Journal of Religion* 90 (2010) 407–506, also published as "Karl Barth on the Old Testament as Christian Scripture," Chapter 4 in this volume (pages 139-71, below).

to ask, What other criteria are available to us besides the norms of human rationality?[84]

Childs is certainly correct to specify that a theological exegesis not only attends descriptively to what the text says but also seeks to engage normatively with what it means: "The object of biblical exegesis is the text itself as well as the subject matter of which the text speaks."[85] But we can surely engage in a theological exegesis in this sense without adopting Childs's larger canonical program. Take, for instance, the question of the literal sense of Gal 2:16 ("a human being is not justified by works of the law but through faith in Jesus Christ," my translation). Clearly, the literal sense of the text is independent of whatever was going on in Galatia or Antioch since it makes a theological claim about how persons are appropriately related to God. According to Childs's own statement, a theological exegesis of Gal 2:16 would be less interested in reconstructing the original historical situation that occasioned Paul's letter and more interested in exploring the meaning and truth of Paul's claim about human existence *coram Deo*. Childs would no doubt agree that to understand this claim we might have to do some historical labor to grasp clearly not only what Paul meant by terms such as "justified," "works of the law," and "faith," but also why he drew this sharp contrast at all. Nonetheless, the major focus of a theological exegesis is to place this yeoman labor in the service of interpreting the text's normative theological claims.[86] This, of course, was the pivotal point made by Bultmann in the epilogue to his *Theology of the New Testament*.

---

84. Brevard S. Childs, "Old Testament in Germany 1920–1940: The Search for a New Paradigm," in *Altes Testament, Forschung und Wirkung: Festschrift für Henning Graf Reventlow*, ed. Peter Mommer and Winfried Thiel (Frankfurt: Lang, 1994) 233–46 at 246; in spite of his affirmation that God's revelation in scripture transcends the canons of human rationality, Childs does not hesitate to criticize those whose "subjective, confessional stance" leads them to a "construal" of scripture's witness that "lies outside all critical criteria and can be neither proven nor disproven by rational argument." "Toward Recovering Theological Exegesis," 23. David Kelsey is a thorn in Childs's side since Kelsey has shown how theologians, including Barth, make a prior theological decision regarding what the Bible is all about and then proceed to interpret it in the light of that construal. *Proving Doctrine: The Uses of Scripture in Modern Theology* (Harrisburg, PA: Trinity, 1999); reprint of *The Uses of Scripture in Recent Theology* (Philadelphia: Fortress, 1975). Childs dismisses Kelsey's views as "liberal." "Toward Recovering Theological Exegesis," 20n8.

85. Childs, "The *Sensus Literalis* of Scripture," 92.

86. Childs even concedes that there would be serious theological consequences for the interpretation of Galatians "if it could be shown historically that Paul had basically misunderstood his opposition," adding that "such a discovery would certainly call into question Paul's witness." *The New Testament as Canon*, 306. Of the three scholars here under discussion, Childs is the one who is most committed to historical criticism but also the one who is most troubled by its possible theological implications.

> Since the New Testament is a document of history, specifically of the history of religion, the interpretation of it requires the labor of historical investigation. The method of this kind of inquiry has been worked out from the time of the Enlightenment onward and has been made fruitful for the investigation of primitive Christianity and the interpretation of the New Testament. Now such labor may be guided by either one of two interests—that is, reconstruction of past history or interpretation of the New Testament writings. Neither exists, of course, without the other, and they stand constantly in a reciprocal relation to each other. But the question is: which of the two stands in the service of the other? Either the writings of the New Testament can be interrogated as the "sources" which the historian interprets in order to reconstruct a picture of primitive Christianity as a phenomenon of the historical past, or the reconstruction stands in the service of the interpretation of the New Testament writings under the presupposition that they have something to say to the present.[87]

For Bultmann, the Bible is of more than mere historical interest because it addresses the existential question of how we are to understand ourselves religiously as subjects in relation to God and morally as agents in the world. That is why its main religious and moral insights can be grasped apart from expertise in historical-critical method. Anyone who has ever preached a sermon knows that the question with which the preacher approaches the biblical text is not that of a historian writing a Hermeneia commentary.[88]

---

87. Rudolf Bultmann, *Theology of the New Testament*, 2 vols., trans. Kendrick Grobel (New York: Scribner, 1951, 1955) 2:251. What Bultmann says about the relation between historical and theological interpretation of New Testament texts could just as easily be said about the relation between historical and theological interpretation of texts from the postbiblical tradition of the church. After all, Protestant theologians who are interested in the texts of Luther and Calvin primarily for normative purposes are not indifferent to the question of historical accuracy in their analysis of these texts. The same, of course, could be said about the debates among contemporary theologians concerning how to interpret the texts of Barth or Tillich. Hence, there need be no special hermeneutic in order to build a bridge between then and now when interpreting historical texts, whether biblical or otherwise.

88. We must distinguish the question of a theological exegesis of scripture at two levels: First, at the level of the ordinary believer or church member who hears a sermon or attends a Bible study and, second, at the level of the minister or theologian who has the professional responsibility for reflecting critically on the content and truth of the church's preaching. While historical criticism is obviously not necessary at the first level, it is necessary at the second level. The only way it can be otherwise is if one is willing to surrender all claims of a historical nature in one's theological interpretation of the meaning of Christian faith.

Schubert M. Ogden develops Bultmann's point by clarifying that a "theological interpretation of the biblical writings is a way of understanding and explicating their meaning that is oriented by the same existential question to which they themselves intend to give answer."[89] Ogden adds that this notion of a theological exegesis provides "a way of construing the Bible that is authentically theological and yet respects the integrity of critical biblical scholarship."[90]

Yet Childs will have none of it, even though Bultmann's statement and its elaboration by Ogden correspond exactly to the formal requirements of Childs's own definition of what constitutes a theological exegesis: "The object of biblical exegesis is the text itself as well as the subject matter of which the text speaks."[91] Much to my amazement, Childs asserts, "The literal sense of the text is the plain sense witnessed to by the community of faith. *It makes no claim of being the original sense, or even of being the best.*"[92] Would the Reformers ever have agreed that the meaning of the literal sense was neither its original nor its best sense? This statement does, however, reveal why Childs judges all attempts to base a theological exegesis upon historical criticism as a series of brilliant failures. For Childs as for Seitz, the orthodox tradition dictates what the literal sense is: "the church's *regula fidei* encompasses both text and tradition in an integral unity as the living Word of God."[93] Childs is forthright in "calling biblical studies back to confessional roots,"[94] and thus he has to set strict limits to the theological implications of historical criticism precisely because it has dissolved the theological unity of the canon that was an essential presupposition of the Reformers' method of basing doctrine on "scripture alone." Jon Levenson has portrayed the dilemma now faced by Protestants as vividly as anyone can when he notes that Matthew, or at least the Sermon on the Mount, "is guilty of the heresy of 'Judaizing' . . . And so the possibility emerges that the church has canonized a heretic," in which case "the Pauline doctrine

---

89. Schubert M. Ogden, "Theology and Biblical Interpretation," in *Doing Theology Today* (Valley Forge, PA: Trinity, 1996) 36–51 at 48. Note that this way of putting it does not entail that we accept whatever answer any particular biblical writer happened to give to this question! In this vein, I once heard Ogden explain to a group of students at the University of Chicago Divinity School: "When I preach a sermon using a text from Matthew, I'm not preaching *on* Matthew; rather, I'm preaching the gospel *with* Matthew."

90. Ogden, "Theology and Biblical Interpretation," 51.

91. Childs, "The *Sensus Literalis* of Scripture," 92.

92. Childs, "The *Sensus Literalis* of Scripture," 92, emphasis added.

93. Childs, "The *Sensus Literalis* of Scripture," 93.

94. Childs, "Old Testament in Germany," 244.

of justification through faith by grace alone, so central to Protestantism ... stands indicted *sola scriptura*."⁹⁵ Levenson correctly notes that "historical criticism of the Christian Bible has shattered the Protestant dream of an orthodox church founded on biblical authority alone."⁹⁶ The proposal of Childs is, in truth, more classically Catholic than Protestant insofar as his reversal of Semler's legacy requires prior acceptance of the ancient church's authority in establishing the canon.⁹⁷

Although Martin is not concerned to uphold biblical authority so much as to open up new vistas of biblical interpretation, it is surprising how traditional his view of theology is in spite of his postmodern mode of argument. For him, a theological exegesis means "interpreting the text of the Bible *as Scripture*, as 'the word of God.'"⁹⁸ To be sure, Martin candidly admits that it is an important theological question in itself to ask "What do we mean by 'the word of God'?"⁹⁹ Still, whatever it means, theological exegesis requires that we view the Bible as "a divine communication" and not merely as "a historical artifact."¹⁰⁰ He goes on to say that "Scripture lives in different and constantly new meanings in the readings of Christians led by the Holy Spirit."¹⁰¹ Nonetheless, in spite of this robust affirmation of pneumatically inspired diversity and novelty of interpretations, there is a countervailing undercurrent that rises to the surface in Martin's repeated—and puzzling—use of phrases such as "a Christian reading of the Bible," "to

---

95. Levenson, *The Hebrew Bible*, 6.

96. Levenson, *The Hebrew Bible*, 6–7.

97. Luther's opponent John Eck anticipates the position of Childs on the relation of the canon to tradition: "Scripture is not authentic without the Church's authority ... Let the objection immediately be raised against [Luther]: how does he know that these Scriptures are canonical except from the Church?" *Enchiridion of Commonplaces against Luther and Other Enemies of the Church*, trans. Ford Lewis Battles (Grand Rapids: Baker, 1979) 13. Note what the Council of Trent says about how the texts of the Bible are to be interpreted: "no one relying on his own judgment shall ... presume to interpret them contrary to the sense which holy mother Church, to whom it belongs to judge of their true sense and interpretation, has held and holds, or even contrary to the unanimous teaching of the Fathers." "The Canons and Decrees of the Council of Trent," in *Creeds of the Churches*, 3rd ed., ed. John H. Leith (Louisville: John Knox, 1982) 400–439 at 403–404. See also Seitz, *Word without End*, 17.

98. Martin, *Pedagogy of the Bible*, 21, emphasis original.

99. Martin, *Pedagogy of the Bible*, 21.

100. Martin, *Pedagogy of the Bible*, 21. Note how Martin, like Childs, sets up a false dichotomy that obfuscates the full range of alternatives before us: Either the Bible is a mere period piece or divine revelation. One does not have to believe in the divine inspiration of the Qur'an or the Upanishads to acknowledge that these texts are much more than mere artifacts of history!

101. Martin, *Pedagogy of the Bible*, 40.

interpret Scripture Christianly," or "the Christian meaning of the text."[102] I have to confess that I do not know what a "Christian reading" of a text is. Presumably this means something like a "special hermeneutic" as distinct from a "general hermeneutic." Although he restricts his discussion to the Bible, is Martin willing to grant the applicability of a "Christian reading" to other texts besides the Bible, say, non-Christian or secular texts?[103] What exactly is the content of the adjective "Christian"? Who defines it and how? For me, a troubling feature of Martin's particular brand of theological postmodernism is the similarity of his rhetoric to the authoritarian and hegemonic tones sounded by Childs and Seitz. All three speak about the church or Christians in highly idealized terms, as though in principle there was and is one and only one true Christianity that yesterday could have been realized had it not been for ancient heretics and today should be realized were it not for modern theologians under the spell of the Enlightenment. Time and again Martin employs certain characteristic locutions ("a Christian could argue . . ."; "Christians legitimately derive correct Christian meanings . . ."; "For Christians, the meaning of the psalm . . ."; "Christians have legitimately refused . . .") that are striking for the monolithic presumptions they imply and reinforce. Have Christians always been and are they now of one mind as to what constitutes a "Christian reading" of the Bible? Do they invariably derive the same "Christian meanings" from it? Which readings of scripture are "led by the Holy Spirit" and which are not?

Whereas Childs at least insists that a historical reading of the Bible is necessary if not sufficient for theological exegesis, Martin denies this. Furthermore, Martin never tells us what criteria are to be used in discerning what constitutes a "legitimate reading," nor does he ever spell out what an "ethical use" of a text is and why.[104] Prior to reading Martin I was uncertain as to where I should place myself on the modern/postmodern divide since I fully share the moral and political concerns of postmodern thinkers; yet I am too much of a historian to say that we can dispense with the historical meaning altogether when considering the question of a theological exegesis. Consider this illustration given us by Martin.

> From the point of view of respectable historical criticism, it is a mistake to read New Testament authors as teaching an explicit and orthodox doctrine of the Trinity. In fact, some of their writings sound so un-Trinitarian that they would have been treated

102. Martin, *Pedagogy of the Bible*, 43, 80, 109.
103. By extension of the same logic, we can ask whether there are distinctively Christian readings (i.e., interpretations) of the "texts" (i.e., data) of biology or geology.
104. Martin, *Pedagogy of the Bible*, 33, 38.

as heretics in later ages. Paul, for example, innocently portrays Christ as "subordinate" to God the Father, a view that would later be declared heretical . . . [A]lthough Paul's own understanding of the 'spirit' is rather hard to clarify, Paul never comes close to treating the spirit in the later terms of orthodox Trinitarian doctrine, as the third person of the Trinity.

In my view, however, none of these historical "facts" should dissuade Christians from reading the Bible in Trinitarian terms. Christians have legitimately refused to limit the meaning of Scripture to its supposed original meaning locked in the ancient past, or to the meaning thought to be intended by the original author. The meaning of Scripture cannot be so circumscribed.[105]

I wonder how Michael Servetus would have responded to such a comment after he had been sentenced to be burned at the stake for trying to argue, on Calvin's own terms, precisely this historical point that Martin has just conceded! There is something morally offensive about this statement when one considers just how many people suffered exile or lost their lives trying to argue against an orthodox interpretation of scripture, whether Catholic or Protestant. While I certainly agree that "premodern exegetical interpretation was anything but arbitrary," it is impossible for me to think the same about Martin's statement.[106] Moreover, one can surely question the adequacy of Martin's portrayal of both premodern and modern interpretation when he locates the source of our present troubles in our "Cartesian anxiety" about getting it right.[107] Martin tells us that premodern exegesis "helps us imagine how Christians read Scripture without suffering from our normal anxiety about finding the right meaning of the text."[108] Aside

---

105. Martin, *Pedagogy of the Bible*, 40. Note how Martin, in postmodernist fashion, puts the word "facts" in quotation marks.

106. Martin, *Pedagogy of the Bible*, 47.

107. Martin says that the "modernist" approach consists in treating the Bible as "basically an answer book or source of information" (*Pedagogy of the Bible*, 58). Yet I can think of no major liberal or neo-orthodox Protestant theologians in the last two centuries whose handling of the Bible could ever be so characterized. Karl Barth explicitly repudiates this view: "we cannot expect or demand a compendium of solomonic or even divine knowledge of all things in heaven and earth" from the Bible. *The Doctrine of the Word of God*, trans. G. T. Thomson and Harold Knight; *Church Dogmatics*, vol. I/2 (New York: Scribner, 1965) 508. Schleiermacher, Harnack, Troeltsch, Bultmann, Tillich, and the Niebuhrs would endorse Barth's statement without reservation!

108. Martin, *Pedagogy of the Bible*, 58. Martin criticizes "the rejection of the use of allegory" as "overly modernist and Protestant" (85). Admittedly, my sympathies are both Protestant and modernist (or liberal). I might add that what Levenson says is certainly true in my case: "not every liberal Protestant values the adjective more than the noun" (*The Hebrew Bible*, 98).

from the observation that Martin's likening of historical-critical inquiry to modern philosophical "foundationalism" is an instance of what Aristotle meant by a *metábasis eis állo génos*, I seriously doubt that either Athanasius or Calvin would have found their exegetical practices mirrored in Martin's postmodern *jouissance*.[109]

As a historian I have to ask, Do the dead have any rights? When Martin reminds us that "no text has ever spoken," he neglects to mention that no text has ever written itself.[110] All texts were written by someone who wanted to communicate something to somebody else. While I would not defend historical interpretation by appeal to a shaky psychological notion of authorial intention, I cannot dismiss the idea that every author had a communicative purpose in writing a text. Hence, I have to reject Martin's assertion that texts do not constrain their meanings.[111] In her explication of an "ethics of historical reading" Elisabeth Schüssler Fiorenza rightly insists that

> The number of interpretations that can legitimately be given to a text are limited. Such a historical reading seeks to give the text its due by asserting its original meanings over and against later dogmatic usurpations. It makes the assimilation of the text to our own experience and interest more difficult and thereby keeps alive the "irritation" of the original text by challenging our own assumptions, world views, and practices. In short, the methods of historical- and literary-critical scholarship and its diachronic reconstructions distance us in such a way from the original texts and their historical symbolic worlds that they relativize not only them but also us.[112]

A few years ago the school where I teach invited Martin to deliver a lectureship on biblical interpretation. After one of his lectures someone asked him what he thought of Mel Gibson's movie *The Passion of the Christ* that had just been released and was unleashing a storm of controversy, not least on account of its presentation of the role played by the Jews in Jesus' crucifixion. Surprisingly, Martin criticized Gibson's film for its lack

---

109. "We cannot in demonstrating pass from one genus to another." Aristotle, "Posterior Analytics," 1, 7, 75a, in *The Basic Works of Aristotle*, ed. Richard McKeon (New York: Random House, 1941) 110–86 at 121. The category mistake consists in likening the laudable aspiration for accuracy in one domain of knowledge (history) to a philosophical doctrine that claims to have set forth the indubitable first principles of all knowledge whatsoever (epistemology).

110. Martin, *Pedagogy of the Bible*, 30.

111. Martin, *Pedagogy of the Bible*, 30.

112. Elisabeth Schüssler Fiorenza, "The Ethics of Biblical Interpretation: Decentering Biblical Scholarship," *Journal of Biblical Literature* 107 (1988) 3–17 at 14.

of historical accuracy even though there was nothing in his lectures about interpretation that would have prepared a listener for this critique.[113] After all, Martin insists on the nonnecessity of historical criticism for correct exegesis, on the legitimacy of multiple readings, on blurring the distinction between exegesis and eisegesis, on the lack of constraint exercised by texts over their possible interpretations, and on the inability of historical criticism to deliver "the Christian meaning" of the text. So what is wrong with Gibson's ultraconservative Catholic reading of the Passion story? In its own way it, too, is a theological exegesis, designed to narrate an ancient story so that its immediate religious relevance to contemporary moviegoers is made fully transparent. On Martin's own grounds, I fail to see how he can object to it. If, however, he had invoked his category of an ethical use of a text in order to accuse Gibson of slandering the Jews as a consequence of violating historical truth, Martin would have found himself backed into a corner. Either there is a moral obligation to tell the truth about history or there is not. In spite of Martin's many fresh observations about the processes of interpretation, his theoretical arguments are confusing in the extreme.

Martin charges those who insist upon the necessity of historical-critical method with "reading" premodern Christians out of the church since that was not how they read the Bible. But this is completely illogical.[114] If "ought implies can," as is clearly the case, then premodern persons cannot be held accountable to the requirements of historical-critical exegesis since they had no access to a mode of interpretation that had to await modernity for its emergence. This is no different from saying that premodern people were not stupid simply because they believed that the sun revolves around the earth, but that does not justify us in holding that belief today given what we know through modern astronomy.

Martin also fears that an insistence upon the necessity of historical criticism for theological interpretation leaves students preparing for the

---

113. Martin's 2004 Gustafson Lectures were recorded and are available in the library of United Theological Seminary of the Twin Cities.

114. Martin's charge depends upon his premise that it makes sense to speak of "the Christian meaning" of the Bible, but I question this as has already been pointed out. Another example where I detect a failure of logic is provided by Martin when, in the course of criticizing other scholars for their equivocal use of the words "history" and "historical," he makes this rather bizarre statement: "there is no particular reason that a religion, just because it arose in history, must have its authoritative texts or Scripture submitted to the analysis of modern historical criticism, a method that, after all, itself arose only in the modern period and long after these religions had been flourishing quite well for centuries. If historical criticism is necessary for studying historical religions, how does one explain the happy existence of those religions before the rise of historical criticism?" (*Pedagogy of the Bible*, 41).

ministry with the false impression that premodern exegesis was arbitrary. Since Martin is primarily concerned with theological education, it will not be inappropriate here if I draw on some of my own experiences as a theological educator. Every year I teach a required course for first-year seminarians titled Introduction to Historical Theology. At the top of my syllabus is a maxim from Gerhard Ebeling that serves as the motto for the course: "The history of the church is the history of its interpretation of scripture."[115] If students enter my classroom thinking that the classical theologians were stupid or weird, they certainly do not believe that after completing the course. As they engage the classic texts of the Christian tradition, they learn both the exegetical methods and the hermeneutical principles informing premodern interpretations of the Bible. Moreover, they come to understand the interrelation between doctrinal conflicts and their roots in divergent exegetical warrants. But I ask Martin, What is the proper method for teaching this course so as to engender in my students a genuine appreciation of the premodern tradition about which he cares so much if not the historical-critical method? Are we free to give an allegorical exegesis of Augustine's or Calvin's texts? Or is it only the Bible that we are permitted to interpret allegorically?

As Martin well knows, one of the biggest issues in contemporary New Testament study is whether Luther correctly interpreted Paul. Yet how are we to answer a question like that apart from strict application of historical-critical method? Is it obligatory to apply historical criticism to the exegesis of Luther but optional in the case of Paul? I should add that I am in complete agreement with Martin regarding the absolute importance of being able to formulate a cogent theological argument for one's positions, and thus my class is not only about the history of theology but also about how to think systematically as a theologian. Students learn the distinction between a historical question and a theological question so as to become aware when they are moving from one logical type of inquiry and mode of argumentation to the other. Hence, the question cannot be avoided: What is—or should be—the relation between historical description and explanation, on the one hand, and normative theological interpretation, on the other hand? If on strictly historical grounds we should become convinced that Luther misunderstood Paul, do we continue to read Paul through the lens of the Lutheran Confessions? Lest I be misunderstood, let me hasten to add that this need not entail a categorical rejection of Luther's interpretation of Paul, which is surely one of the most insightful in the history of exegesis. Students can

---

115. The motto is drawn from the title of Ebeling's essay, "Church History is the History of the Exposition of Scripture," in Gerhard Ebeling, *The Word of God and Tradition: Historical Studies Interpreting the Divisions of Christianity*, trans. S. H. Hooke (Philadelphia; Fortress, 1968) 11–31.

learn how someone asking a sixteenth-century question found his answer in a new reading of a first-century Jew, and Luther's example can stand as a model of creative yet responsible appropriation of an inherited tradition given the intellectual possibilities available to him in his time and place. But the crucial difference for us has to be our explicit awareness of the distinction between historical exegesis of Paul and a normative theological argument about Paul's significance today, a distinction of which Luther or any other premodern interpreter was innocent.[116]

When Martin argues in defense of christological readings of the Old Testament, he avoids the question whether such readings are justified today if we no longer share the exegetical methods, hermeneutical principles, and theological beliefs on the sole basis of which such christological readings were once intelligible.[117] My students realize that they can expect to flunk

116. We could also point to Tillich's creative adaptation of Luther's doctrine of justification to address the question of modern unbelief, a question as far removed from Luther's mind as Luther's question was from Paul's mind; yet Tillich was well aware that he was doing something new with Luther's idea that went beyond Luther's own intention: "Luther applied the doctrine of justification only to the religious-moral life ... Tillich applies the doctrine to the religious-intellectual sphere also." James Luther Adams, "Tillich's Concept of the Protestant Era," in Paul Tillich, *The Protestant Era*, trans. James Luther Adams (Chicago: University of Chicago Press, 1948) 273–316 at 292. But I do not conclude from this fact of ever-new appropriations of inherited traditions that texts per se have multiple meanings (though some might, e.g., Apuleius, *Metamorphoses*, which is an allegory intended to be read on two levels at once); rather, I would say that ideas within texts can be further developed to address situations or challenges their original formulators never imagined. Whether such new developments are to be seen as authentic continuations or inauthentic distortions of an inherited tradition cannot itself be decided in a purely historical manner since it involves an evaluative judgment. So, for instance, we might conclude that Luther's exegesis of Paul is not historically accurate and yet still judge that Luther's theology represents a valid reconfiguration of certain Pauline themes and ideas. Heiko Oberman proposes "contextual" readings of history that "place ideas in their context and point to their characteristics and their changing structures." *Forerunners of the Reformation: The Shape of Late Medieval Thought Illustrated by Key Documents* (Philadelphia: Fortress, 1981) 39. The goal of such a contextual reading is to provide "a perspective for measuring the changes in the configuration of questions and answers." This is a good description of my pedagogical aims in teaching historical theology.

117. Jewish biblical scholar Marvin A. Sweeney asks, "To what extent does Christianity have the right unilaterally to impose Jesus Christ and the New Testament on the reading of the Old Testament without acknowledging the continuing theological validity of Judaism and its reading of biblical texts?" Review of Christopher R. Seitz, *Prophecy and Hermeneutics: Toward a New Introduction to the Prophets* in *Toronto Journal of Theology* 24 (2008) 115–17 at 116. Since none of my three scholars would deny the continuing validity of Judaism altogether, I have to wonder what claims they are really making on behalf of a christological interpretation of the Old Testament. Should Jews accept such an interpretation? Why or why not? Childs tries to hold together both a non-Christianizing reading that does "justice to the discrete voice of the Old

their Old Testament classes if they exegete the texts of the Jewish Bible the way Paul did. But they do not think that Paul was weird or stupid. They understand that he was different from us because he lived in a cultural and religious world far removed from our own. Does Martin really believe that there is a divine intentionality behind the biblical texts that allows us to interpret scripture as Paul did? On the one hand, he disavows any aim "to argue for divine intention as providing the meaning of the scriptural text."[118] On the other hand, however, he sets up as a condition of theological exegesis the premise that the Bible is "a divine communication."[119] If Martin truly believes it is a divine communication, he should have no hesitation affirming that the divine intention is what the Bible communicates. But is this really Martin's view? I doubt it, but if so, he should be forthright about this belief. His claim, then, becomes an explicitly theological one, no different in principle from that of Childs regarding scripture's divine inspiration or that of Seitz about the Bible as privileged speech articulating the perspective of God. Such a theological claim for the Bible hardly depends for its force upon postmodern theories of interpretation. Indeed, I have difficulty imagining that nontheological postmodern theorists would ever endorse a claim granting supernatural authority to a text.

Martin asks us to be aware of the metaphors we use when speaking about what goes on in interpretation. My chief metaphor is that of "conversation" or "dialogue," which I derive from the hermeneutical tradition of Bultmann, Gadamer, Ricoeur, and Tracy.[120] The conversation between reader and author is focused on the subject matter of the text (*die Sache*

Testament according to its true historical context" and a canonical reading that treats both testaments as "a unified witness bearing testimony to one Lord, Jesus Christ." Then he asks, "Are not these two approaches in irreconcilable conflict?" ("Toward Recovering Theological Exegesis," 20–21). My answer is, "Yes, they are in conflict." Note the utter confusion in the equivocal use of the word "context" in this statement by Childs: "The Old Testament within the context of the canon is not a witness to a primitive level of faith, nor does it need to be Christianized. Within its historical context it is a witness to Jesus Christ." *Biblical Theology in Crisis*, 111.

118. Martin, *Pedagogy of the Bible*, 40.

119. Martin, *Pedagogy of the Bible*, 21.

120. I agree with the position on hermeneutics set forth by David Tracy: "When all historical work completes its judgments of historical probability, we do not end but begin anew our proper task of interpreting. For interpreters, now historically informed, must return to the task of understanding by conversing with the claim to attention of classic texts and events. No amount of historical reconstruction can spare us that further effort. If all classic claims to attention are not to become historical period pieces, then history . . . must have the first but not the last word in all interpretation." *Plurality and Ambiguity: Hermeneutics, Religion, Hope* (San Francisco: Harper & Row, 1987) 39. Why cannot Martin affirm this statement?

selbst), not on the world behind the text. When one teaches at a seminary, even a liberal one as I do, it is necessary to justify why the historical study of religion is important given the antihistorical bias of American culture shared equally by theological students on both the right and the left. Yet two concerns dear to the hearts of my students provide me with examples with which to illustrate what is involved in historical method and why they should care about learning it. The first is related to cultural diversity and interreligious dialogue. Appreciation for non-Western cultures and non-Christian religions is a deeply held value at my school. I explain to students that what we are trying to do as historians is similar to what goes on when trying to understand people from another culture. Unless we can learn to speak their language and to see the world through their eyes, we will always be in danger of misinterpreting them through our own lenses and preconceptions. The difference, of course, is that we cannot travel to ancient Rome or medieval Germany to meet these people whose texts we are reading so as to ask them if we are correctly interpreting them.

The second illustration comes from pastoral care. Martin objects to the presumed passivity implied in the metaphor of listening for what a text is saying, but I think he misunderstands what is involved in real listening to another person. The kind of listening that goes on in pastoral care is anything but passive; it is active in the sense of being attentive both to what a person is saying and not saying so that the pastor can ask just the right questions to move the conversation forward. Any seminarian who does a unit of Clinical Pastoral Education learns that listening is a skill that has to be mastered. To use language rejected by Martin and other postmodernists, the reason why historical interpretation is "foundational"—or, in my terms, "constitutive"—is that there can be no genuine dialogue with premodern theologians about the normative questions of theology if they are not allowed to speak for themselves. Thus the chief task of a historian is to insure that the dead get to have their say in our contemporary conversations. I fail to see how a postmodernist can argue against this insistence upon the necessity of historical interpretation since a nonnegotiable commitment of postmodernism is respect for the other as other and not as just another instance of more of the same. Scholars who lift up the value of difference, the ambiguity of language, suspicion of grand metanarratives, and concern for those whose voices have been silenced in official accounts of the past have every reason to insist upon the utter necessity of a truly historical understanding of our traditions with all of the critical implications for the evaluation of these traditions such understanding implies.

IN DEFENSE OF A HISTORICIZED UNDERSTANDING OF THEOLOGY

All three of the scholars treated here seek to dethrone historical criticism on account of its alleged negative impact on a theological approach to scripture, yet they fail to substantiate this charge. Since they are troubled by the normative conclusions that other scholars have reached on the basis of historical criticism, they assert—or at least imply—the superiority of premodern exegesis. Moreover, they resort to a special hermeneutic that, in effect, allows tradition to set the parameters within which the Bible is to be read normatively in the church. In spite of their overall agreement, however, there are some differences between them. Seitz states as clearly as anyone does the position of the (nonfundamentalist) theological right just as Martin is the most forceful spokesperson for the theological left in contemporary biblical studies. By comparison with these two, Childs is the middle figure who, as heir to both the German tradition of historical-critical scholarship and Barthian theology, strives valiantly to do justice to this dual heritage. I judge, however, that his proposed synthesis is inherently unstable, as I have sought to show. By contrast, Seitz is much less nuanced and subtle than his teacher, but precisely for that reason he is more internally consistent. Martin's position is the most difficult to understand. Though my ethical and political sympathies lie with him, I fail to see that he has articulated a sufficiently cogent theological rationale that explains how he can insist on the need for ideology critique while denying the necessity of historical interpretation for theological and ethical uses of the Bible. The latter is the condition of the possibility of the former, since only a fully historicized approach both to the biblical authors and to exegetes of the Bible allows us to raise the question of ideological biases reflecting their social and cultural locations. Indeed, it would be interesting to observe how Martin might try to persuade Seitz to take ideology critique seriously given their similar negative evaluations of historical criticism and their high views of the Bible as a communication from God.

Martin doubts that it is possible to provide a compelling theological rationale for the necessity of historical criticism. He is both right and wrong. The evaluation of historical criticism as positive or negative depends upon what one thinks a theological exegesis (or biblical theology) is supposed to accomplish. Yet one's definition of what is meant by theological interpretation of the Bible is simply a more precise application to a specific case of how one defines theology in general. In this sense, Martin is correct: There can be no compelling theological rationale in defense of historical criticism given definitions of theology that are beholden to the doctrinal contents of the premodern classical tradition. Each of these men presumes that theology's task consists primarily or solely in securing the orthodoxy or Christian character of contemporary doctrine and practice by appeal to a way of reading the Bible designed to serve that normative purpose.[121] Since historical criticism obviously cannot accomplish their desired end, they are compelled by the logic of their views about theology to deny or severely to circumscribe any normative implications it might otherwise have upon doctrine and practice. While welcoming their interest in contributing to theology as biblical scholars, I deem all three to be guilty of collapsing the distinction between descriptive and normative claims. One has to wonder what has become of the concern of the Reformers to free the Bible from the hegemony of the church's tradition. If in the consistent pursuit of that concern some of the Reformers' cherished assumptions (say, of the theological unity of the Bible) have had to be set aside, is that a tragedy or a betrayal of the faith? I hardly think so.[122]

---

121. Martin's understanding of theology is difficult to grasp. In one place Martin says: "Theology is thinking about how faith statements are true—or not. Or even more accurate: theology is the explanation of how faith statements may be sensible or rational" (*Pedagogy of the Bible*, 72). In another place he states that the task of theology is "to make Christian, rational sense out of Christian beliefs" (89). The former statement suggests that Martin may be willing to subject the truth of Christian beliefs to critical challenges arising from nontheological perspectives as represented by other disciplines in the university (e.g., science, history, philosophy). By contrast, the latter statement implies the opposite view that theology is solely an internal affair of the church and thus immune from external challenges, as when Martin speaks of how an interpretation can be "Christianly true" or "Christianly false" (90) Since he defines "theological hermeneutics" as addressing "how to interpret Scripture Christianly," I assume that in his view theology is beholden only to criteria of rationality and truth that are already defined by Christians themselves (80). But my confusion increases all the more when I later read that theology does not have to presuppose faith since "I have known agnostics and even atheists who make, in my opinion, quite good theologians" (117). I wish Martin had taken greater care to be more precise.

122. B. A. Gerrish helpfully clarifies that Luther and Calvin gave a twofold answer to the question: "Wherein lies the authority of Scripture?" On the one hand, they can say that "Scripture is authoritative because it bears witness to God" and, on the other hand, that "Scripture is authoritative because it is the verbally inspired Word of God." The former answer represents the new element in the Reformers' theology whereas the latter answer is a continuation of the medieval tradition: "And if there is no necessary contradiction between the two answers, neither is there any necessary connection between them: they do not stand or fall together." "The Word of God and the Words of Scripture: Luther and Calvin on Biblical Authority," in *The Old Protestantism and the New: Essays on the Reformation Heritage* (Chicago: University of Chicago Press, 1982) 51–68 at 56, 64. This distinction is important for understanding how the seeds of both conservative and liberal Protestantism were sown in the Reformation. Whereas conservative Protestants held fast to what the Reformers had in common with the medieval tradition, liberal Protestants seized upon what was new in their doctrine of the Bible

But this is not the only way to define theology. Upholding the liberal Protestant option rejected by them, I believe that theology is obligated not only to ask whether the church's doctrines and practices cohere with our best critical understanding of the gospel, but also to ask whether these doctrines are true and these practices are good regardless of whether they are taught in the Bible or the postbiblical tradition.[123] Since the truth about history is simply one aspect of what is meant by truth in general, a liberal Protestant cannot accept a view of theology that insulates the Bible and the tradition from the critical challenges that a fully historical understanding of religion might occasion, just as any view of theology that excludes the secure results of the natural sciences is unacceptable.[124] By insisting upon the insights of historical study as constitutive of any normative interpretation of Christian faith today, I do not imply any disrespect for the classical tradition and its ways of reading the Bible, nor do I thereby disqualify premodern Christians from membership in the church. Nevertheless, I do not see how we can in good conscience rehabilitate premodern ways of reading the Bible after two centuries of historical-critical labor. In showing the Bible to be fully explicable as a human product of the history of religion, historical criticism has made it very difficult for post-Enlightenment persons to continue to regard the Bible as the repository or criterion of all religious and moral truth. Hermann Gunkel made the point well when articulating the

since it provided a theological rationale for the Bible's importance that allowed for the unreserved appropriation of the results of historical criticism.

123. In this respect I share completely what Franklin I. Gamwell calls interchangeably "the modern commitment" or "the humanistic commitment," which is the "affirmation that our understandings of reality and ourselves in relation to it cannot be validated or redeemed by appeals to some authoritative expression or tradition or institution. In other words, our understandings can be validated only by appeal in some sense to human experience and reason as such. Because it is identified by this latter appeal, the modern commitment may also be called the humanistic commitment." *The Divine Good: Moral Theory and the Necessity of God* (San Francisco: HarperSanFrancisco, 1990) 3–4. For the sake of obviating possible misunderstanding, Gamwell distinguishes "between the modern commitment in the formal or minimal sense I have identified and any material or substantive convictions that claim to be justifiable or valid. To affirm that understandings of reality and ourselves in relation to it can be redeemed only by humanistic appeal leaves open to further deliberation and argument the material understandings that can be so redeemed" (7).

124. A moral consequence of this commitment to the historical study of religion is the requirement that Christians tell the truth about other religious traditions. So, for example, I believe that what the best historical scholarship teaches us about Judaism should profoundly alter traditional Christian beliefs about Jews and their religion, even if these beliefs have the sanction of the New Testament behind them. I cannot imagine a responsible theological exegesis of the New Testament for our time that looks upon such scholarship as optional.

basic premise of all historical-critical investigation: "the Bible is in the first instance a book produced by human means in human ways . . . Research has brought it down from heaven and set it up in the midst of the earth."[125] On this view, claims for the Bible's divine character or authority are nothing short of idolatrous. In all honesty, this is exactly what I think of Seitz's claim that the Bible speaks from the perspective of God.[126] This is not to deny, of course, that there is truth, wisdom, and insight to be found within its covers. Indeed, the very act of taking the Bible seriously as a religious and theological document implies that its meaning is not locked in the ancient past, just as philosophers today continue to read Plato and Aristotle on account of their enduring contributions to philosophical debate and not as mere period pieces. But this recognition of the Bible's permanent value and existential significance for later generations need not depend in any way upon doctrines of biblical inspiration or even a special theological hermeneutic.

I realize this rationale for the indispensability of historical criticism is not going to carry any weight with Childs, Seitz, or Martin, but that is not because it is incoherent in itself; rather, it presupposes a notion of theology that is rejected by them from the outset. For my part, I judge their main failing to be an inability or unwillingness to think through consistently the normative implications for theology (and ethics) of a thoroughgoing historical approach to the study of religion, including Christian religion. Such an approach acknowledges that understandings of Christian faith have changed over the centuries, and that not even within the New Testament is there unanimity as to its proper interpretation.[127] Moreover, the later doctrinal positions articulated in the ecumenical creeds or the Protestant confessions cannot be drawn directly out of the New Testament, as Martin has conceded in the case of Paul's relation to later trinitarian doctrine and

125. Hermann Gunkel, "Why Engage the Old Testament?" in *Water for a Thirsty Land: Israelite Religion and Literature*, ed. K. C. Hanson, Fortress Classics in Biblical Studies (Minneapolis: Fortress, 2001) 1–30 at 4.

126. Given this premise, Seitz must seek to exonerate the Bible from any complicity in American slavery. *Word without End*, 324–25n4.

127. I fully agree with Levenson when he suggests that Christians could learn something of great value from Judaism in this regard: "I suspect that Judaism is somewhat better situated to deal with the polydoxy of biblical theology than is Christianity . . . [M]ost of the Talmud is a debate, with both majority and minority positions preserved and often unmarked. This is very different from most of the theological literature of Christianity. A tradition whose sacred texts are internally argumentative will have a far higher tolerance for theological polydoxy (within limits) and far less motivation to flatten the polyphony of the sources into a monotony." *The Hebrew Bible*, 56. Such an approach to pluralism within the Christian tradition could occasion a new spirit of theological debate that moves away from the traditional "orthodoxy/heresy" model that has been so destructive of genuine conversation and even argument.

as critics of Luther's exegesis of Paul have argued. In this insistence upon an understanding of theology's task that fully incorporates the results of historical labor, I follow Troeltsch, who observed that "the application of historical criticism to religious tradition must result in a profound change in one's inward attitude to it and in one's understanding of it."[128] John J. Collins has aptly stated what the implementation of Troeltsch's insight would entail for biblical theology:

> The History of Religion approach . . . is not an alternative to be avoided but an ally to be utilized. While it may be difficult for any Christian to avoid dogmatic prejudices and apologetics in addressing theological questions, it is an ideal worthy of our aspirations. Such an approach will not satisfy those who see theology as an essentially confessional enterprise, but it does affirm the possibility of a Biblical Theology that is consistent with the regnant historical-critical method.[129]

And so, until better instructed, I see no reason to abandon liberal Protestantism's classic commitment to a mutually enriching dialogue between the ongoing and thus corrigible traditions of the Reformation and the Enlightenment for the sake of both a self-critical understanding of faith and a self-critical understanding of reason—including historical reason.

---

128. Troeltsch, "Historical and Dogmatic Method in Theology," 13. Ironically, Seitz appears to agree with Troeltsch's assessment of the implications of historical criticism for theology (*Word without End*, 35n11). He quotes this statement from Troeltsch: "Historical method, once . . . applied to biblical study, is a leaven that transforms everything, and finally shatters the whole framework of theological method as this has existed hitherto" (Troeltsch, "Historical and Dogmatic Method," 12; reproduced here in the translation used by Seitz). Seitz then comments, "Whether one judges this a good thing is another matter, of course."

129. John J. Collins, "Biblical Theology and the History of Israelite Religion," in *Encounters with Biblical Theology* (Minneapolis: Fortress, 2005) 24–33 at 33.

3

Friedrich Schleiermacher on the Old Testament as Jewish Scripture

IN THE NINETEENTH CENTURY the unrestricted application of the historical-critical method posed an unprecedented challenge to inherited Christian notions about the Bible. While this challenge was eventually to be felt most acutely in the study of the New Testament once the distinction between the "Jesus of history" and the "Christ of faith" had firmly established itself, traditional viewpoints on the Old Testament were actually the first to be called into question. As a consequence of historical investigation, it became increasingly difficult for theologians to claim that the gospel is already taught in the Old Testament. Regarding this matter, Friedrich Schleiermacher (1768–1834) made a bold proposal. He argued against the canonical standing of the Old Testament on the grounds that it expresses Jewish, not Christian, religion. For him this conclusion was the unavoidable result of the advancing critical scholarship that was undermining the christological exegesis used to defend the church's claim to the Old Testament against the synagogue's counterclaim to its sole rightful possession. Opposing such "christianizing" readings, Schleiermacher broke ranks from Christian theologians and championed the side of the Jews in this historic debate. His only predecessors in this regard were Marcion and the Socinians, although his proposal for relegating the Old Testament to noncanonical status was later endorsed by Adolf von Harnack.

Surprisingly, there has been very little scholarship devoted to Schleiermacher's stance toward the Old Testament.[1] In a recent monograph, Klaus

---

1. Hans-Joachim Kraus insists, "For the basic understanding of the Old Testament

Beckmann takes note of this deficiency and seeks to reignite theological discussion on the Christian relation to the Old Testament in light of historical research by exploring in detail Schleiermacher's argument.[2] Since Beckmann believes that Schleiermacher's position is inadequate, he investigates five other German Protestant theologians from the nineteenth century who also sought to come to grips with historical study of the Old Testament in order to ascertain whether their conclusions are more adequate. While I agree that Schleiermacher's view is inadequate, I disagree with the reasons Beckmann gives for this judgment. Beckmann is convinced that the problems with Schleiermacher's position can be traced to his abandonment of the supposedly "biblical" model of *Heilsgeschichte* (prophecy and fulfillment) that was revived by the real hero of Beckmann's tale, J. C. K. von Hofmann. While Hofmann acknowledged the relative right of historical methods to display the meaning of the Old Testament on its own terms, he insisted that in the final analysis the Old Testament must be interpreted through the lens of the New Testament's christological *kerygma*. As Beckmann indicates, Hofmann's position anticipates that of Karl Barth, who proposed to rescue the Old Testament from a purely historical exegesis by reasserting a distinctly theological hermeneutic that regards the Old Testament as a witness to Jesus Christ.[3] Clearly, Beckmann is engaged in an *external* criticism: the only way to avoid Schleiermacher's conclusion is to work from a different set of premises. But the odd thing about Beckmann's recommendation of Hofmann's (and Barth's) proposal is that it is an instance of precisely the sort of christianizing interpretation Schleiermacher opposed. Beckmann has thus not addressed Schleiermacher's argument but simply bypassed it.

Beckmann does not consider the possibility that Schleiermacher's argument might be subject to criticism and, hence, modification along the very methodological lines that Schleiermacher recognized as in keeping with his commitment to a thoroughgoing historical-critical exegesis of the Bible and its revisionary implications for theology. In this respect Beckmann is typical

---

in the nineteenth century, Schleiermacher's statements were of no small importance." *Die Geschichte der historisch-kritischen Erforschung des Alten Testaments von der Reformation bis zur Gegenwart,* 2nd ed. (Neukirchen-Vluyn: Neukirchener, 1969) 170.

2. Klaus Beckmann, *Die fremde Wurzel: Altes Testament und Judentum in der evangelischen Theologie des 19. Jahrhunderts,* Forschungen zur Kirchen- und Dogmengeschichte 85 (Göttingen: Vandenhoeck & Ruprecht, 2002) 31, 33.

3. Karl Barth exclaimed, "A religio-historical understanding of the Old Testament in abstraction from the revelation of the risen Christ is simply an abandonment of the New Testament and of the sphere of the church in favor of that of the synagogue, and therefore in favor of an Old Testament . . . understood apart from its true object and content." *The Doctrine of the Word of God,* vol. I/2 of *Church Dogmatics,* trans. G. T. Thomson and Harold Knight (Edinburgh: T. & T. Clark, 1956) 489.

of many theologians who grant a limited role to historical methods while invoking theological categories derived from the New Testament so as to make the Old Testament serviceable for the purposes of Christian faith. But the enduring question Schleiermacher's argument poses is whether there are compelling reasons to retain the Old Testament in the church's Bible without resorting to christological readings that deprive Judaism of its claim to it. Two important values are at stake here: the Old Testament as a part of the Christian canon, on the one hand, and the intellectual integrity of Old Testament exegesis and Christian theology, on the other. Unless his challenge can be met directly, the Christian claim to the Old Testament cannot be justified theologically apart from a christological exegesis imposed on it from without.

As an exercise in historical theology this essay undertakes three distinct yet interrelated tasks: first, to analyze Schleiermacher's proposal in its own historical context; second, to offer a criticism of it drawing upon contemporary biblical scholarship; third, to propose an alternative theological construal of Christian faith and of the Old Testament's importance for it. In contrast to Beckmann's, however, my argument with Schleiermacher is an *internal* criticism that does not adopt a standpoint extrinsic to his point of departure. Precisely because his theological method requires any interpretation of Christian faith "to be subject to a process of continuous checking against the whole history of Christianity, as presented by contemporary historical research,"[4] his own position on the Old Testament is subject to critique insofar as it assumes a view of Judaism and of early Christianity's relation to it no longer substantiated by historical research. Since, moreover, some of his material doctrinal conclusions are not required by his theological method, other conclusions can be defended as more appropriate without abandoning his model of theology for another.

SCHLEIERMACHER'S ARGUMENT ABOUT THE OLD TESTAMENT

Endorsing Semler's call for a "free investigation of the canon" unfettered by doctrinal constraints, Schleiermacher rejected the notion that "the sacred books require a hermeneutical and critical treatment departing from the generally valid rules" of interpretation.[5] For him, this freedom was an

---

4. Stephen Sykes, *The Identity of Christianity: Theologians and the Essence of Christianity from Schleiermacher to Barth* (Philadelphia: Fortress, 1984) 99.

5. Friedrich Schleiermacher, *Der christliche Glaube nach den Grundsätzen der evangelischen Kirche im Zusammenhang dargestellt*, ed. Martin Redeker, critical ed. based on

inviolable bequest from the Reformers, whose aim was to let the Bible speak for itself apart from the yoke of ecclesiastical tradition. "It is thoroughly Protestant," he contended, "to allow everyone the free application of the exegetical art as based on philology."[6] He realized that this would occasion revision, and in some cases rejection, of certain cherished Protestant beliefs about the biblical canon, though he predicted that historical scholarship would prove to be more problematic for the Old Testament than for the New Testament.[7] Although the Documentary Hypothesis had yet to receive its classic formulation from Wellhausen, there was already by Schleiermacher's time a well-established tradition of doubting Mosaic authorship of the Pentateuch. Furthermore, critical scholarship was questioning the view that the prophets had predicted the coming of Christ and was beginning to look upon the prophetic oracles as messages addressed to the particular historical circumstances of their own times.[8]

Schleiermacher was convinced that the Christian effort to prove Jesus' messianic status on the basis of Old Testament prophecy was a mistake, and that the New Testament's appeal to it was strictly an intra-Jewish affair of the first century. He conceded that while a Jew of that time might well have become persuaded that the prophecies referred to Jesus, such an opinion necessarily presupposed faith in the inspiration of the Jewish scriptures that a Gentile convert could not have been expected to possess. Indeed, such proof had not really been decisive even for Jewish believers whose conversion was brought about by the powerful impression the personality of Jesus made upon them, not by arguments about prophecy. Hence, far from being troubled by the negative results of historical scholarship, Schleiermacher sought to put them to good theological use. The lesson to be learned is that faith in Jesus can stand on its own apart from appeals to the Old Testament.[9]

---

the 2nd German ed. (Berlin: de Gruyter, 1960) §130.2 (henceforth abbreviated as *Gl.* and cited by section and paragraph); ET, *The Christian Faith*, ed. H. R. Mackintosh and J. S. Stewart, English translation of the 2nd German ed. of 1830–31 (Philadelphia: Fortress, 1976). Translations of Schleiermacher's and other German texts are mine unless otherwise indicated.

6. *Gl.* §27.3.

7. Friedrich Schleiermacher, *Schleiermachers Sendschreiben über seine Glaubenslehre an Lücke*, ed. Hermann Mulert (Giessen: Töpelmann, 1908) 41–43; ET, *On the Glaubenslehre: Two Letters to Dr. Lücke*, trans. James Duke and Francis Fiorenza, American Academy of Religion Texts and Translations Series 3 (Chico, CA: Scholars, 1981) 65–67 (henceforth, page references to the English translation will be placed in parentheses).

8. *Gl.* §14, postscript.

9. Schleiermacher, *Sendschreiben*, 42 (*On the Glaubenslehre*, 66).

Schleiermacher believed the time had come for the church to acknowledge that the Old Testament is a "superfluous authority" for dogmatics. He justified this departure from Christian tradition by arguing that a doctrine taught only in the Old Testament but not in the New Testament could hardly be said to possess a genuinely Christian character; by contrast, a doctrine taught only in the New Testament would not be questionable because nothing about it was to be found in the Old Testament.[10] While there are few doctrines which at one time or another have not been justified by appealing to the Old Testament, he was of the opinion that such appeals had done damage to the intellectual integrity of exegesis by foisting an alien meaning upon the text.[11] Moreover, they had unnecessarily muddied the later development of Christian doctrine: "we have to thank the dogmatic attachment to the Old Testament for much that is bad in our theology; and if Marcion had been correctly understood and not denounced as a heretic, our doctrine of God would have remained much purer."[12] Hence, both subdisciplines of theology—exegesis and dogmatics—have a stake in the question of the Old Testament.[13]

Yet Schleiermacher did not actually call for the excision of the Old Testament from the Bible. He recognized that the Old Testament is the indispensable source for understanding the history of the Jewish people from which Jesus and his first disciples descended. For that reason alone, a thorough acquaintance with the Old Testament is essential for grasping the many literary references and linguistic idioms of the New Testament writings, and Schleiermacher fully expected ministerial candidates to know Hebrew and Aramaic as well as Greek.[14] His point, rather, is theological. He distinguished the historical fact of Christianity's origin in the Jewish milieu from the normative question of appealing to the Old Testament in support of Christian doctrine. Since only the New Testament writings were produced under the influence of Jesus' ministry, they are the first in the series of presentations of Christian faith which alone can serve as the norm for all subsequent presentations of it.[15] Hence, however important its historical

---

10. *Gl.* §27.3.

11. *Gl.* §132.2.

12. Friedrich Schleiermacher, *Aus Schleiermacher's Leben in Briefen*, 4 vols., ed. Ludwig Jonas and Wilhelm Dilthey (Berlin: Reimer, 1860–1863) 4:394.

13. In Schleiermacher's model of theology, biblical exegesis is the first part of historical theology. See *Kurze Darstellung des theologischen Studiums zum Behuf einleitender Vorlesungen*, ed. Heinrich Scholz, critical ed. (Hildesheim: Olms, 1961) §85; ET, *Brief Outline on the Study of Theology*, trans. Terrence N. Tice (Atlanta: John Knox, 1977).

14. Schleiermacher, *Kurze Darstellung*, §141.

15. *Gl.* §132; see also *Gl.* §129.

value for understanding the context of the New Testament, the Old Testament should not be taken as canonical: "To include the Jewish codex within the canon means to view Christianity as a continuation of Judaism and is at odds with the idea of the canon."[16]

For Schleiermacher, early Christianity was a completely new religion and stood in the same relation, religiously speaking, to Judaism as to paganism, notwithstanding its historical ties to the former.[17] Whereas conversion to Christianity required that Gentiles abandon their idolatrous worship, it required that Jews relinquish the Mosaic legislation. Accordingly, the step from Judaism to Christianity was as much a transition to another religion as the step from paganism to Christianity. Schleiermacher anticipated the objection that there was a far greater leap "from the side of paganism, insofar as it first had to become monotheistic in order to become Christian."[18] He countered this objection by pointing out that the Gentiles had long been inclined toward monotheism through the influence of their own philosophers, who for centuries had criticized Greco-Roman polytheism. Furthermore, Judaism at this time "was no longer based exclusively on Moses and the prophets" as a result of the many foreign influences it had incorporated since the Babylonian exile.[19] Seen in this light, the sharp dichotomy between Judaism and Hellenism breaks down, and it is evident that the church was a new formation in the religious sphere: "if Christianity is related in the same way to Judaism as to paganism, then it can no more be a continuation of Judaism than a continuation of paganism."[20]

In opposition to the rationalism of the Enlightenment with its "natural religion," Schleiermacher set out to rehabilitate "positive" (i.e., historically given) religion, each instance of which is a unique entity with its own distinct identity or "essence." In order to identify the essence of any positive religion, it is necessary to specify four features: (1) its stage of religious development, (2) the type of religion it represents, (3) its central idea, and (4) its originating event.[21] Each positive religion has an "outward unity," reflect-

---

16. Schleiermacher, *Kurze Darstellung*, 47n2 (*Brief Outline*, 53n2).
17. *Gl.* §12.
18. *Gl.* §12.2.
19. *Gl.* §12.1.
20. *Gl.* §12.2.
21. According to Schleiermacher, the definition of a religion's essence is designated a "critical inquiry" because the constant element in a historical phenomenon cannot be "ascertained in a merely empirical manner." He called this task "philosophical theology" (*Kurze Darstellung*, §32; see also *Gl.* §21). Ernst Troeltsch correctly understood that the attempt to define the essence was a response to the dissolution of dogma's authority in the light of historical consciousness. Troeltsch, "What Does 'Essence of

ing a definite origin in history, and an "inward unity," which is a peculiar modification of the elements it shares with other faiths at the same stage and of the same type. Christianity's essence can thus be formulated as follows:

> Christianity is a monotheistic mode of faith, belonging to the teleological type of piety, and essentially distinguishes itself from other such modes of faith in that everything in it is related to the redemption accomplished by Jesus of Nazareth.[22]

Once the essence is ascertained, the relations of Christianity to other religions can be set forth with precision. Unlike premodern theologians Schleiermacher did not assume that monotheism was the earliest form of religion, although he did consider it to stand at the apex of human religious development. Judaism, too, is monotheistic and belongs to the "teleological" (or moral) type. Greco-Roman polytheism, however, not only reflects a lower stage of development but also belongs to the "aesthetic" type wherein the sense of moral obligation is not constitutive of the religious consciousness. Still, the contrast between Judaism and paganism with respect to stage and type of religion did not lead Schleiermacher to conclude that Christianity is related to Judaism in more than a merely external historical manner. He detected in Judaism an affinity with a less developed stage of religion ("fetishism") since its monotheism is corrupted by nationalism, whereas Christian monotheism is free of this defect.[23] And while the teleological character of Judaism is expressed in the form of obedience to law, in Christianity it assumes the form of exhortations, indicating how moral action springs forth from the consciousness of redemption. So even in those respects that the two religions share in common, there are profound differences between them.[24] Since everything in Christianity is related to the redemptive efficacy of Jesus, "Christian piety, as it emerged right from the start, is not to be

---

Christianity' Mean?," in *Ernst Troeltsch: Writings on Theology and Religion*, ed. Robert Morgan and Michael Pye (Atlanta: John Knox, 1977) 124–81 at 158, 177. Sykes comments, "Schleiermacher stumbles on a theological tool, namely that of the critical definition of the essence of Christianity, which meets the future exigencies of the impact of the biblical-critical movement on doctrinal theology" (*The Identity of Christianity*, 99).

22. *Gl.* §11.

23. Schleiermacher wrote, "Christianity is the purest formation of monotheism to have emerged in history" (*Gl.* §8.4). See Erhard Lucas, "Die Zuordnung von Judentum und Christentum von Schleiermacher bis Lagarde," *Evangelische Theologie* 23 (1963) 590–607, esp. 590–93; also Ernst Katzer, "Schleiermacher und die alttestamentlich-jüdische Religion," *Neues Sächsisches Kirchenblatt* 26 (1919) 721–28, 737–44, 759–62.

24. Schleiermacher characterized "the two chief concepts of the Jewish religion" as "the divine election of the nation and divine retribution" (*Gl.* §103.3).

understood by means of the Jewish piety of that or of an earlier time: thus in no way can Christianity be viewed as a reshaping or a renewal of Judaism."[25]

Since the Old Testament reflects Jewish religion, confusion as to the essential nature of Christianity necessarily arises from the traditional practice of placing both testaments on an equal footing as two parts of one canon of scripture. The Old Testament cannot be for Christians what it is for Jews, namely, an indivisible whole.[26] The Old Testament contains elements that are foreign to the church so that "whatever is most definitely Jewish has least value" for Christians, and even those passages in it that appear compatible with Christian piety are only "of a more general nature and not distinctively Christian."[27] Aside from the fact that the Old Testament can be claimed as a Christian book only when exegetical violence is done to the plain historical meaning of its literal-grammatical sense, placing the Old Testament on the same level as the New Testament diminishes the central significance of Jesus in an Ebionite (Jewish-Christian) manner. Moreover, those Christians who are especially fond of the Old Testament evince a legalistic mentality not in keeping with the Christian conception of the moral life.[28]

Although his assessment of the Old Testament is negative in its import for the church, it is necessary to recognize its double-sided character. The clear implication of Schleiermacher's argument is that Christians should acknowledge the integrity of Judaism as a distinct religion that is to be

---

25. *Gl.* §12.2.

26. The force of this observation is qualified when Schleiermacher insists upon the need for a critical investigation into the New Testament canon: "The Protestant Church necessarily claims to be continually occupied in determining the New Testament canon more exactly. The New Testament canon has obtained its present form through the decision of the Church," though "[t]his is not a decision to which we attribute an authority exalted above all inquiry." "It must be permissible, then . . . to have the canon in two forms: that which has been handed down historically and that which has been separated out critically" (*Brief Outline*, §§110, 114).

27. *Gl.* §12.3. Schleiermacher sometimes preached on Old Testament texts. For analysis of these sermons, see Joachim Hoppe, "Altes Testament und alttestamentliche Predigt bei Schleiermacher," *Monatschrift für Pastoraltheologie* 54 (1965) 213–20; and Wolfgang Trillhaas, "Schleiermachers Predigten über alttestamentliche Texte," in *Schleiermacher und die wissenschaftliche Kultur des Christentums*, ed. Günther Meckenstock, Theologische Bibliothek Töpelmann 51 (Berlin: de Gruyter, 1991) 279–89.

28. *Gl.* §132.2. Schleiermacher said that "law is not originally a Christian term" (*Gl.* §66.2). In his understanding of Christian ethics the imperative mood is replaced by a descriptive account of how Christians act in accordance with their religious consciousness. Though his statement implies that Judaism is "legalistic," the primary target of his criticism is the extremely conservative use of the Old Testament by some Christians such as his Berlin colleague Hengstenberg, who appealed to the Old Testament to defend the institution of monarchy and to oppose the modern liberal state. See Beckmann, *Die fremde Wurzel*, 239–70.

understood on its own terms quite apart from any relation to Christianity. As Joseph Pickle points out, "Schleiermacher's appreciative assessment of Judaism recognizes the uniqueness of Judaism and rejects attempts to treat it or the Old Testament as a *preparatio evangelii*."[29] Hence, Schleiermacher conceded that the Old Testament really belongs to the synagogue, and not to the church, after all. The most important theologian of the nineteenth century thus departed from the classical Christian tradition by upholding the Jewish character of the Old Testament. But precisely because the Old Testament is Jewish, it cannot also be Christian.

CRITIQUE OF SCHLEIERMACHER'S PORTRAYAL OF JUDAISM AND EARLY CHRISTIANITY

Schleiermacher's methodological insistence upon the distinctiveness of each positive religion cleared the way for the possibility of an impartial historical treatment of Judaism in its own right. Nevertheless, his interpretation of Judaism betrays certain prejudices that reflect his own Christian starting point. Consequently, his reconstruction of the history of religion invites criticism to the extent that it fails to meet the requirements of a genuinely historical interpretation. Since his proposal regarding the Old Testament is so closely tied to his view of the church's relation to Judaism, of chief concern here is his argument that Christianity is not to be understood as a continuation or development of Judaism.

The characterization of the Old Testament as "Jewish" is subject to some important qualifications not made by Schleiermacher himself. He apparently assumed that Judaism was the religion of Israel even before the exile.[30] Yet modern study has shown that Judaism first began to take shape during the exilic crisis of Israel's earlier national religion and so is not identical with preexilic religion. This insight has ramifications for Schleiermacher's critique of Jewish monotheism as bearing an affinity with a lesser form of religion ("fetishism") on account of its ties to a particular nation. By comparison with Judaism, preexilic Israelite religion was not a thoroughgoing monotheism but, rather, a "henotheism" since Israel's national deity was not yet conceived consistently in radical terms as the creator and sovereign

---

29. Joseph W. Pickle, "Schleiermacher on Judaism," *Journal of Religion* 60 (1980) 115–37 at 115.

30. It appears as though Schleiermacher viewed Moses as the founder of Judaism: "By 'Judaism' is understood primarily the Mosaic institutions, but also, as preparation for these, every earlier usage which abetted the segregation of the people" (*Gl.* §12.1–2). He also characterized the religion of the pre-Mosaic period as "Abrahamitic Judaism," which is obviously anachronistic.

of the entire world. Accordingly, a genuine monotheism developed in concert with the emergence of Judaism, not in spite of it! While vestiges of the premonotheistic Israelite religion are embedded in older strata of the Old Testament, these traditions were subject to reinterpretation from the monotheistic perspective of the Jewish redactors of the Old Testament. Hence, Schleiermacher's criticism of Jewish monotheism as less than pure results in part from his lack of adequate knowledge of the actual historical relations between preexilic Israelite religion and postexilic Jewish religion as well as of the theological struggle between monotheism and henotheism that is reflected in the literature of the Old Testament. But this is not the entire explanation for his view. Curiously, Schleiermacher's critique of Judaism as particularistic shows the unwitting influence upon him of the Enlightenment's preference for a universal, rational religion. The irony here is that he thereby betrayed his own groundbreaking recognition of the irreducibly particular nature of actual religion, which he articulated in his polemic against "natural religion" as an artificial intellectual construct.[31] Judaism is constituted by the twin poles of universality (reflecting its monotheism) and particularity (rooted in its special vocation to bring all peoples to monotheism). But particularity is not the same as "particularism," just as universality is not identical with "universalism." Christianity is just as particular as and no less prone to particularism than Judaism.[32]

Schleiermacher's portrait does not, moreover, sufficiently differentiate the postexilic Judaism that put its indelible stamp upon the final form of the Old Testament from the Judaism of the rabbis after the destruction of the second temple. Judaism as classically defined is a post-Christian development that cannot be simply identified with the Jewish religion evident in the later formative period of the Old Testament. Prior to the rabbinic period, there was no such thing as a monolithic or "orthodox" Judaism

---

31. Pickle points out that the emancipated Jews whom Schleiermacher knew held to these same views of Judaism on account of their commitment to the Enlightenment's ideal of a purely rational religion: "The uncompromising critic of natural religion sees, and tries to appreciate, Judaism in the guise formulated by passionate devotees of natural religion." Pickle, "Schleiermacher on Judaism," 137. Pickle concludes that Schleiermacher's view of Judaism was not really negative so much as it was ambivalent.

32. Schleiermacher's comparison of Jewish and Christian monotheisms results from an unfair juxtaposition of an actual Judaism and an idealized Christianity. Christianity has been particularistic (as distinct from historically particular) in its own way on account of the belief that "outside of the church there is no salvation." Finally, doubt must surely be cast on Schleiermacher's claim that monotheism has found its purest expression in Christianity when it is recalled that Jews and Muslims alike have traditionally looked upon trinitarianism as a relapse into polytheism. That he was sensitive to this criticism is evident from his plea for reconsideration of the Sabellian way of interpreting the trinitarian doctrine. See *Gl.* §§170–72.

commanding the allegiance of all Jews. In fact, there were varieties of Judaism, each of which claimed to embody the authentic continuation of Israel's religious heritage. The crucial point is that the Bible (Tanakh/Old Testament) does not belong to rabbinic Judaism in any simple sense. Indeed, the results of historical criticism have been no less troubling for traditional Jewish beliefs about the Bible.[33] While the Old Testament is certainly Jewish, it is not to be equated with classical Judaism as though the latter were the inevitable outcome of the former.[34]

Since the religion we now call Christianity began its existence as one variety of Judaism, it is anachronistic to describe it as a new religion in its original phase, as Schleiermacher did; indeed, it is difficult to identify at what stage in its history we can speak of it as a different religion from Judaism. Yet if this is the case, must we not grant that the New Testament, too, is in a real sense a document of Jewish religion? In his critique of Schleiermacher, Barth correctly understood that humanly speaking the entire Bible is

> a product of the Israelitish, or to put it more clearly, the Jewish spirit. This is true ... of the whole Bible, even of the whole of the New Testament Bible ... If we want it otherwise, we will have to strike out not only the Old but all the New Testament as well ... The Bible is a Jewish book, the Jewish book.[35]

Although the New Testament is full of polemics against non-Christian Jews as well as against other Christians (Jewish and non-Jewish), it breathes throughout the spirit of genuine Jewish piety.[36]

33. Tikva Frymer-Kensky writes, "The Bible is the source of halakic [legal] authority, but it does not function on its own and is not an independent source of authority in traditional Judaism ... [T]he Christian church was explicitly 'supersessionist.' It showed honor to and interest in the Hebrew Bible and claimed it as its own heritage, but it considered the New Testament as its foundational Scripture ... Judaism was almost equally supersessionist, but it did not make its supersessionism apparent. It behaved ritually as if the Torah was the central facet of Judaism, but it dictated the way that the Torah should be read." Frymer-Kensky, "The Emergence of Jewish Biblical Theologies," in *Jews, Christians, and the Theology of the Hebrew Scriptures*, ed. Alice Ogden Bellis and Joel S. Kaminsky, SBL Symposium Series 8 (Atlanta: SBL Press, 2000) 109–21 at 111.

34. Matthias Wolfes makes this pointed observation: "The equation of the Old Testament and Jewish religion carried out by Schleiermacher has, however, a fatal consequence for the theological evaluation of Judaism. For it denies to Judaism a capacity for renewal and development beyond the historical religious development attested in the biblical writings." Matthias Wolfes, *Öffentlichkeit und Bürgergesellschaft. Friedrich Schleiermachers politische Wirksamkeit* (Berlin: de Gruyter, 2004) 2:374.

35. Barth, *The Doctrine of the Word of God*, I/2:510. See also Julie Galambush, *The Reluctant Parting: How the New Testament's Jewish Writers Created a Christian Book* (San Francisco: HarperSanFrancisco, 2005).

36. Since incipient Christianity was not homogenous, Wayne A. Meeks insists that

The historical picture is further complicated by the insight that all of these varieties of Judaism, including Christianity, were profoundly influenced by Hellenism. Wayne Meeks argues that "'Judaism' was in some senses a Hellenistic religion . . . Like the other varieties of Judaism, the earliest Christian groups were simultaneously Jewish and Hellenistic."[37] Yet Schleiermacher did not view Christianity as either Jewish or Hellenistic, and certainly not as simultaneously Jewish *and* Hellenistic, since for him it was a completely new formation equidistant from both Judaism and Hellenism. Although he perceived the influence on Judaism of what would later be called syncretism, his mode of conceiving each religion as a distinct entity implies a view of the religions as having only external or accidental relations to one another. Even if we should wish to allow for a more dynamic model of their mutual relations, Schleiermacher's thesis that Christianity stood in the same relation of religious discontinuity to Judaism as to paganism is hardly persuasive. It is not clear, moreover, what we are to make of this rather surprising assessment given his classification of paganism as a polytheistic religion of the aesthetic (i.e., nonmoral) type. On his own terms, this means that paganism not only represented a lower stage of religious development than Judaism but also differed in kind from it. Indeed, he invoked Greco-Roman paganism as his chief illustration of an aesthetic religion:

> What [in the history of religion] is most apparent to us, as being sharply opposed in this respect to Christianity, is not coordinate with it, but belongs to a lower level, namely, Greek polytheism. In this religion the teleological direction retreats completely; neither in their religious symbols nor in their mysteries is there any discernable trace of the idea of a totality of moral ends and of a relation of all human situations to this . . . *Christianity, even apart from the fact that it occupies a higher level, is in the sharpest way opposed to this type.*[38]

It is pertinent to recall Schleiermacher's view that the "inward unity" of any positive religion is to be understood as a "peculiar modification" of that which is shared with religions of the same type and at the same stage of

---

we formulate better questions: "The questions that have to be asked are more particular: Which parts of the Jewish tradition were being assumed and reinterpreted by this or that group of early Christians? Which institutions were continued, which discarded?" Meeks, "Judaism, Hellenism, and the Birth of Christianity," in *Paul beyond the Judaism/Hellenism Divide*, ed. Troels Engberg-Pedersen (Louisville: Westminster John Knox, 2001) 17–27 at 26.

37. Meeks, "Judaism, Hellenism, and the Birth of Christianity," 24–26.

38. *Gl.* §9.2, emphasis added.

development.³⁹ Yet what else can this mean other than that early Christianity was a peculiar modification of Jewish religion?⁴⁰ In his lectures on hermeneutics where he attempted to sort out the differing relations of dependence upon Hebrew and Greek evident in the New Testament, Schleiermacher concluded:

> It is undeniable that the influence of Hebrew in the really religious terms is particularly great. For in what was originally Hellenic—particularly to the extent that it was known to the [New Testament] writers—the religious aspect which was to be newly developed (not only) found no point of contact, but even what was similar was rejected via its connection to polytheism.⁴¹

Here there appears to be an inconsistency in Schleiermacher's argument. From the perspective of hindsight, we know that what began as a Jewish sect developed into a distinct religious community whose self-definition had to be hammered out in polemics against incipient rabbinic Judaism as well as against paganism. But from this fact of history it does not follow that the material substance of Christian religion is as discontinuous with Judaism as with the Hellenistic religions from which the church drew the majority of its converts. Schleiermacher was right to point out the philosophical developments on Greek soil that had prepared for the reception by non-Jews of a monotheistic and ethical religion. Yet his comparison of pagan converts to Jewish converts is misleading since the latter did not understand themselves as rejecting the legacy of Israel for a new religion but, rather, as embracing its fulfillment. This was clearly true of the apostle Paul.⁴²

The conclusion is unavoidable that the historical foundation of Schleiermacher's argument about the Old Testament is inadequate inasmuch as it presupposes an undifferentiated view of prerabbinic Judaism as well as an interpretation of early Christianity as only accidentally related to the religious heritage of Judaism. For this reason, Pickle has rendered the following ironic verdict: "The advocate of historical-critical understanding

---

39. *Gl.* §9.2.

40. For an early critique of Schleiermacher's thought along these lines, see J. C. F. Steudel, "Über Schleiermacher's und Marheineke's Ansicht über das Alte Testament," in *Vorlesungen über die Theologie des Alten Testaments*, ed. G. F. Oehler (Berlin: Reimer, 1840) 539–43 at 540–42. Steudel represented the supernaturalist orthodox theology.

41. Schleiermacher, *Hermeneutics and Criticism and Other Writings*, ed. and trans. Andrew Bowie, Cambridge Texts in the History of Philosophy (Cambridge: Cambridge University Press, 1998) 42.

42. Krister Stendahl cautions against speaking of "conversion" with respect to the apostle Paul since it implies that he joined another religion. Krister Stendahl, *Paul among Jews and Gentiles and Other Essays* (Philadelphia: Fortress, 1976) 7–23.

accepts a view of Judaism that is utterly ahistorical."[43] While Schleiermacher cannot be held responsible for not having had the benefit of recent biblical scholarship at his disposal, it is nonetheless the case that his commitment to the historical-critical method invites these criticisms of his own historical reconstruction. In this connection, we are brought back to the idea that Christianity, like every other positive religion, has a distinguishing "essence" that identifies it as a unique entity in the religious realm. This idea was much debated in the nineteenth century. In the wake of the widespread acknowledgment of the demise of the orthodox doctrine of scripture, it answered the need for a conceptual tool to bridge the empirical study of history and the normative task of theology. And yet, the notion of a distinguishing "essence" presented its own problems. The ambiguity inherent in this notion is whether the essence of a religion is an abstraction from history intended merely to characterize a set of related phenomena, or whether it is also meant to serve a critical purpose in relation to them.[44] In practice, it appears to do double duty in this regard, although this is not objectionable provided that the proper conceptual distinctions are made between these two functions.[45]

Schleiermacher reasoned that the essence of Christianity can be determined in a scholarly manner only by comparing Christianity to the other positive religions. In this he was surely correct. Two questions must be asked, however. The first is whether such a concept is not too static to do justice to the dynamic character of a movement in history. Given that religious traditions undergo real change and development over time, does

---

43. Pickle, "Schleiermacher on Judaism," 137. Pickle goes on to say, "One can only wish that Schleiermacher's theological dispositions had been matched with an equally comprehensive awareness of Jewish piety, tradition, and insight . . . Since theology is never a closed book, however, it falls to his admirers to improve—in his own spirit—upon his view of Judaism."

44. The ambiguity involved in the idea of an "essence" is that it is not merely descriptive in intent but prescriptive as well. Its purpose, according to Troeltsch, is not only to indicate what distinguishes Christianity from other religions but also "to make possible an evaluation of what is essential [within Christianity], on the basis of which the inessential can be ignored and that which is contrary to the essence can be condemned" (Troeltsch, "What Does 'Essence of Christianity' Mean?" 144). The central problem in its deployment, as Troeltsch indicated, lies in "this unavoidable transition from an abstracted concept to an ideal concept" (158). Troeltsch thus called for a more careful distinction between "the properly historical" and "the philosophically historical, normative element."

45. A helpful analogy may be found in thinking about the reasons why the United States was founded, such as democracy, freedom of religion, human rights, and so forth. This descriptive-historical judgment obviously entails normative implications for judging America as a nation in relation to these ideals.

not the assumption of an essence hamper our appreciation of their dynamic character? This objection is valid whenever an abstract conception of a phenomenon is mistaken for the concrete phenomenon itself. But this confusion is not inevitable. Indeed, we cannot even speak of movements in history (say, the Renaissance or the Reformation) apart from the application of abstract concepts to the interpretation of the historian's empirical data. And all historians who are more than mere chroniclers necessarily hazard some general characterizations of broad movements in history and culture. This commonplace has to be stressed in response to those scholars who reject the very notion of an essence on the grounds that such an idea is foreign to temporal phenomena. No doubt, a large part of the problem stems from the connotations the word "essence" has acquired in our postmodern intellectual situation where "essentialisms" of one kind or another are rightly suspected of falsifying the complexity of reality. Yet it is erroneous to think that Schleiermacher intended to reify an abstraction. Although it may be desirable to come up with new terminology to designate such a conceptual operation, this does not obviate the need to specify wherein the enduring identity of a religious tradition consists if we wish to avoid a complete nominalism in historical interpretation.[46]

This recognition of the legitimacy, even indispensability, of inquiring into the essence leads to our second question, namely, whether the quest to define what makes Christianity distinctive must depend upon a comparison with the other religions that implies their inferiority. As I see it, there is no reason, for instance, why the identity of Christianity has to be purchased at the cost of a sharp contrast or opposition between it and Judaism given their inextricably close historical relations and substantial material overlaps. While Schleiermacher's concept of an essence can be defended in principle, his use of it in fact is vulnerable to this criticism.[47] Hence, an updated attempt to implement this task must renounce any apologetic motive when attempting to define the essence of Christianity in relation to Judaism. But in itself there is nothing wrong with his formal definition of Christianity's

---

46. The German word *Wesen* can be translated either as "essence" or "nature." For my own constructive purposes in the next section, I employ the term "nature" to distinguish the material content of Schleiermacher's understanding of Christian faith from his formal statement of its "essence."

47. John B. Cobb Jr. criticizes the tradition of Schleiermacher: "[T]he question of the distinctive essence of Christianity was subordinated to that of its superiority to other religions in such a way that the former question was inadequately treated." Cobb, *The Structure of Christian Existence* (Philadelphia: Westminster, 1967; reprint, New York: Seabury, 1979) 14.

essence: like Judaism, it is an ethical monotheism; but unlike Judaism, its central figure is Jesus and its central idea is redemption from sin.[48]

THE JEWISH JESUS AND THE NATURE OF CHRISTIAN FAITH

Schleiermacher posed the question: "Was Christianity something new or not?" In light of the foregoing discussion, the question should not be formulated so starkly as "new or not," since on historical grounds alone we have to say that Christianity was relatively new even if not absolutely so. Yet Schleiermacher disagreed. To his mind, Christianity represents an absolutely new beginning in the religious realm that cannot be explained by what preceded it historically. Here, however, we are dealing with more than a strictly historical judgment on his part since a particular theological construal of Christian faith codetermines his argument. He said as much in his lectures on hermeneutics: "The question cannot be decided in an immediately hermeneutic manner and therefore shows itself as a matter of conviction."[49] To be sure, in the final analysis how we think about Christianity's relation to Judaism (and, hence, to the Old Testament) is a theological question, the answer to which is indicative of a theologian's entire construal of the nature of Christian faith. While one cannot move directly from history to theology in positivistic fashion, there is nonetheless a critical interrelation between the two, especially for a theologian who affirms without qualification the results of historical-critical study. Yet in moving from the empirical questions of the historian of religion to the normative questions of the theologian, a shift is being made from a standpoint "external" to Christianity to one that is "internal" to it.[50] Whereas the essence must be determined through comparative study, theology (in the sense of dogmatics or systematic theology) requires that the theologian stand within the church, sharing its distinctive religious experience, and seeking to give as accurate a description of it as possible.[51]

---

48. For an example of this sort of inquiry on the part of a liberal Jewish thinker, see Leo Baeck, *The Essence of Judaism*, trans. Victor Grubenwieser and Leonard Pearl (New York: Schocken, 1976).

49. Schleiermacher, *Hermeneutics and Criticism*, 43, 41.

50. *Gl.* §11.5, 28.2.

51. Faith in Christ, according to Schleiermacher, is "a purely factual certainty, but a certainty of a fact which is entirely inward" (*Gl.* §14.1). Elsewhere he states, "This exposition is based entirely on the inner experience of the believer; its only purpose is to describe and elucidate that experience" (*Gl.* §100.3).

Though Schleiermacher is most often remembered for his famous redefinition of religion as "the feeling of absolute dependence," of greater importance perhaps was his proposal of a historicized model of dogmatics (*Glaubenslehre*) designed to transcend the dichotomy beyond supernaturalism and rationalism occasioned by the Enlightenment's challenge to the Reformation heritage. The components of this model are the following: first of all, faith is not an assent to doctrinal propositions, but a matter of the heart or, to use his terminology, the religious affections. Indeed, one may share Schleiermacher's affective view of faith without endorsing his theory of religion in every detail. Second, doctrines are understood as intellectual attempts to explicate the understanding of human existence in the world before God implicit in the Christian religious affections.[52] Third, historical study teaches that the church's doctrines have changed over the course of time. Fourth, the task of dogmatics is to discern the logical or systematic connection between the various doctrinal *loci* as representing in their totality the historically particular experience of redemption through Christ that constitutes the church as a distinctive religious community.[53] Fifth, since dogmatics concerns the state of Christian doctrine in the present moment, it must be open to further doctrinal revision for the sake of the best contemporary understanding of the Christian religious affections wherein faith consists. Formal agreement with Schleiermacher's model and method of dogmatics does not, however, entail endorsing all of his material conclusions. This distinction between the formal and material elements in Schleiermacher's dogmatics is crucial if there is to be an internal criticism of his positions that does not—as in the case of an external criticism such as Beckmann's—presuppose a completely different conception of the theological enterprise.[54] In my judgment, there are three interrelated doctrines to be interrogated for the sake of proposing a revision of Schleiermacher's construal of the nature of Christian faith. These are christology, soteriology, and the multiple meanings of revelation.

We cannot fail to notice what many scholars have labeled as Schleiermacher's "christocentrism." Of course, all Christian theology is christocentric in some sense inasmuch as the person of Jesus is the central revelation of God that constitutes the church as a distinct religious community. But Schleiermacher's theology is christocentric in a much stronger sense on

---

52. Schleiermacher exposited each doctrine in a threefold manner as a statement about the self, the world, and God (*Gl.* §30).

53. "Dogmatic propositions arise only from logically ordered reflection upon the immediate utterances of the religious self-consciousness" (*Gl.* §16, postscript).

54. Richard R. Niebuhr makes exactly the same point. *Schleiermacher on Christ and Religion: A New Introduction* (New York: Scribner, 1964) 16–17.

account of his conviction that redemption from sin is mediated through Jesus alone. Schleiermacher affirmed that Jesus, by virtue of his incomparable relation to God, quite simply *is* the new element that cannot be explained by any historical antecedents. He conceived of Jesus as a person whose consciousness of God was unbroken by sin; indeed, the religious ideal for human existence became an actual fact in this one individual.[55] Here we meet the sole miracle in Schleiermacher's theology.[56] For him, denial of this claim would spell the end of Christian faith.[57] Still, he was certain that his view of Jesus was a necessary inference about who he really must have been given his actual redemptive influence upon the present religious experience of Christian believers. In spite of his assurance in this regard, however, there are grave problems with such an idea. For one thing, it is exceedingly difficult to imagine what it would mean to say of a real human being that he or she was entirely without sin.[58] It is easy to suspect a "docetic" strain at work here, notwithstanding Schleiermacher's explicit rejection of this ancient heresy.[59] Moreover, the admittedly imperfect consciousness of God on the part of Christians does not require a perfect consciousness of God as its sufficient source, but merely a more powerful and vivid one.[60] Also, this conception has negative implications for the question of Jesus' relation to Judaism. In Susannah Heschel's analysis, Schleiermacher

> lifted Jesus from the realm of the human to a superhuman, if not supernatural, pedestal, by virtue of his extraordinary inner

---

55. *Gl.* §93. Schleiermacher added that this perfect God-consciousness was "a veritable existence of God in him" (*Gl.* §94). He thereby wished to indicate his continuity with the Alexandrian tradition.

56. *Gl.* §93.1–3.

57. *Gl.* §93.2.

58. Leander E. Keck adds that there is no need to "presuppose 'sinless perfection' (to speak with Schleiermacher) in the event of Jesus." Keck, *A Future for the Historical Jesus: The Place of Jesus in Preaching and Theology* (1971; reprint, Philadelphia: Fortress, 1981) 217.

59. For Schleiermacher the two opposing christological heresies are the Ebionite (or "Nazarean") and the docetic; the former denies that Jesus is absolutely superior to all other persons by virtue of his God-consciousness and the latter denies that there is an essential likeness between him and all other persons (*Gl.* §22.2). Docetism originally referred to the denial that Jesus had a real body and later to the denial that he had a rational human soul. Schleiermacher, of course, did not deny either of these; but his assertion of Jesus' absolutely perfect God-consciousness makes him categorically unlike everyone else.

60. Schleiermacher acknowledged this point as a possible criticism of his doctrine but rejected it (*Gl.* §93.1).

life . . . As a result, Jesus' life as a Jew became fundamentally irrelevant to the crux of his exceptional role.⁶¹

Schleiermacher feared that if Jesus had not perfectly embodied the religious ideal, then he was "only a more or less original and revolutionary reformer of the Jewish law."⁶²

It is pertinent to recall Schleiermacher's calm predication that historical-critical scholarship would be more damaging for the traditional Christian assessment of the Old Testament than for that of the New Testament. Yet in no wise has the historical basis of Schleiermacher's theology been more badly shaken than by the subsequent course of research into the gospels as sources for our knowledge of who Jesus was. Schleiermacher was confident that John's gospel provides us with a reliable report of Jesus' teaching from which we can form a picture of his inner life.⁶³ Accordingly, the message proclaimed by Jesus was about his own unique relation to God. This assumption that the christological teaching of John's gospel accurately depicts what Jesus taught about himself in turn accounts for the antithetical relationship between Jesus and Judaism in Schleiermacher's interpretation.⁶⁴ But this view founders on the later insight of critical study that the synoptic gospels, not John, contain the most authentic reminiscences of Jesus' teachings. In his survey of the nineteenth century's quest for the historical Jesus, Albert Schweitzer concluded:

> Schleiermacher is not in search of the historical Jesus, but of the Jesus Christ of his own system of theology; that is to say, of the historic figure which seems to him appropriate to the self-consciousness of the redeemer as he presents it . . . What is chiefly fatal to a sound historical view is his one-sided preference for

---

61. Susannah Heschel, *Abraham Geiger and the Jewish Jesus*, Chicago Studies in the History of Judaism (Chicago: University of Chicago Press, 1998) 145.

62. *Gl.* §93.2.

63. Schleiermacher defended the historical veracity of John's gospel in a note added to the third edition of the *Speeches* in 1821. Schleiermacher, *On Religion: Speeches to Its Cultured Despisers*, trans. John Oman (1958; reprint, Louisville: Westminster John Knox, 1994) 262–63. In another place, Schleiermacher speculated on John's relation to Jesus: "In John's Gospel the interest is historical: was the author a contemporary witness?" Schleiermacher, *Hermeneutics and Criticism*, 212.

64. Horst Dietrich Preuss writes, "The opposition of Moses and Christ Schleiermacher takes from the Gospel of John which is also in other respects for him the most highly prized [of the gospels], and perhaps this even played a role in determining his attitude to 'the Jews.'" Preuss, "Vom Verlust des Alten Testaments und seinen Folgen dargestellt anhand der Theologie und Predigt F. D. Schleiermachers," in *Lebendiger Umgang mit Schrift und Bekenntnis*, ed. Joachim Track (Stuttgart: Calwer, 1980) 127–60 at 144.

the Fourth Gospel. It is, according to him, only in this Gospel that the consciousness of Jesus is truly reflected.⁶⁵

If Schleiermacher had been constrained to base his view of Jesus' preaching on the evidence of the synoptic evangelists instead of relying on John, he would have been forced to confront head-on what became the major problem of New Testament scholarship in the nineteenth century: the relation between the Jesus of history and the Christ of faith.

The only figure to the left of Schleiermacher analyzed in Beckmann's study is David Friedrich Strauss.⁶⁶ It was in the work of Strauss that this distinction became crucial for the scholarly study of the New Testament. Strauss, too, faulted Schleiermacher for teaching "not an historical, but an ideal Christ."⁶⁷ In sharp contrast to Schleiermacher, Strauss clearly saw that in his religion Jesus was a Jew, and that the church's christology as reflected, for example, in John's gospel attests to what Christians later taught about Jesus after his death.⁶⁸ Yet Strauss understood that even in its christological faith the church was still primarily a Jewish phenomenon. The New Testament's witness to Jesus as the messiah was born of a lively continuation of religious motifs found in the Old Testament.⁶⁹ Hence, for Strauss, the Old Testament and its interpretation in second-temple Judaism were the formative influences upon the presentation of Jesus in the gospels. Two consequences follow from this distinction between the historical Jesus and

---

65. Albert Schweitzer, *The Quest of the Historical Jesus*, trans. W. Montgomery (New York: Macmillan, 1968) 62, 66.

66. Beckmann, *Die fremde Wurzel*, 197–239.

67. David Friedrich Strauss, *The Life of Jesus Critically Examined*, ed. with an introduction by Peter C. Hodgson, trans. George Eliot, Lives of Jesus Series (Philadelphia: Fortress, 1972) 773.

68. Beckmann, *Die fremde Wurzel*, 206.

69. Beckmann, *Die fremde Wurzel*, 206. Beckmann is troubled by the application of "myth" to the exegesis of the Bible as well as by the Hegelian interpretation of it given by Strauss, yet he correctly formulates the import of this hermeneutic for Strauss: "In his 'mythical' criticism of the gospels Strauss expressed in radical fashion the literary unity of the Old and New Testaments. In his view, the evangelical narratives arose from the living Jewish tradition. Since the New Testament writers intended to prove the messianic character of Jesus, the Jewish Bible was seen [by Strauss] as the decisive formative influence upon the evangelical texts. The Jewish–Old Testament myth about the messiah determined for Strauss not only the 'how' but already the 'that' of the narratives about Jesus as the Christ" (208). If Beckmann had been willing to follow Strauss down this path, he could have claimed that Strauss, not Hofmann, provided the best alternative to Schleiermacher's position. One need not endorse the Hegelianism of Strauss as a condition for recognizing the importance of myth as a category of biblical interpretation.

the Christ of faith. First, Jesus did not teach the gospel that Christians later taught about him, as Schleiermacher mistakenly assumed.[70] Second, the actual content of Jesus' message can only be understood in relation to his Jewish context. This means that Jesus was a Jew, not a Christian.[71]

These considerations would require Schleiermacher to rethink the historical basis of his christological doctrine. More importantly, they would most certainly entail revision of his historical reconstruction of Jesus' teaching in the direction of what he pejoratively called "Ebionitism," i.e., a view that qualifies the absolute uniqueness of Jesus by stressing his continuity rather than discontinuity with Judaism. Schleiermacher well understood what this would mean for his theological position:

> If Christ was so constrained by the limitations of what was given at the time of his appearance, then even he and not least his entire work have to be capable of explanation from what was historically given to him; hence, Christianity as a whole could be understood to have emerged from Judaism at the particular stage of its development that it had attained at that time, the stage at which a person like Jesus could have come forth from its womb.[72]

This alternative view which was rejected by Schleiermacher is, however, completely in keeping with the results of contemporary scholarship on Jesus. Hence, if we are in earnest about the historical Jesus, as Schleiermacher was in principle, we have to surrender unhistorical claims that insulate Jesus' religiosity from his Jewish milieu.[73] We may properly seek to delineate Jesus' distinctiveness in relation to his milieu, but this is not to deny that the religion he taught was a form of Judaism. Though Schleiermacher insisted upon the Jewish character of the Old Testament, he did not view it as a document of equal religious value to the New Testament.[74] This assessment reflects his conviction that Christianity is not only a different religion from Judaism but also superior to it. He further assumed that this view

---

70. Rudolf Bultmann, *Theology of the New Testament*, 2 vols., trans. Kendrick Grobel (New York: Scribner, 1951, 1955) 1:3.

71. Hans Dieter Betz, "Wellhausen's Dictum 'Jesus was not a Christian, but a Jew' in Light of Present Scholarship," *Studia Theologica* 45 (1991) 83–110.

72. *Gl.* §93.2.

73. Schleiermacher was the first to offer a course of lectures on the life of Jesus, in 1819, thereby helping to launch the nineteenth century's quest for the historical Jesus. *The Life of Jesus*, ed. Jack C. Verheyden, trans. S. MacLean Gilmour, Lives of Jesus Series (Philadelphia: Fortress, 1975).

74. Beckmann, *Die Fremde Wurzel*, 133n530.

was consonant with what Jesus taught. This claim is now undermined by the insight that Jesus, however distinctive, was wholly rooted in the Jewish tradition.

Strauss clearly saw that it is no longer possible to assume an identity between the church's proclamation *about* Jesus and the proclamation *of* Jesus. But if the church's *kerygma* represents a development beyond what the historical Jesus taught, the question arises as to how we are to understand the material relation between them.[75] Although the christological faith of the church is not based directly on the teachings of Jesus, it nonetheless first arose in response to his distinctive embodiment of Jewish faith.[76] His central message concerned the coming of God's sovereign reign ("the kingdom of God"), and he called upon his fellow Jews to be prepared to receive it. As such, his preaching was about God, not about himself.[77] Without rejecting the Torah in principle, he differentiated between greater and lesser commandments in it. He continued aspects of the prophetic tradition in his concern for the poor and the oppressed. He pointed to evidence of God's providential care in the ordering of nature as had Israel's wisdom teachers before him. In all these respects, Jesus' teaching and ministry were firmly rooted in the Old Testament/Jewish tradition. H. Richard Niebuhr spoke of the faith that came to expression in Jesus' words and deeds as a paradigmatic illustration of Israel's "radical" or thoroughgoing monotheism. The historic significance of early Christianity, as Niebuhr noted, is that it made this faith available to non-Jews without requiring of them conversion to Judaism.[78] This crucial step obviously required a critical sifting of the

---

75. When I employ the phrase "historical Jesus," I simply mean the earliest layers of the synoptic tradition that have the greatest claim to reflect the authentic words of Jesus, although these can never be completely reconstructed with absolute assurance. Such historical judgments are always matters of probability. Schubert M. Ogden helpfully points out that the earliest, nonchristological stratum of the synoptic tradition has a *kerygmatic* intent inasmuch as it seeks to confront the hearer/reader with the same decision for God called for by Jesus' words. *The Point of Christology* (San Francisco: Harper & Row, 1982) 112–15.

76. This way of posing the question of the material continuity between the historical Jesus and the Christ of faith was the signal contribution of the post-Bultmannian "New Quest" initiated by Ernst Käsemann. See Ernst Käsemann, "The Problem of the Historical Jesus," in *Essays on New Testament Themes*, trans. W. J. Montague (Philadelphia: Fortress, 1982) 15–47.

77. Adolf von Harnack correctly understood that Jesus "desired no other belief in his person and no other attachment to it than is contained in the keeping of his commandments." *What Is Christianity?*, trans. Thomas Bailey Saunders, Fortress Texts in Modern Theology (Philadelphia: Fortress, 1986) 125.

78. H. Richard Niebuhr, *Radical Monotheism and Western Culture* (New York: Harper, 1970) 39–40.

Jewish scriptures for the purpose of discerning what was still valid for the new community under altered circumstances. But this development did not negate the material connection between Jesus' faith in God and the faith of Israel to which he was heir. Rudolf Bultmann emphasized that no matter how critical Jesus may have been in relation to the other Jewish teachers of his day, the content of his preaching was

> nothing else than true Old Testament-Jewish faith in God radicalized in the direction of the great prophets' preaching . . . [T]he concepts of God, world, and man, of Law and grace, of repentance and forgiveness in the teaching of Jesus are not new in comparison with those of the Old Testament and Judaism, however radically they may be understood. And his critical interpretation of the Law, in spite of its radicality, likewise stands within the scribal discussion about it.[79]

Even the love-command that has been so important in Christian ethics is derived from Jesus' summary of the Torah. Correctly understood, then, the faith of Christians is not opposed to the Jewish faith of Jesus; rather, it is trust in and loyalty to God *through* Jesus.[80] "Christian faith is not belief in a miracle," not even the miracle of Jesus' sinless perfection, but "the confidence that Jesus' witness [to God] is a true one."[81] Hence, Christian faith cannot be construed as standing in a completely antithetical relationship to Judaism without pitting itself against Jesus' own faith as a devout Jew.

Claude Welch is correct in characterizing Schleiermacher's position as representing only a "halfway" solution to the modern problem of christology. Unlike the classical problem of trying to affirm Jesus' humanity given the prior assumption of his self-evident divinity, the modern problem was to ask in what sense Jesus could be divine given his genuine humanity.[82] But it is possible to go further than Welch does by arguing that even this

---

79. Bultmann, *Theology of the New Testament*, 1:34–35. Bultmann says that this continuity between Jesus and his Jewish heritage explains why "modern liberal Judaism can very well esteem Jesus as teacher."

80. Troeltsch wrote, "In the absence of historical-critical thinking, Jesus was naturally identified with God in order that he might be the immediate object of faith; with critical thinking, the God of Jesus becomes the object of faith, and Jesus is transformed into the historical mediator and revealer." "The Dogmatics of the History-of-Religions School," in *Religion in History*, trans. James Luther Adams and Walter F. Bense (Minneapolis: Fortress, 1991) 87–108 at 98.

81. Van A. Harvey, *The Historian and the Believer: The Morality of Historical Knowledge and Christian Belief* (Philadelphia: Westminster, 1966) 274.

82. Claude Welch, *Protestant Thought in the Nineteenth Century*, 2 vols. (New Haven: Yale University Press, 1972–1985) 1:83–84.

new formulation of the christological problem is flawed insofar as it asks "about the being of Jesus in himself, as distinct from asking about the meaning of Jesus for us."[83] Instead of asking about Jesus' own relation to God (about which we could know next to nothing in any case), we should be asking another question: What does Jesus mean for those persons who have experienced redemption as a result of their encounter with him? Christological reflection thus properly begins, not with a question about the being of Jesus in relation to either divinity or humanity, but with the given fact of his salvific impact upon those who call themselves Christians. The question "What does Jesus actually do for Christians?" is, as Brian Gerrish rightly notes, "the crucial one to ask in any Christian community, if the christological project is to be duly launched."[84] It is this aspect of Schleiermacher's approach—namely, his insistence that christology arises from reflection upon Jesus' redemptive influence—that remains worthy of development since, if pursued consistently, it would allow us to state the meaning of Jesus for contemporary Christian experience while leaving behind untenable claims about the historical Jesus and his supposedly sinless relation to God.

If we ask how Jesus is efficacious in a redemptive manner today, we have to address the role of preaching in the church. Although Schleiermacher affirmed that the faith of Christians in every age is none other than that experienced by Jesus' original disciples, he did acknowledge a difference in the medium through which this faith has been evoked and sustained:

> To us is given, instead of [Jesus'] personal efficacy, only that of his community insofar as even the picture (*Bild*) of him found in the Bible likewise only came into being and persists because of it.[85]

After Jesus' death, it is the New Testament's portrait of him that serves as the occasion for an experience of redemption. This biblical picture of Christ thus takes the place that Jesus once had in relation to those who came into personal contact with him. In this respect, the church's proclamation can be understood as a continuation of Jesus' ministry. Such a focus on the New Testament's depiction of Jesus and its actualization in the church's preaching does not require assertions about Jesus that exempt him from the contingencies of his own historical circumstance as well as from our common humanity.

---

83. Ogden, *The Point of Christology*, 16.

84. B. A. Gerrish, *Saving and Secular Faith: An Invitation to Systematic Theology* (Minneapolis: Fortress, 1999) 98. Gerrish likens this logic of christological reflection to that found in Athanasius and Luther.

85. *Gl.* §88.2.

This modification of Schleiermacher's proposed avenue to christological reflection need not entail the problematic conclusion that redemption from sin can be attained only through an encounter with Jesus, an assumption he shared with the classical tradition that he in other ways sought to revise. Not only is redemption for Schleiermacher the central idea in the Christian religion, but Jesus is its only mediator.[86] He spoke of "the conviction, which we assume every Christian to possess, of the exclusive superiority of Christianity" without, however, giving a satisfactory explanation as to why we should be convinced of this.[87] A paradox in Schleiermacher's thought is precisely how this "absolutist" conception of christology and soteriology is to be related to his celebration of diversity in religion.[88] Whereas the premodern tradition had seen in religious diversity a symptom of sin, Schleiermacher viewed it as reflecting the varying historical circumstances in which religions originate and develop. It appears, however, as though he wanted to have it both ways: while an appreciation of diversity is ingredient in a genuinely historical understanding of religion, all Christians are nonetheless agreed that redemption can come only through Jesus. But this latter assertion reflects an absolutizing of what is historically relative and thus is contrary to a truly historical viewpoint. We must find some distinction that will allow us to extricate ourselves from this contradiction while still acknowledging the legitimate motive that misled Schleiermacher to fall victim to it. A descriptive account of the Christian religious experience rightly emphasizes what Schleiermacher understood, namely, that Christians are those who are certain that their own experience of redemption is constituted by a relation to Jesus. Indeed, the Christian religious affections do have a necessary connection to the figure of Jesus as mediated by the church's gospel. Yet it does not follow that a redemptive experience of God must always be constituted by a relation to Jesus. Such a claim exceeds the bounds of Schleiermacher's method of dogmatics, which cannot render judgments about non-Christian religious experience.

Wesley Wildman, tracing what he calls "the Absolutist Principle" back to the church's earliest stages of christological reflection, explains the basic confusion here:

---

86. *Gl.* §11.3.

87. *Gl.* §7.3.

88. Wesley J. Wildman defines the "Absolutist Principle" as "the proposition that Jesus Christ is absolutely, universally, uniquely, unsurpassably significant for revelation and soteriology." "Basic Christological Distinctions," *Theology Today* 64 (2007) 285–304 at 299.

> The origins of the Absolutist Principle are understandable, as Christians sought to account for their powerful experiences of salvation in Jesus Christ. Nevertheless, there were never any compelling reasons for absolutizing the interpretation of those transforming experiences. The significance of Jesus Christ could be adequately and accurately expressed without the aid of the Absolutist Principle.[89]

This brand of christocentrism and its corollary that salvation is a human possibility solely in connection with Jesus are, in Wildman's view, the major doctrinal factors that have also created the problem of the church's relation to Judaism. The church's traditional polemic against the synagogue is a consequence of universalizing its historically particular religious experience so that those who stand in other streams of religious history are viewed as simply bereft of anything like the redemptive benefits that accrue to Christians as a result of their relation to Jesus. In place of absolutism, Wildman proposes a "modest" christological conception that does not make such exaggerated claims.

> Modest christologies have tremendous advantages over their absolutist counterparts because they are not required to adopt the view that cosmic history and religious insight reach their culmination in the figure of Jesus and in his reception as the Christ.[90]

Niebuhr, who was conscious of his formal continuity with Schleiermacher's method, made virtually the same point: "A critical historical theology cannot ... prescribe what form religious life must take in all places and all times beyond the limits of its own historical system."[91] By declaring that apart from Jesus the consciousness of God is tainted and impure, Schleiermacher violated the strictures of his own theological method, which only allows for a descriptive account of the *Christian* religious experience.[92]

Schleiermacher did not derive all knowledge of God exclusively from Christ in Barthian fashion. The revelation in Christ has a "point of contact" (*Anknüpfungspunkt*) in the innate awareness of God given with human

---

89. Wildman, "Basic Christological Distinctions," 302.

90. Wildman, "Basic Christological Distinctions," 303.

91. H. Richard Niebuhr, *The Meaning of Revelation* (New York: Macmillan, 1941) 13. Niebuhr's work is an example of how a theologian employing a "confessional" theological method quite similar to that of Schleiermacher can nonetheless put different material content into it.

92. *Gl.* §94.2.

self-consciousness simply as such.[93] Moreover, in Schleiermacher's usage, "revelation" is not a theological principle that stands in an oppositional relation to the mode of understanding to be derived from the historical interpretation of religion, as is the case with Barth (and presumably also Beckmann). Revelation, for Schleiermacher, refers either to the original revelation of God to human self-consciousness or to the historical revelation in Christ that is the basis of the church's proclamation. Still, it may be asked whether there is not also a third sense in which we can and should speak of revelation in reference to that religious development wherein the original revelation, which in itself may be quite inchoate, did in fact become a clear monotheistic consciousness of God. Paul Tillich, a theologian who was quite explicit about his indebtedness to Schleiermacher, made precisely this point when he differentiated between three senses of revelation as "universal," "preparatory," and "final."[94] Since the meanings of "universal" and "final" are sufficiently similar to the two senses of revelation found in Schleiermacher's thought, we ought to inquire into what Tillich meant by a "preparatory" revelation. Speaking as a Christian for whom Jesus as the Christ is the final revelatory event in history, Tillich nevertheless attributed an unparalleled significance to the history of Israel:

> The revelation through the prophets is the direct concrete preparation of the final revelation, and it cannot be separated from it. The universal revelation as such is not the immediate preparation for the final revelation; only the universal revelation criticized and transformed by the prophetism of the Old Testament is such preparation.[95]

Tillich thus claimed that "the Old Testament is an inseparable part of the revelation of Jesus as the Christ."[96] What is apparent in Tillich, though missing from Schleiermacher, is a deep appreciation of the religious significance of Israel's history as having provided the indispensable presupposition of the church's faith in Jesus.[97]

   93. Schleiermacher called this "an original revelation of God to the human being" (*Gl.* §4.4).
   94. Hans W. Frei called Tillich "Schleiermacher redivivus." Frei, *Types of Christian Theology*, ed. George Hunsinger and William C. Placher (New Haven: Yale University Press, 1992) 3, 68.
   95. Paul Tillich, *Systematic Theology*, 3 vols. (Chicago: University of Chicago Press, 1951, 1957, 1963) 1:142.
   96. Tillich, *Systematic Theology*, 1:133.
   97. Tillich responded to the charge that Judaism is inherently nationalistic: "The Old Testament certainly is full of Jewish nationalism, but it appears over and over as that against which the Old Testament fights" (*Systematic Theology*, 1:142). Such a

Schleiermacher was right to locate what is new about Christianity in the religious significance Jesus has for Christians. But to say that Jesus is of central importance to Christians is not to say that everything important in Christianity began with him. Nonetheless, there is one respect in which Schleiermacher credited the history of Israel, namely, when he said that a universal redeemer could only have come from a monotheistic people.[98] He also acknowledged that the Christian notion of redemption, presupposing as it does the reality of freedom and consequently of guilt on account of sin, is intelligible solely on the basis of the teleological type of religion that first emerged in Israel. Are these not admissions that, apart from the prior religious development in Israel, the church could never have arisen in the first place? On his own terms, would it not be possible for Schleiermacher to grant the truth in what Tillich said since he well understood that ethical monotheism is an ingredient in the Christian religious experience?[99]

Cumulatively, these various considerations more than suffice to justify the conclusion that Schleiermacher's formal method of theology allows for a revision of his material positions in the doctrinal *loci* of christology, soteriology, and the multiple meanings of revelation. While Schleiermacher was correct to identify the essence of Christian faith as monotheistic and ethical and focused on the figure of Jesus for the purpose of redemption from sin, he was wrong to draw such a sharp antithesis between Israel's faith and that of the church. Indeed, there is every reason to affirm a strong material connection between the Jewish message of Jesus and the church's proclamation of his ongoing significance. Christians need not deny the indispensable role played by the Israelite-Jewish tradition in establishing precisely those presuppositions without which neither Jesus nor the church would have been possible, and on the sole basis of which their fundamental import is intelligible. Of course, to say that these alternatives to Schleiermacher's own views are allowed by his method is not to imply that he personally would have agreed with them. The point is simply that another theologian working from the same model for theological inquiry initially proposed by Schleiermacher can arrive at a different construal of the nature of Christian faith that likewise claims to be a faithful rendering of the religious affections evoked and sustained by the church's preaching. It is not necessary to demonstrate more than this in order to make a convincing case that Schleiermacher's material interpretation of doctrine can be criticized according

nuanced approach is absent from Schleiermacher's portrayal.

98. *Gl.* §12.1.

99. In a handwritten marginal comment, Schleiermacher did attribute the emergence of monotheism to "revelation" (*Gl.* §2:502, 504, notes to §§10 and 15 from the first German edition of 1821–1822).

to the methodological criteria he set forth as adequate to the unprecedented responsibilities of modern theology. All the same, this alternative proposal has the advantage that it coheres with the best historical scholarship in a way no longer true of Schleiermacher's theology.[100]

HISTORICAL CRITICISM AND THE CANON OF SCRIPTURE

The question of the Old Testament's right to a place in the Christian Bible did not first arise with historical criticism. Quite early in the church's history, the Old Testament became problematic because it was also the Bible of the synagogue (Tanakh). Since Marcion believed that Jesus taught an altogether new religion antithetical to Judaism, he was completely consistent in arguing that the church should dispense with the Jewish Bible in favor of a canon of distinctively Christian writings. Yet he was alone in his categorical rejection of all spiritualizing modes of exegesis. When the proto-orthodox church repudiated Marcion's proposal by retaining the Old Testament as the first part of its canon, it simultaneously rejected his insistence upon the literal sense of the text.[101] The church thereby secured its christological exegesis of the Old Testament, which backed up its claim that Israel's scriptures belong to the Christians, not to the Jews. For this reason, the anti-Marcionite church never refuted Marcion on his own terms, but rather implicitly accepted his formulation of the crucial issue: if the Old Testament is not Christian, it cannot be canonical.

Although Schleiermacher shared Marcion's view of the absolute novelty of Christianity in relation to Judaism, he did not defend it on the mythological grounds that Jews and Christians worship two distinct deities. On the basis of historical scholarship, he recognized the real differences between the Old Testament and the New Testament that had been smoothed over by premodern forms of exegesis; as a result, he was right in criticizing previous theologians for trying to make the Old Testament say something about Jesus that it does not say. His argument underscored the legitimate rationale for historical criticism, namely, that it alone makes possible an understanding

---

100. Not only could Schleiermacher's method have allowed him to paint a more positive portrait of Judaism, but Jewish theologians could easily avail themselves, *mutatis mutandis*, of his formal model of theology.

101. Jaroslav Pelikan notes, "The Old Testament achieved and maintained its status as Christian Scripture with the aid of spiritual exegesis. There was no early Christian who simultaneously acknowledged the doctrinal authority of the Old Testament and interpreted it literally." *The Emergence of the Catholic Tradition 100–600*, vol. 1 of *The Christian Tradition* (Chicago: University of Chicago Press, 1971) 81.

of the biblical texts free from the distortions of anachronism.[102] Indeed, it is to his credit that he frankly acknowledged the Jewish character of the Old Testament and pleaded for an end to the church's historic polemic against the synagogue over its rightful possession. He was, moreover, prescient in his prediction that critical scholarship would occasion difficult problems for the church's inherited theology.

For the sake of arriving at a different conclusion than Schleiermacher's about the Old Testament's place in the Christian canon, must we abandon the strictly historical perspective in favor of a special theological or "sacred" hermeneutic that treats the Bible as a unique case to which the general rules of interpretation do not apply? Should these turn out to be in fact our only options, then modern Protestant theology has certainly been brought to an impasse by historical criticism. But there is another option beyond this impasse that has not been sufficiently considered. Beckmann's inadequacy is that he never thinks of arguing against Schleiermacher's thesis on the basis of the latter's own hermeneutical presuppositions. This failing mirrors that of nascent orthodoxy, which was unable to reply to Marcion except by evading his direct challenge. Like Hofmann and Barth, Beckmann tips his hat to the legitimacy of historical-critical readings of the Bible in principle but only to shift the grounds of discussion by appealing to dogmatic categories of interpretation derived from the New Testament in order to argue for the canonical status of the Old Testament. The irony here is that Beckmann has tacitly accepted Schleiermacher's neo-Marcionite formulation of the basic issue: either the Old Testament is not strictly speaking a Christian book, in which case the church should hand it back to the synagogue, or the true meaning of the Old Testament consists in its prophetic witness to Jesus as

---

102. Today, historical-critical readings of scripture have to be defended against attacks from both ends of the theological spectrum. From the right, Christopher R. Seitz, seeking to rehabilitate a traditional view of biblical authority, denies that historical-critical study has any constitutive significance for theology. Seitz, *Word without End: The Old Testament as Abiding Theological Witness* (Waco, TX: Baylor University Press, 2004) 97. John J. Collins provides a cogent rejoinder to this type of conservative argument; see Collins, "Biblical Theology and the History of Israelite Religion," in *Encounters with Biblical Theology* (Minneapolis: Fortress, 2005) 24–33. On the left, Dale B. Martin, working from a "postmodern" position, argues against "the notion that Christians should insist on the *necessity* of historical criticism." Martin, *Sex and the Single Savior: Gender and Sexuality in Biblical Interpretation* (Louisville: Westminster John Knox, 2006) 9, emphasis original. For a critique of this type of argument, see Collins, "Historical Criticism and Its Postmodern Critics," in *The Bible after Babel: Historical Criticism in a Postmodern Age* (Grand Rapids: Eerdmans, 2005) 1–25. I have also responded to these two types of criticism of the historical approach to biblical study; see Paul E. Capetz, "Theology and the Historical-Critical Study of the Bible," *Harvard Theological Review* 104 (2011) 459-88, published under the same title as Chapter 2 in this volume (pages 70-104).

Israel's messiah, in which case the Jews' claim to it is invalidated by their lack of faith in its christological referent. After his otherwise admirable recounting of the story of historical-critical research into the Old Testament, Beckmann concludes with this pronouncement: "For the sake of the faith affirmed in the New Testament, Christian theologians must insist against the Jewish 'no' that Jesus of Nazareth is the messiah promised in the Old Testament."[103] But it can be asked of Beckmann why Christian theologians must continue to press this claim. Not only has historical research into the Old Testament undermined the traditional "proofs" of Jesus' messianic status, but even the very idea of a "messiah" appears to be a mythological or symbolic one, as Strauss clearly understood.[104] Moreover, the early Christians, by ascribing this title to Jesus, radically redefined its content in light of his nonmessianic fate. Drawing a very different conclusion from historical study, Rabbi Michael Hilton calls upon Jews and Christians to revise their theological traditions on the basis of a "more accurate understanding . . . of the relationship between the two faiths":

> We cannot afford the two faiths an equal and distinct right to exist while we continue to regard Judaism as the unchanged word of the Bible from which Christianity deviated, or Christianity the true fulfillment of the prophets which the Jews rejected.[105]

Hilton's proposal thus points the way beyond that untenable impasse of either an Old Testament historically interpreted as a document of Jewish religion and, hence, antithetical to Christianity (Marcion, Schleiermacher, Harnack) or an Old Testament spiritually interpreted as a witness to Christian faith and, hence, denied to Judaism (Hofmann, Barth, Beckmann).

The modern impasse in Protestant theology with respect to the Old Testament results from the dual legacy of the Reformation. The Reformers insisted that the Bible be allowed to speak in its own voice and that the Bible should be the sole norm of Christian doctrine. Their rejection of the allegorical method and correlative insistence upon a literal exegesis undergirded their use of the Bible as the critical principle for testing the medieval tradition. Prior to modernity, these two commitments could be affirmed simultaneously because it was axiomatic that the Bible as a whole provided an unambiguous foundation for doctrine. But in the modern period, these

---

103. Beckmann, *Die fremde Wurzel*, 349.

104. Many modern Jews also acknowledge the mythological or symbolic character of the messianic idea. See the Prayer Book of Conservative Judaism, *Sabbath and Festival Prayer Book* (New York: The Rabbinical Assembly of America and the United Synagogue of America, 1973) ix.

105. Michael Hilton, *The Christian Effect on Jewish Life* (London: SCM, 1994), 2.

two aspects of the Reformation heritage came into conflict. Historical scholarship not only separated Old Testament and New Testament into distinct fields of study but also identified within each testament diverse theological traditions that could not easily be harmonized. Perceiving the problem, Schleiermacher fought against an uncritical use of the Bible as a proof text for doctrine. For him, this entailed three departures from the inherited approach to the scriptures: first, the "true" or normative New Testament canon has to be critically distinguished from its received historical form; second, the New Testament should not be used to support Protestant doctrine against Catholicism; and, third, the Old Testament cannot be invoked to defend Christianity against Judaism. The first two points are relatively noncontroversial in theology today. Still, his handling of the Old Testament continues to be denounced. Yet the usual alternative to it, illustrated by Beckmann, is even more problematic. Schubert Ogden locates the problem here in the assumption that the Old Testament is to be judged by the same critical norm as is the New Testament.

> The usual view on this point in recent Protestant theology is, in effect, this: just as the New Testament is to be used by theology only under the control of the New Testament message, so the Old Testament's authority for theological reflection and argument is subject to that of the New. But . . . this familiar view of the use of the Old Testament is now scarcely less untenable than the views of the Reformers and of the orthodox dogmaticians of which it is a revision . . . That the New Testament is to be used in theology only under the authority of the Jesus-kerygma poses no particular difficulty, since the New Testament's writings . . . expressly have to do with the subject-term of this kerygma, that is, with Jesus . . . However, we now recognize that it is historically false as well as theologically misleading to claim that the Old Testament writings, too, are expressly about Jesus . . .
>
> [R]ecognizing that the Old Testament does not bear witness to Christ prophetically in the sense in which the early church understood it to do and, therefore, at the crucial point is *not* like the New, forces the question whether the Old Testament may be properly used as a theological authority at all.[106]

Here Ogden formulates the theological question of the Old Testament in the only way it can be taken seriously on the basis of Schleiermacher's premises. This question can be rephrased by asking whether Schleiermacher's

---

106. Schubert M. Ogden, "The Authority of Scripture for Theology," *On Theology* (San Francisco: Harper & Row, 1986), 45–68 at 65–66, emphasis original.

perfectly sound argument against an illicit use of the Old Testament in Christian theology precludes altogether the possibility of an admissible use therein.

Since Schleiermacher acknowledged the necessity of a theological criticism (*Sachkritik*) of the New Testament scriptures, there is no reason in principle not to insist upon a similar approach to the Old Testament. Only in this case the theological criterion should not be the *kerygma* as in the New Testament, but rather the indispensable monotheistic-ethical presuppositions on the sole basis of which the New Testament's christological and soteriological affirmations are intelligible and apart from which they are easily distorted in a dualistic and polytheistic manner. Accordingly, the Old Testament's enduring import for the church is to insure that its faith is never interpreted in such a manner that explicitly contradicts or even implicitly denies these presuppositions which are contained in all authentic proclamation of the gospel.[107] That the ethical monotheism to which the Old Testament bears definitive witness has as a matter of fact actually functioned in this sense as a necessary—though not sufficient—norm by which to test the adequacy of the various interpretations of the gospel found in the New Testament and the postbiblical tradition is ample warrant for deeming the Old Testament to be of indispensable *religious* and *theological* value to Christian faith.[108] This rationale for attributing a definite sort of canonical status to the Old Testament—different from that of the New Testament but no less important—does not sidestep the challenge of historical criticism to traditional theology. It also validates the legitimate motive at work in the ancient church's retention of the Old Testament without endorsing the inadequate argumentation on which it based this decision.[109] Not the least advantage of this alternative systematic proposal for formulating both the

---

107. Schleiermacher said of the less distinctively Christian doctrines elaborated in the first part of his dogmatics that they are "both presupposed by and contained in every Christian religious affection" (*Gl.* §32).

108. Rolf P. Knierim asks "whether the understanding of Christ as expressed in diverse theological interpretations triggered by the New Testament is at times so controversial among Christians, today as throughout history, that they reflect a polytheistic more than a monotheistic Christology or Christianity." *The Task of Old Testament Theology: Substance, Method, and Cases* (Grand Rapids: Eerdmans, 1995) 7n5.

109. Neither Marcion and nor the Gnostics were monotheists. Hence, the decision to retain the Old Testament was simultaneously a reassertion of monotheism as the indispensable presupposition of Christian faith. For an example of how the Old Testament's witness to monotheism functioned as a constraint upon the development of trinitarian doctrine, see Gregory of Nyssa, "Concerning We Should Think of Saying that There Are not Three Gods to Ablabius," in *The Trinitarian Controversy*, trans. William G. Rusch, Sources of Early Christian Thought (Philadelphia: Fortress, 1980) 117–26 at 151.

question and its answer is that it is not constrained to secure its positive valuation of the Old Testament by diminishing the import of historical criticism, thus pitting a special theological hermeneutic against a so-called general hermeneutic.[110] Moreover, it does not entail a denial of the synagogue's equally valid claim to possession of Israel's scripture.[111]

Ernst Troeltsch, who pursued the theological implications of a consistently historical approach to religion more fully than anyone either before or after him, noted that "the strictly historical interpretation of Christianity has made tremendous strides and has furnished a historical-critical picture very different from that which lay before . . . Schleiermacher."[112] Regarding the Old Testament, Troeltsch affirmed, "To acknowledge Christianity . . . is also to recognize the religion of Israel as its prior stage and presupposition, for without it, Christianity is incomprehensible."[113] Nonetheless, he gave this positive assessment of Schleiermacher's new departure for modern theology: "His program simply needs to be carried out consistently. Hardly any change is necessary."[114] While Schleiermacher's execution of his self-appointed task is justifiably subject to criticism, we must look upon his program for theology as *an unfulfilled possibility* and not as an accomplishment forever witnessing to the errors following from his methodological starting point."[115]

Perhaps the true service of historical theology consists not only in providing new angles of vision that illuminate the ambiguities of our religious past, but also in reminding us of unfinished business that has to be on any agenda for future constructive work.

110. James Barr identifies the usual false dichotomy at work here: "It is sometimes said that the historical relation between the Old and New Testaments is not in question, but that the problem lies in stating a theological relation. The theological relation, however, cannot be the formation of connections *other than* the historical; it must rather be the seeing of theological values *in* the historical connections." *Old and New in Interpretation: A Study of the Two Testaments*, Currie Lectures (London: SCM, 1966) 31.

111. Ogden submits that "the key" to answering the question of the Old Testament lies in "the insight that the writings of the Old Testament contain the most fundamental presuppositions . . . of the Jesus-kerygma . . . But if this is correct, there is no doubt that the Old Testament, in its way, is also a theological authority, nor does using it as such pose any particular difficulty." Ogden, "The Authority of Scripture for Theology," 66–67.

112. Troeltsch, "The Dogmatics of the History-of-Religions School," 93.

113. Ernst Troeltsch, *The Christian Faith*, trans. Garrett E. Paul, Fortress Texts in Modern Theology (Minneapolis: Fortress, 1991) 85. Though Troeltsch's dogmatics follows Schleiermacher's model, it includes a discussion of "The Religious Significance of the History of Israel" (85–86).

114. Troeltsch, "The Dogmatics of the History-of-Religions School," 108n5.

115. Van A. Harvey, "A Word in Defense of Schleiermacher's Theological Method," *Journal of Religion* 42 (1962) 151–70 at 153, emphasis original.

4

Karl Barth on the Old Testament as Christian Scripture

WITH THE ADVENT OF historical-critical exegesis of the Bible, the Old Testament became a problem for inherited Christian interpretations of it. Whereas the classical tradition had proceeded from the assumption that the Old Testament bears prophetic testimony to Jesus as Israel's messiah, modern scholars sought to uncover its historical meaning through their reconstructions of Israel's religious development. When viewed in this light, the Old Testament could no longer be invoked to support Christian claims about Jesus against Jewish interpretations of the texts. (To be sure, the conclusions of historical criticism did not sit well with many traditional Jewish beliefs about the Bible, but that is a different story.) The issues raised by critical scholarship came to the fore in an especially dramatic fashion in modern Protestant thought for two reasons. First, the Bible had been elevated to a unique status as the sole measure of correct doctrine during the Reformation. Commitment to *sola scriptura* entailed repudiation of the Latin Vulgate in favor of reading the Bible in Hebrew and Greek as well as rejection of every allegorical or spiritualizing hermeneutic so that exegesis might uncover the literal sense of scripture according to the rules for interpreting ancient texts espoused by the humanist scholars of the Renaissance. Second, modern historical-critical methods were pioneered almost exclusively by Protestant scholars, whose newly won historical consciousness intensified this focus on the literal sense in order to avoid the danger of anachronistic readings of the Bible.[1] But increasingly the effort to understand the biblical

---

1. There has been much discussion in recent years as to what exactly the Reformers

text on its own terms called into question the Reformers' assumption of a unified biblical theology capable of providing the church with its single source and norm of doctrine. The division of exegetical labor represented by the separation of Old and New Testament study into distinct disciplines and the sharp distinction between exegesis as a historical discipline and dogmatics (or theology) as a normative discipline clearly illustrate how critical study of the Bible, while upholding one aspect of the Reformation heritage, actually undermined the other aspect of it. It is thus no exaggeration to say that the exegetical methods and hermeneutical principles of the Reformers set the stage for the rediscovery of the Jewish character of the Old Testament by their modern-day heirs.[2]

---

understood by the "literal" sense of the Bible and to what degree it is or is not identical with what came to be understood as the "historical" sense in the modern era. Hans W. Frei, to whom this discussion owes so much of its original impulse, characterizes premodern readings of the Bible in the West as "strongly realistic, i.e., at once literal and historical, and not only doctrinal or edifying." *The Eclipse of Biblical Narrative: A Study in Eighteenth and Nineteenth Century Hermeneutics* (New Haven: Yale University Press, 1974) 1. Frei explains, "The preeminence of a literal and historical reading . . . received new impetus in the era of the Renaissance and the Reformation, when it became the regnant mode of biblical reading. From it, modern biblical interpretation began its quest, in continuity as well as rebellion." Discontinuity resulted "once literal and historical reading began to break apart. Literal reading came increasingly to mean two things: grammatical and lexical exactness in estimating what the original sense of the text was to its original audience, and the coincidence of the description with how the facts really occurred" (6–7). Accordingly, one can say with assurance that the Reformers assumed that the literal sense was identical with its historical sense. Yet there is more to be said than that. The Reformers combined their insistence upon the literal-historical sense of the Bible with the inherited belief in its divine inspiration. In a fine study of Calvin's interpretation of the Old Testament, David L. Puckett points out that since Calvin's stated goal in biblical exegesis was to decipher the author's intention, the question naturally arises: "Is the genuine meaning that of the human writer or that of the Holy Spirit?" *John Calvin's Exegesis of the Old Testament*, Columbia Series in Reformed Theology (Louisville: Westminster John Knox, 1995) 32. But the answer is not as clear-cut as the question itself: "Calvin is unwilling to divorce the intention of the human writer from the meaning of the Holy Spirit. It is difficult to escape the conclusion that for him, the intention, thoughts, and words of the prophet and of the Holy Spirit in the production of scripture are so closely related there is no practical way to distinguish them" (36–37). Hence, the break with the past represented by the rise of historical criticism was not merely the loss of the Reformers' assumption that the literal sense was historically accurate but also the demise of their belief in the Bible's divine inspiration, which they shared with the medievals. It was only when this belief was set aside that it became possible to understand the Bible historically in our modern sense.

2. A. H. J. Gunneweg makes the point more strongly: "It was only with the resolute return to the literal sense at the time of the Reformation that the veil spread over the Old Testament by allegorical interpretation, dogma, tradition and the authority of the church was ripped away. As a result, it could once again be seen just how alien this collection of writings was." *Understanding the Old Testament*, trans. John Bowden, Old

While very conservative theologians such as Hengstenberg opposed critical methods of biblical study, prominent liberal theologians, most notably Schleiermacher and Harnack, argued that the Old Testament should no longer be deemed canonical, since historical criticism had demonstrated its character as a document of Israelite-Jewish religion. Hence, the Old Testament cannot be a source or norm of the church's doctrine, because its content was not shaped by the distinctively Christian faith in Jesus to which only the New Testament bears witness. Ironically, then, historical criticism led these liberal theologians to champion the side of the Jews in the historic dispute between church and synagogue as to whom the scriptures of Israel properly belong. But their main goal was to purify Protestantism of all elements originating in the pre-Christian history of religion not in keeping with the true essence of Christianity. This criticism of the canon was thus intended to stand in the service of furthering the cause of the Reformation for a new day.[3]

In sharp opposition to this reduction of the canon was Karl Barth, who gave a resounding endorsement of the Old Testament as Christian scripture. In continuity with the premodern exegetical tradition, he affirmed that the Old Testament's real meaning lies in its witness to Jesus Christ as God's unique self-revelation. Yet his was by no means a straightforward

---

Testament Library (Philadelphia: Westminster, 1978) 147. The historical picture is actually a bit more complicated, since the Reformers were never able to free themselves from the assumption that the Old Testament foretells Jesus as Israel's messiah. For Luther, the literal sense of the Old Testament is prophetic in a christological sense. "The combination of literal, historical, and christological elements is especially noticeable in Luther's treatment of the prophets . . . History here includes knowledge of Hebrew, yet Luther also affirms that the chief message of all the prophets is to prepare the faithful for the coming of Christ, and he does not hesitate to impose a christological interpretation on some biblical passages in a way that could only be called 'allegorizing.'" Irena Backus, "Biblical Hermeneutics and Exegesis," in *The Oxford Encyclopedia of the Reformation*, 4 vols., ed. Hans J. Hillerbrand (New York: Oxford University Press, 1996) 1:152-58 at 154. Calvin exercised greater caution by veering farther away from christological readings, thereby bringing upon himself the charge of "Judaizing." But Calvin did not always agree with Jewish exegetes, either; Puckett, *John Calvin's Exegesis of the Old Testament*, 1, 16, 53.

3. See Friedrich Schleiermacher, *The Christian Faith*, trans. H. R. Mackintosh and J. S. Stewart (Philadelphia: Fortress, 1976) §132; Paul E. Capetz, "Friedrich Schleiermacher on the Old Testament," *Harvard Theological Review* 102 (2009) 297–325, also published as "Friedrich Schleiermacher on the Old Testament as Jewish Scripture," Chapter 3 in this volume 105-138; Adolf von Harnack, *Marcion: The Gospel of the Alien God*, trans. John E. Steely and Lyle D. Bierma (Durham, NC: Labyrinth, 1990) 134. For a recent discussion of Hengstenberg, see Klaus Beckmann, *Die fremde Wurzel: Altes Testament und Judentum in der evangelischen Theologie des 19. Jahrhunderts*, Forschungen zur Kirchen- und Dogmengeschichte 85 (Göttingen: Vandenhoeck & Ruprecht, 2002) 239–70.

disagreement with Schleiermacher and Harnack about the historical meaning of the Old Testament. The truth is that Barth sought to transcend the opposition between conservative and liberal theologies by completely redefining the terms of the debate. His point of departure lay in rejecting the high value attributed to historical-critical scholarship in liberal theology.[4] Still, his position should not be misunderstood as though it were a complete rejection of such study in the manner of the reactionary Hengstenberg. Barth's theology is thoroughly modern in its acknowledgment of the right of historical scholars to apply the tools of their trade to the investigation of ancient Israel and the origins of the church. In this respect, Barth stood closer to the intellectual milieu of his liberal teachers than to any defensive antimodern polemics. The problem for Barth was that the Bible had become of interest to scholars chiefly as a source for reconstructing the history of ancient religion and in the process had lost its power to speak to contemporary persons with a message that transcends the particularities of time and place. As an antidote, Barth called for a return to the sort of theological exegesis of scripture exemplified by Luther and Calvin.[5] Just as Hengstenberg, Schleiermacher, and Harnack all professed allegiance to the Reformation heritage, so too Barth saw himself as retrieving the Reformers' view of the unified canon of Old and New Testaments as the indispensable vehicle of God's address to humanity.

On account of his endeavor to read the biblical text in a manner that moves decidedly beyond the concerns of historical criticism, Barth has been hailed by some for his rediscovery of the canon as the proper context for exegesis[6] and claimed by others as a forerunner of a "postmodern" hermeneutic that breaks with the intellectual constraints of modernity.[7] Certainly,

---

4. "Both Liberalism and orthodoxy are children of the same insipid spirit, and it is useless to follow them. For after all, there seems no good reason why the Bible as the true witness of the Word of God should always have to speak 'historically.'" Karl Barth, *The Doctrine of Creation*, vol. III/1 of *Church Dogmatics*, trans. J. W. Edwards, O. Bussey, and Harold Knight (Edinburgh: T. & T. Clark, 1958) 82.

5. In his groundbreaking commentary on Romans Barth illustrated his point by referring to Calvin's exegetical practice: "how energetically Calvin, having first established what stands in the text, sets himself to rethink the whole material and to wrestle with it, till the walls which separate the sixteenth century from the first become transparent! Paul speaks, and the man of the sixteenth century hears." "Preface to the Second Edition," in *The Epistle to the Romans*, trans. from the 6th ed. by Edwyn C. Hoskyns (London: Oxford University Press, 1933; reprint 1976) 7.

6. Brevard S. Childs, "Old Testament in Germany, 1920–1940: The Search for a New Paradigm," in *Altes Testament—Forschung und Wirkung: Festschrift für Henning Graf Reventlow*, ed. Peter Mommer and Winfried Thiel (Frankfurt: Lang, 1994) 233–46 at 235.

7. In his survey of the history of hermeneutics, David Jasper mentions scholars

a broad consensus now exists among biblical scholars and theologians alike that the meaning of a biblical text cannot be restricted solely to its original historical context. Whatever meaning it may once have had for its original addressees, biblical texts assume new meanings unintended by their original authors throughout the history of their reception. It is, furthermore, widely recognized that the diverse questions and presuppositions interpreters bring to the Bible inform, initially at least, the interpretation to be derived from the process of reading. Notwithstanding the import of these insights for our reading of texts, ambiguity remains as to how Barth's christocentric construal of the Old Testament on the theological level coheres with his admission of the relative legitimacy of historical-critical interpretations of the text. What exactly is the relation between them? Do historical-critical insights have any bearing upon how the church ought to read the Bible, or are they to be set aside as being of minor import once the really momentous task of theological exegesis begins? With Barth it certainly appears that the latter is the case. But if this is so, it can be asked what point there is in acknowledging the validity of historical criticism in principle if its results do not in fact limit the range of responsible theological readings of the Bible for our time.

While we can surely heed Barth's call for a mode of interpretation that approaches the Bible as something other than merely an artifact of antiquity, we can also challenge his notion that an adequate theological exegesis of scripture has to construe the Old Testament as a witness to Jesus Christ as the necessary condition of its canonical status alongside the New Testament. Yet it is not only the problematic relation of historical to theological exegesis in Barth's thought that occasions critical scrutiny of his handling of the Old Testament. His position has negative ramifications for the Christian assessment of how Jews read their scriptures (Tanakh) that move in a different direction from the postmodern insight into the myriad ways a text may plausibly be recontextualized and thereby assume new meanings. Apparently Barth wanted to have it both ways. While opposing the hegemony of historical-critical readings of the Bible in the name of a theological exegesis, his insistence upon the sole validity of a christological construal of the Old Testament is hegemonic in its own right. From other perspectives than that recognized as valid by Barth, whether Christian or Jewish, it surely

---

who "have seen Karl Barth as anticipating elements of a *postmodern* hermeneutics" and adds that "in some respects this is the case, for both Barth and the postmodern constitute radical turns from the whole Enlightenment movement and a disregard for the elaborate structures and claims of historical criticism. On the other hand, nothing could be farther than Barth from the relativities of postmodern hermeneutics." *A Short Introduction to Hermeneutics* (Louisville: Westminster John Knox, 2004) 101, 119.

appears as though his christocentric theology purchases its defense of the Old Testament at the very high cost of doing damage to the biblical text itself. If, however, we should reject Barth's christocentrism, then the ground can be cleared for a new inquiry into the possibility of a theological exegesis of the Old Testament as the church's scripture that neither minimizes the implications of historical criticism nor denies to the Jews their legitimate right to claim the scriptural heritage of ancient Israel equally on behalf of the synagogue.

BARTH ON THE OLD TESTAMENT

Barth's defense of the canonical status of the Old Testament is of a piece with his larger program to reestablish what he called the "scriptural principle" in Protestant theology. This principle gave expression to the Reformers' conviction that "the word of God for them lay only in the Old and New Testaments . . . the whole Scriptures and not a part of them."[8] By overthrowing the "tyranny" of historicism, Barth aimed to rehabilitate the Reformers' estimate of biblical authority without reverting to a premodern doctrine of biblical inspiration. In the preface to his Romans commentary, he explained:

> The differences between then and now, there and here, no doubt require careful investigation and consideration. But the purpose of such investigation can only be to demonstrate that these differences are, in fact, trivial. The historical-critical method of Biblical investigation has its rightful place: it is concerned with the preparation of the intelligence—and this can never be superfluous. But, were I driven to choose between it and the venerable doctrine of Inspiration, I should without hesitation adopt the latter, which has a broader, deeper, more important justification . . . Fortunately, I am not compelled to choose between the two.[9]

Barth thus sought to redirect the focus back to the issues of greatest concern to the biblical writers themselves, which he believed should be foremost on the hearts and minds of readers today. In the broadest sense, this is what is meant by a "theological exegesis" of scripture: one need not oppose the genuine insights won by historical scholarship to recognize that the real task of interpretation begins only when criticism has done its preliminary

---

8. Karl Barth, "The Doctrinal Task of the Reformed Churches," in *The Word of God and the Word of Man*, trans. Douglas Horton (1928; reprint, Gloucester: Smith, 1978) 218–71 at 240–41. Barth explained that the "scriptural principle" is identical with what is otherwise called "the formal principle of the Reformation."

9. Barth, "Preface to the First Edition," in *Epistle to the Romans*, 1.

work. Such interpretation should revolve around the subject matter (*Sache*) of the text: "The conversation between the original record and the reader moves round the subject matter, until a distinction between yesterday and to-day becomes impossible."[10] Indeed, Barth rejected the assumption that the object of biblical exegesis is to understand the historical development of Israel and the early church. For him, this assumption is anthropocentric, since its primary interest is human religion, not divine revelation: "When we do take the humanity of the Bible quite seriously, we must also take quite definitely the fact that as a human word it points away from itself."[11] The Reformers understood that the Bible "does not speak of itself, but of God's revelation."[12] For Barth, then, the task of exegesis is to hear the Word of God in and through the human words of the Bible.

In Barth's theology, revelation is the epistemological principle that excludes all forms of "natural theology" (by which is meant not only philosophical arguments for God's existence but also the deliverances of religious and moral experience), since the only route to knowledge of God is that made available through God's free decision to be known. This principle grounds the unique authority ascribed to the Bible in Barth's theological method and accounts for the sharp antithesis set up between divine revelation and human religion. Barth went further, however, and insisted upon a radically christocentric doctrine of revelation according to which Jesus Christ is the sole locus where genuine knowledge of God is to be found. These two premises are essential to Barth's theology and, consequently, his interpretation of scripture: first, the Bible is the human witness to the self-revelation of God, and, second, God has chosen to be revealed only in Jesus Christ, who is the very Word of God.[13] Barth distinguished his view from Protestant orthodoxy by specifying a threefold form of the Word of God: God's self-revelation in Christ, which is primary, along with scripture and preaching, which are subordinate witnesses to this divine revelation.[14] Hence, the Bible itself is not, strictly speaking, to be equated with revelation; still, without the biblical witness and its contemporary actualization in the

---

10. Barth, "Preface to the Second Edition," in *Epistle to the Romans*, 7.

11. Karl Barth, *The Doctrine of the Word of God*, vol. I/2 of *Church Dogmatics*, trans. G. T. Thomson and Harold Knight (Edinburgh: T. & T. Clark. 1956) 464.

12. Barth, *The Doctrine of the Word of God*, I/2:468. Barth was opposed to any hermeneutical procedure "in which attention is paid to the biblical expressions but not to what the words signify" (466).

13. "Word of God" and "revelation" refer to the same reality: "God's Word is God himself in his revelation." Karl Barth, *The Doctrine of the Word of God*, vol. I/1 of *Church Dogmatics*, trans. G. W. Bromiley (Edinburgh: T. & T. Clark. 1936) 295.

14. Barth, *The Doctrine of the Word of God*, I/1:121.

sermon, there would be no access to God's revelation.[15] Important in this regard is Barth's conviction that the Old Testament is to be considered as Christian scripture in equal measure alongside the New Testament. Both testaments bear witness to the one event of God's self-revelation in Christ, even though there is an important distinction in their temporal sequence: "Genuine expectation and genuine recollection are testimonies to revelation, mutually as different as expectation and recollection are different, but one in their content."[16] The Old Testament bears prophetic witness to the expectation of God's revelation in Christ, whereas the New Testament is the apostolic witness to this same revelatory event through recollection: "We cannot speak of the time of revelation without also speaking of its pre-time. It, too, is revelation-time, although in the sense of expecting revelation . . . The Old Testament is the witness to the genuine expectation of revelation."[17] The New Testament writers were completely unanimous in affirming that the truth of their proclamation concerning Jesus was validated by what the Old Testament has to say. Hence, the message of the New Testament cannot be properly understood apart from its essential connection with the Old Testament writings. The ancient church correctly grasped this dimension of the gospel when it rejected Marcion's proposal to dispense with the scriptures of Israel altogether in favor of a canon of distinctively Christian writings. "Without the Word of God in the Old Testament," Barth explained, "the Church would be believing in a different Christ from the New Testament witnesses."[18] The corollary of the New Testament's necessary dependence on the Old, however, is the recognition that the Old Testament cannot stand alone apart from the New. This means that the Old Testament receives its character as a witness to God's revelation only by virtue of its relation to the

---

15. "Scripture is holy and the Word of God because by the Holy Spirit it became and will become to the Church a witness to divine revelation." Barth, *The Doctrine of the Word of God*, I/2, 457. David H. Kelsey describes Barth's use of scripture in functional terms: "The texts are authoritative not in virtue of any inherent property they may have, such as being inerrant or inspired, but in virtue of the function they fill in the life of the Christian community. To say that scripture is 'inspired' is to say that God has promised that sometimes, at his gracious pleasure, the ordinary human words of the biblical texts will become the Word of God, the occasion for rendering an agent present to us in a Divine–human encounter." *Proving Doctrine: The Uses of Scripture in Modern Theology* (Harrisburg, PA: Trinity, 1999) 47–48; orig. pub. as *The Uses of Scripture in Recent Theology* (Philadelphia: Fortress, 1975).

16. Barth, *The Doctrine of the Word of God*, I/2:70.

17. Barth, *The Doctrine of the Word of God*, I/2:70. "The Old and the New Testament both have as their distinctive feature to attest in the one case the Messiah who is to come, and in the other case the Messiah who has already come . . . It is only in this unity that the biblical witness is the witness of divine revelation" (481–82).

18. Barth, *The Doctrine of the Word of God*, I/2:93–94.

gospel. It does not have this character on its own. Since the birth, death, and resurrection of Christ demarcate the time of revelation, the light it sheds allows us retrospectively to affirm the Old Testament as a witness to this once-and-for-all revelatory event, albeit in the mode of expectation: "Apart from this revelation breaking in from without or from above . . . we cannot speak of revelation in the Old Testament."[19]

Since revelation is by definition a miracle, faith in God's miraculous self-revelation through Christ has to be presupposed before we approach the Old Testament, because we can never move from history as the historical-critical method conceives it to the confession that revelation has truly occurred in the history of Israel: "That one must speak of God's revelation in the Old Testament . . . cannot be proved by the fact that . . . we can show the peculiarity of Old Testament piety to be historically unique. For this uniqueness is only of a relative kind and can be described as revelation only in the improper sense of the concept. However brilliantly and happily conceived, the 'history of Israelite religion' is not the 'biblical theology of the Old Testament.'"[20] Given the naturalistic assumptions behind historical criticism, there is no basis for believing that revelation has occurred in Israel but not in Babylon or Persia. Barth is, of course, correct that the category of revelation has no place in a purely historical account of Israel's religious development. For this reason, the theologian who speaks of revelation in the Old Testament does not mean "this or that attribute supposed to belong as such and in itself to the Old Testament or to the stories attested in the Old Testament."[21] For Barth, the modern problem occasioned by historical criticism of the Bible rests on a failure to understand properly the relation between history and revelation: "Revelation is not a predicate of history, but history is a predicate of revelation."[22]

With this axiom firmly in mind, the witness of the Old Testament to the revelation of God in Christ can be affirmed again today, just as it had been in the scriptural principle of the Reformers. Still, Barth conceded that this has become more difficult for us "because the eyes and methods with which we seek to read and understand the texts of the Old Testament today have been

---

19. Barth, *The Doctrine of the Word of God*, I/2:71. "Revelation itself takes place from beyond the peculiar context and content of the Old Testament." Barth affirmed that the same holds true for the New Testament as well, "but with this difference that the completed event of revelation does not lie before but behind the witness to it" (103).

20. Barth, *The Doctrine of the Word of God*, I/2:79.

21. Barth, *The Doctrine of the Word of God*, I/2:71.

22. Barth, *The Doctrine of the Word of God*, I/2:58. "The modern problem of 'revelation and history' . . . rests upon a portentous failure to appreciate the nature of revelation" (56).

changed by the host of textual, literary, historical, and in particular religio-historical problems."[23] Nonetheless, recovery of this underlying unity of the two testaments remains the "chief task" of Old Testament scholarship in our time, even though most historical-critical scholars neglect this all-important duty; but theology cannot remain content with the results achieved by modern scholarship on the Old Testament and is thus "compelled to seek its own way itself, conscious of the dangers therein."[24] His own efforts to discern this unity led Barth to delineate "three lines" or thematic connections linking the testaments' witness to revelation in their relations of expectation and fulfillment: covenant, the hiddenness of revelation, and God as both present and future.[25] First, God's covenant with Israel should not be misunderstood in a nationalistic sense since Israel did not exist as a nation at all until God freely elected it to be the instrument through which all the nations would be blessed. This covenant finds its fulfillment in Jesus Christ, who united Jews and Gentiles in one church. The covenant proclaims both gospel and law: as gospel, it expresses God's unmerited mercy; as law, it expresses God's unconditional demand for holiness.[26] Second, although God can be known only when revealed, paradoxically God remains hidden even in revelation. Indications of God's hiddenness are found in Israel's laments, in some of the psalms and prophets and, most dramatically, in Job, before culminating in

---

23. Barth, *The Doctrine of the Word of God*, I/2:78.

24. Barth, *The Doctrine of the Word of God*, I/2:79. Barth "meets Old Testament research . . . critically; he is far from recognizing its presuppositions, methods, and results as the basis for his own research and building upon its foundation . . . He knows that he is at greater risk in relation to Old Testament scholarship than in relation to that on the New Testament." Otto Bächli, *Das Alte Testament in der Kirchlichen Dogmatik von Karl Barth* (Neukirchen-Vluyn: Neukirchener, 1987) 21–22. All translations of German texts are mine unless otherwise indicated.

25. Barth, *The Doctrine of the Word of God*, I/2:80–84, 103–106 (on "covenant"); 84–94, 106–13 (on "the hiddenness of revelation"); and 94–101, 113–21 (on "God as both present and coming").

26. The formulation "gospel and law" represents Barth's inversion of the Lutheran "law–gospel" dichotomy and is rooted in Calvin's belief that the "third use" of the law (i.e., instruction in the Christian life) is its primary purpose. See John Calvin, *Institutes of the Christian Religion* (1559), 2 vols., ed. John T. McNeill, trans. Ford Lewis Battles, Library of Christian Classics (Philadelphia: Westminster, 1960) 2.7.12 (1:360–61); also Karl Barth, *Evangelium und Gesetz*, Theologische Existenz Heute 32 (Munich: Kaiser, 1935). Barth (*The Doctrine of God*, vol. II/2 of *Church Dogmatics*, ed. G. W. Bromiley and T. F. Torrance [Edinburgh: T. & T. Clark, 1957] 509) thus employs the term "law" with positive connotations in his ethics: "As the doctrine of God's command, ethics interprets the Law as the form of the Gospel, i.e., as the sanctification which comes to man through the electing God." By contrast, Schleiermacher (*The Christian Faith*, §112, par. 5) dropped the category of law from his conception of theological ethics on the grounds that it is not originally a Christian term.

the cross of Jesus. Third, God's presence always points to the eschatological future: just as the Old Testament prophets looked ahead to the revelation of God in Christ recollected by the New Testament writers, so too the apostles proclaimed not only the past event of Jesus' death and resurrection but also his future coming in glory. In each of these three respects, then, the Old Testament is related to the New "as the question correctly put is to the answer correctly given."[27]

By means of this theological framework for comprehending the unity of the Bible's twofold witness to Christ, Barth completely redefined the terms of the debate concerning the Old Testament's canonical status. Whereas Schleiermacher and Harnack sought to decanonize the Old Testament since, as a document of Israelite-Jewish piety, it teaches a different religion from Christianity, Barth countered that the issue is not about "religion" and, therefore, not about the relations of Judaism and Christianity as religions: "The whole concern is neither 'Judaism' nor 'Christianity,' neither Old Testament nor New Testament piety, but Jesus Christ as the object of the Old Testament and the New Testament witness. Therefore it is not a matter of an historical relation between two religions . . . but of unity of revelation in both cases which connects the two so-called religions."[28] From the second century, when the church rejected Marcion, up until the seventeenth century, it was axiomatic that the Old Testament is essential to the gospel and the gospel essential to it. For that reason, were the Protestant church to accept the neo-Marcionite proposals of Schleiermacher and Harnack, it would sever its ties not only with the New Testament and the postbiblical tradition but also with its own Reformation heritage.[29]

This does not mean, however, that Barth absolutely refused to reopen the question of the canon: "The canon is not absolutely closed."[30] He acknowledged that the Reformers curtailed the scope of the Old Testament when they rejected the Apocrypha and decided in favor of the Masoretic text and canon of the synagogue, even though that decision put them at odds with both the Roman Catholics and the Eastern Orthodox. He also

27. Barth, *The Doctrine of the Word of God*, I/2:120. "It is often said that hindsight is one hundred percent accurate. As far as understanding the [Old Testament's] history is concerned, Barth would agree. If one knows where a particular series of events is leading, the events have a greater meaning than they would if that end were not known." Roger R. Keller, "Karl Barth's Treatment of the Old Testament as Expectation," *Andrews University Seminary Studies* 35 (1997) 165-79 at 178. See also John Marsh, "Christ in the Old Testament," in *Essays in Christology for Karl Barth*, ed. T. H. L. Parker (London: Lutterworth, 1956) 41-70.

28. Barth, *The Doctrine of the Word of God*, I/2:79.
29. Barth, *The Doctrine of the Word of God*, I/2:74.
30. Barth, *The Doctrine of the Word of God*, I/2:478.

pointed to the well-known example of Luther, who had raised critical questions about the New Testament canon when he expressed doubts not only about James ("an epistle of straw") but also about Hebrews, Jude, and 2 and 3 John.[31] Furthermore, Barth admitted that the church "does not in fact and practice treat all parts of the Bible alike."[32] Hence, Barth's scriptural principle did not preclude for him the possibility of valid theological questioning of the canon. But the radical proposal to reduce the church's canon to the New Testament alone undermines the very faith it allegedly aims to support by denying what the New Testament explicitly affirms about the Old Testament: "We cannot even try to do what Marcion and after him the Socinians and Schleiermacher . . . and Harnack tried to do, without substituting another foundation on which the Christian Church is built. The Old Testament is not an introduction to the real New Testament Bible, which we can dispense with or replace."[33] It is right, therefore, that their proposal should be rejected by the church, because, in abandoning the Old Testament, "they had abandoned not something but everything, namely the New Testament itself as well and the whole New Testament at that."[34] The question of the Old Testament, then, is not merely a formal question regarding biblical authority but also a material issue concerning the true meaning of Christian faith.

It has to be remembered that Barth's own historical context saw the rise of the National Socialists and the Nazification of German Protestantism. In fact, Barth was the guiding light of the movement of the so-called Confessing Church that resisted the infiltration of Nazi ideology into the church's preaching and teaching. When seen against this backdrop, Barth's christological appropriation of the Old Testament and his uncompromising insistence upon its retention within the church's canon represented, among other things, a heroic effort to rescue it from the virulent anti-Semitism of its detractors, who sought an Aryan Christianity freed of all elements of Judaism.[35] In response to the objection that the Old Testament should be

31. Barth, *The Doctrine of the Word of God*, I/2:476; Martin Luther, "Preface to the New Testament," in *Luther's Works*, 55 vols., ed. Jaroslav Pelikan and Helmut T. Lehmann (St. Louis: Concordia; Philadelphia: Fortress, 1955–86) 35:357–65 at 362.

32. Barth, *The Doctrine of the Word of God*, I/2:478.

33. Barth, *The Doctrine of the Word of God*, I/2:488. Emil G. Kraeling explains the view of the Socinians: "These Protestants, though conceding the divine character of the Old Testament, claimed that it now had only a historical interest and was not essential for Christian doctrine." *The Old Testament since the Reformation* (London: Lutterworth, 1955) 40.

34. Barth, *The Doctrine of the Word of God*, I/2:74.

35. "Already in the first edition of the 'Epistle to the Romans' Barth constantly equated the concepts 'Israel' and 'church,' and by making them synonyms Barth

expunged from the Bible on account of its Jewish character, Barth replied that the same objection could be brought against the New Testament: "The Bible as the witness of divine revelation is in its humanity a product of the Israelitish, or to put it more clearly, the Jewish spirit. This is true . . . of the whole Bible, even of the whole of the New Testament Bible . . . If we want it otherwise, we will have to strike out not only the Old but all the New Testament as well . . . The Bible is a Jewish book, the Jewish book."[36] Barth characterized the disdain for the Bible's Jewish character as a modern instance of the ancient Docetic heresy that denied Jesus' real humanity. By extension Barth looked upon the Bible, in analogy with Christ, as both fully human and fully divine: "the word of man, the Jewish word of the Bible, heard and accepted as the Word of God."[37]

Nonetheless, we cannot escape the ambiguity of Barth's christocentric approach to the Old Testament, especially as it influences how the church understands its relation to non-Christian Judaism. To Barth's mind, Jewish scholars such as Martin Buber and Hans-Joachim Schoeps are "instructive to listen to on our question, both in what they say as earnest Jews, and in what they cannot say as unconverted Jews."[38] As "pure" students of the Old Testament, they exhibit the "grim unredeemedness" with which unconverted Judaism reads the Old Testament in isolation from the New. Yet "in and for itself, the Old Testament . . . is not a reality at all, but a Jewish abstraction."[39] This is precisely what the historical-critical scholar does: by treating the Old Testament apart from the New, the Ebionite (Jewish-Christian) heresy that denied Christ's divinity is established anew: "A

---

countered the view that the Old Testament does not belong in the canon of the church since the church has nothing to do with Israel. Proponents of Jewish emancipation as well as anti-Semites had championed this thesis . . . With the year 1933 Barth's understanding of Israel begins to undergo a decided change: in the face of the escalation of anti-Semitism, Barth increasingly argues in a philo-Semitic fashion." Dieter Kraft, "Israel in der Theologie Karl Barths," *Communio Viatorum* 27 (1984) 59-72 at 61, 64.

36. Barth, *The Doctrine of the Word of God*, I/2:510.

37. Barth, *The Doctrine of the Word of God*, I/2:511.

38. Barth, *The Doctrine of the Word of God*, I/2:80. In spite of Barth's positive assessment that the philosophy of "I and Thou" correctly articulates the true meaning of authentic co-humanity, Buber noted this caveat: "Nevertheless, [Barth] can't really admit that such an interpretation of humanity could have arisen on some basis other than the christological." Martin Buber, *Die Schriften über das dialogische Prinzip* (Heidelberg: Schneider, 1954) 303. The correspondence between Barth and Schoeps is published in Gary Lease, "Der Briefwechsel zwischen Karl Barth und Hans-Joachim Schoeps (1929–1946)," *Menora: Jahrbuch für deutsch-jüdische Geschichte* 2 (1991) 105-37. I am indebted to Hans J. Hillerbrand for assisting me in locating this correspondence.

39. Barth, *The Doctrine of the Word of God*, I/2:89.

religio-historical understanding of the Old Testament in abstraction from the revelation of the risen Christ is simply an abandonment of the New Testament and of the sphere of the Church in favor of that of the Synagogue, and therefore in favor of an Old Testament . . . understood apart from its true object and content."[40] For Barth, the crucial question dividing church and synagogue is, "Who possesses, who reads the real Old Testament."[41] Unlike Schleiermacher and Harnack, who answered this question in favor of the synagogue, Barth argued that the Old Testament rightfully belongs only to the church, since its true subject matter is Jesus Christ. The irony here is that Barth, by likening historical readings to Jewish readings of the Old Testament, has tacitly conceded to Schleiermacher and Harnack their main point, namely, that the historical-critical interpretation of the Old Testament does not support the traditional claims of the church against the synagogue. And that is why, in the final analysis, Barth's scriptural principle requires a transcendence of the strictures of historical criticism for the sake of claiming the Old Testament on behalf of Christian faith.[42]

CRITIQUE OF BARTH'S ARGUMENT ABOUT THE OLD TESTAMENT

It is no easy task to disentangle the genuine insights in Barth's work from his adversarial stance toward his liberal predecessors. Indeed, many a scholar has taken umbrage at Barth's portrayal of nineteenth-century Protestant theology.[43] Much to the detriment of conceptual clarity that might have contributed to genuine discussion and argument, Barth's mastery of rhetoric more often than not obscured the real issues at stake between him and other theologians. Hence, taking Barth's challenge seriously does not entail allowing his formulation of the basic points under dispute to dictate the

---

40. Barth, *The Doctrine of the Word of God*, I/2:489. Katherine Sonderegger says of Barth, "He was anti-Judaic, yet not anti-Semitic." *That Jesus Christ Was Born a Jew: Karl Barth's "Doctrine of Israel"* (University Park: Pennsylvania State University Press, 1992) 12.

41. Barth, *The Doctrine of the Word of God*, I/2:93.

42. Regarding Barth's exegesis of the Old Testament, one scholar observes, "The reason for such departures from historical-critical results seems to be a Christological one . . . Loyalty to Jesus Christ will lead one beyond the results that the historical or critical method puts forward for a given passage." Roger Raymond Keller, "The Interpretation of the Old Testament in Karl Barth's *Church Dogmatics*" (PhD diss., Duke University, 1975) 38.

43. For one example, see Richard R. Niebuhr, *Schleiermacher on Christ and Religion: A New Introduction* (New York: Scribner, 1964) 11.

terms of debate. Since his theology is thoroughly modern and not a return to the premodern theology of Protestant orthodoxy, it is entirely appropriate to analyze his position with the questions of modern theology in mind even though he tried valiantly to redefine them.

The strength of Barth's position lies in its clear recognition that the New Testament is not only historically illuminated but also religiously constituted by its relation to what precedes it in the Old Testament. Indeed, so much is this the case that serious damage would be done to the material substance of Christian faith if the gospel were to be uprooted from its Jewish soil. This danger presented itself acutely in the theologies of Marcion and the Gnostics, who were dualists (though for different reasons) and not monotheists. Barth astutely observed that one cannot reject the Old Testament on account of its Jewish character without being forced by the same logic to disown the New Testament also. Moreover, his nonlegalistic interpretation of "law" as a category in Christian ethics accurately reflects modern Old Testament scholarship in viewing the Torah, first, as a gift of God's grace and, second, as a gift that brings with it a demand. On these two points, at least, Barth's argument can surely stand on its own historical-theological merits quite apart from his christocentric rationale for including the Old Testament in the church's canon. (Incidentally, I judge Barth's views on these two matters to be superior to those of either Schleiermacher or Harnack.) Finally, we cannot ignore the virulent anti-Semitism of Barth's context that sharpened his grasp of the religious and moral issues at stake in retaining the Old Testament against its detractors. In these respects, Barth deserves praise for his defense of the Old Testament as an integral part of the church's Bible. The question before us is whether his reasons for its inclusion in the canon are both theologically adequate and exegetically appropriate.

Barth presented his theology as being uniquely faithful to scripture in comparison to both his liberal predecessors and other contemporary theologians such as Brunner, Bultmann, and Tillich, with whom he had sharp disagreements. For that reason, the question how his christological approach to the Old Testament stands up to scrutiny in the eyes of other interpreters of the Bible cannot be avoided. The problem in criticizing Barth, however, is that it is not clear what, to his own mind, could possibly count as evidence against his christological reading of the Old Testament given his critique of historical scholarship. David H. Kelsey, in his careful analysis of the uses of scripture in modern theology, says of Barth's approach, "It is difficult to see how this way of construing scripture can be assessed. It can in principle be neither confirmed nor disconfirmed by historical-critical exegesis of scripture."[44] It cannot be confirmed since historical scholarship has no grounds for claiming that the miracle of revelation has occurred. It cannot be disconfirmed, because historical exegesis, for Barth, is misguided (and, hence, beside the point) in treating the Bible primarily as a source for reconstructing the history of human religion, whereas exegesis in the true sense (i.e., theological exegesis) seeks to understand the text's own subject matter, which is divine revelation.

For Barth, there is no "general" hermeneutics that could adjudicate conflicting interpretations of a biblical text. Barth embraces a "special" hermeneutics that follows from his theological commitments. As Werner G. Jeanrond rightly notes, "Barth's hermeneutics is not an introductory reflection before actual theology begins. It is part of theology proper, and thus part of dogmatics."[45] Modern hermeneutical theories developed outside the context of the church are not serviceable for dogmatic theology on account of their loss of focus upon the text's subject matter in favor of an interest in the text's author. Yet if we take Barth at his word, there would apparently be no need for a special biblical hermeneutics were it not for this deficiency in general hermeneutics: "Biblical hermeneutics must be guarded against the totalitarian claim of a general hermeneutics. It is a special hermeneutics only because hermeneutics generally has been mortally sick for so long that it has not let the special problem of biblical hermeneutics force its attention upon its own problem. For the sake of a better general hermeneutics it must therefore dare to be this special hermeneutics."[46] But we cannot take Barth at his word here. By his time, hermeneutical reflection had left behind the psychological interest of earlier romanticist theories of interpretation as well as the positivist quest for total objectivity in historiography. Barth's hermeneutics is not a purely formal claim that interpretation of any text, including the Bible, must revolve around the text's own subject matter (*die Sache selbst*).[47] It is, first and foremost, a material claim that the subject matter of the entire Bible is God's revelation in Jesus Christ. Unless this premise is granted, the subject matter of the Old Testament cannot be understood for what it really is. This is not what is elsewhere called "the hermeneutical circle" wherein exegesis without presuppositions is recognized as not possible, though the text can and, if we allow it, does challenge our initial

---

44. Kelsey, *Proving Doctrine*, 49.

45. Werner G. Jeanrond, *Theological Hermeneutics: Development and Significance* (New York: Crossroad, 1991) 128.

46. Barth, *The Doctrine of the Word of God*, I/2:472.

47. Although that is precisely what he did claim in his Romans commentary, where his method of interpretation is said to be "applicable also to the study of Lao-Tse and of Goethe." Barth, "Preface to the Second Edition," 12.

presuppositions so that we understand both it and ourselves anew.⁴⁸ Barth's is not an open circle, but a closed one.

If we grant that an adequate interpretation of the Bible must at some point move beyond a strictly historical exegesis to engage the theological claims of the text, we can surely ask of Barth, Why does a theological exegesis of the Old Testament have to be christological? Barth's answer, of course, is that Jesus Christ is God's only locus of self-revelation. But, clearly, this is a dogmatic (i.e., systematic-theological) premise that reflects Barth's distinctive—one might even say idiosyncratic—perspective on Christian faith. According to Barth, apart from this premise the Old Testament forfeits its claim to be a witness to revelation and, therefore, cannot be claimed as Christian scripture. But why must a theology predicated on the axiom that the Bible bears witness to God's revelation assume that a doctrine of revelation has to be christocentric in Barth's sense? There is nothing self-evident about this assumption.⁴⁹ Every seminary student knows that Barth's theology represents the most radical christocentrism to be found in the church's history (with the possible exception of Marcion).⁵⁰ Barth's decision to define revelation in this exclusively christological sense is not the only systematic option available to theology. A more expansive notion of revelation could account for the presumption of the writers of the Old Testament that God was known in various ways throughout Israel's history.⁵¹ Hence, Barth's insistence that a theological exegesis of the Old Testament has to begin by positing that it is a witness to Jesus Christ is both false and misleading.

48. Rudolf Bultmann, "Is Exegesis without Presuppositions Possible?" in *The New Testament and Mythology and Other Basic Writings*, trans. Schubert M. Ogden (Philadelphia: Fortress, 1984) 145–53.

49. For an alternative to Barth's christocentrism, see H. Richard Niebuhr, *The Meaning of Revelation* (New York: Macmillan, 1941). Niebuhr's theology can be read as a sustained effort to address many of Barth's questions and concerns in a non-Barthian manner.

50. Early on, Barth noted that some of his critics had accused him of being a Marcionite. "Preface to the Second Edition," 13. H. Richard Niebuhr (in the series "How My Mind Has Changed") objected to Barth's virtual collapse of theology into christology, dubbing it "a new Unitarianism of the second person of the Trinity." "Reformation: Continuing Imperative," *Christian Century* 77 (March 2, 1960) 248–51 at 250. Ironically, it is here perhaps that Barth was most indebted to the liberal heritage he so wanted to overcome: Barth's "Christocentric account of Christian doctrine . . . stands in direct continuity with Schleiermacher." R. Kendall Soulen, *The God of Israel and Christian Theology* (Minneapolis: Fortress, 1996) 93.

51. According to P. Wernberg-Möller, Barth's theology with its axiom "that Old Testament theology can have nothing to do with historical research . . . defies the explicit and clear evidence of the Old Testament that the will of God was revealed to the Jewish people." "Is There an Old Testament Theology?" *Hibbert Journal* 59 (October 1960) 21–29 at 27.

Most troubling of all, though, is that Barth's christocentric principle of revelation dictates from the outset what he purports to find in the Old Testament. Biblical scholars who insist upon a constitutive—and not merely ancillary—role for historical-critical study in any theological exegesis judge that Barth was able to enlist the Old Testament on his behalf only by first subordinating it to fit the purposes of his dogmatics. James Barr, whose incisive analyses have cleared up much confusion in the study of the Bible and theology, takes stock of the consequences of Barth's principle for biblical exegesis: "The principle thus set up has very important effects in Barth's theology. It controls the methods by which exegesis will be permitted to work . . . [I]t affects the use of historical criticism; and indeed it finally decides all questions of ways in which the text may be able to sustain itself against what is alleged to be its interpretation. In a theology so dependent on close biblical work as Barth's it is therefore extremely fateful that such a principle should be set up."[52] Rolf P. Knierim, whose concern for a theological exegesis of the Old Testament is no less serious than was Barth's, warns that "the claim that the Old Testament is theologically significant only when it is read in light of the New Testament, or of Christ, has imperialistic implications . . . because it censures the Old Testament's theological validity by external criteria."[53] While Barth's return to the Reformers' doctrine of biblical authority secured for him the canonical unity of both testaments in the face of its dissolution by historical criticism, the high price paid for this unity is the loss of the Old Testament's integrity as a text in its own right bearing witness to its distinctive subject matter apart from the dogmatic categories of Christian theology.[54] Here it is the other side of the Reformation heritage that has now been placed in jeopardy, namely, the Reformers' nonnegotiable

---

52. James Barr, *Old and New in Interpretation: A Study of the Two Testaments*, Currie Lectures 1964 (London: SCM, 1966) 90–91.

53. Rolf P. Knierim, *The Task of Old Testament Theology: Substance, Method, and Cases* (Grand Rapids: Eerdmans, 1995) 1n1.

54. Walter Baumgartner spoke of Barth's "disparagement—notwithstanding all his protests to the contrary!—not only of what Old Testament scholarship as a whole has achieved but even of the Old Testament itself. For what the Old Testament really intends, what its words once meant for its time, is consistently set aside as being of no theological value . . . In many respects one is reminded of Hengstenberg. To be sure, it was easier to argue with Hengstenberg than with Barth. With Hengstenberg the debates were about the 'authenticity' of the Pentateuch and Daniel, the existence of Deutero-Isaiah and Deutero-Zechariah, etc. With Barth all critical presuppositions are held in abeyance; the critical results are not negated but, for the most part, accepted only with reservation, now used and now ignored, so that one never knows exactly where one stands and on which turf the battle is being waged." "Die Auslegung des Alten Testaments im Streit der Gegenwart," in *Zum Alten Testament und seiner Umwelt: Ausgewälte Aufsätze* (Leiden: Brill, 1959) 179–207 at 184, 186–87, 194.

commitment to let the Bible speak for itself (*scriptura sui ipsius interpres*) apart from, and even against, if need be, the postbiblical tradition of the church. Walter Brueggemann makes the point as well as anyone can: "Given the intensely and consistently iconoclastic propensity of the Old Testament text, it may be suggested that the Old Testament stands as a critical principle over against any easy claims of New Testament faith . . . [T]he problem is even more acute when one moves from the claims closely linked to Jesus in the New Testament to the developed dogmatic tradition of the church."[55] Rejecting the assertion prevalent in certain theological circles today that the Bible has to be read in the context of the church's "rule of faith" (*regula fidei*) as set forth in the ecumenical creeds, Brueggemann observes that "it is difficult to see how biblical theology can protest against or correct dogmatic claims (a role Reformed faith fully affirms) if it must proceed in such a fashion."[56] With Barth, the Reformers' struggle to free the Bible from its servitude to the theological traditions of the church has thus been abandoned in the name of a theology that claims for itself singular fidelity to the Bible.

Given his axiom that the Old Testament receives its character as a witness to revelation only through the light shed upon it by the gospel, Barth was compelled by the logic of his position to deny the validity of Jewish readings of the Bible. It is the church, not the synagogue, to which the scriptures of Israel rightfully belong: "The Synagogue is corporately, so to speak, the Old Testament *per se* and *in abstracto* stiffened into petrifaction. To that extent it is quite in order for it to claim the Old Testament for itself as an

---

55. Walter Brueggemann, *The Book That Breathes New Life: Scriptural Authority and Biblical Theology* (Minneapolis: Fortress, 2005) 152–53.

56. Brueggemann, *The Book That Breathes New Life*, 170. Such a claim is made by Brevard S. Childs, "Toward Recovering Theological Exegesis," *Pro Ecclesia* 6 (Winter 1997) 16–26 at 20. This claim is often buttressed by the historically correct observation that Luther, Calvin, and their followers did not reject the postbiblical tradition in its entirety (in contrast to the radical Reformers) as is shown by their defense of the Nicene-Chalcedonian formulations against the Unitarians. But this argument rests on a fundamental confusion. In fact, the leaders of the Magisterial Reformation did accept the ecumenical creeds, but only because they believed their content was in accordance with the Bible. As a matter of principle, however, they gave no independent authority to these creeds as controlling how scripture is to be interpreted as was done in the patristic era when the "apostolic tradition" (consisting of the mutual interdependence of the creed [rule of faith], the New Testament canon, and episcopal succession) was defined. Luther radically redefined "apostolic" ("Preface to the Epistles of St. James and St. Jude," in *Luther's Works*, 35:395–97 at 396), and Calvin declared that not only popes but also councils can err (*Institutes*, 4.9.1–14). Hence, according to their own "formal principle," the Reformers would have had to reject the creeds if they had become convinced by exegesis that they were not in accordance with the Bible; see Heinrich Bornkamm, *Luther and the Old Testament*, trans. Eric W. and Ruth C. Gritsch, ed. Victor I. Gruhn (Philadelphia: Fortress, 1969) 114–20.

unfulfilled Old Testament."⁵⁷ It is telling, I think, that Barth accused historical critics of abandoning the church in favor of the synagogue. Clearly, he understood that historical study of the Old Testament lends more credibility to the synagogue's nonchristological interpretation than to the church's christological reading of it. Though Barth defended a theological exegesis against what he perceived to be the hegemonic presumption that the only meaning of a biblical text is its original historical sense, he was apparently untroubled by the hegemonic implications of his own insistence upon only one valid theological exegesis of the Old Testament. If he could have granted that both the church and the synagogue are equally legitimate heirs of Israel's scriptures, then his christocentric construal (while not shared by Jews or non-Barthian Christians) could be appreciated as one way of reading the Old Testament in relation to the New. But since he rejected any theological exegesis that is not christocentric, he had to deny the validity of a Jewish theological exegesis of the Bible.⁵⁸

Yet there is a certain ambiguity, perhaps even ambivalence, in Barth's handling of this question. In all fairness to him, it has to be remembered that he had a much more positive assessment of the Jewish character of both Old and New Testaments than did many other Protestant theologians of his day. Indeed, some Jewish scholars have expressed great admiration for aspects of his theology, not to mention his opposition to anti-Semitism.⁵⁹

---

57. Barth, *The Doctrine of the Word of God*, I/2:93. James Barr comments, "For Barth the strictly Christian doctrines, trinity and incarnation, were basic to any Old Testament interpretation. A Christian interpretation of Old Testament texts could not really agree with a Jewish interpretation." *Holy Scripture: Canon, Authority, Criticism* (Philadelphia: Westminster, 1983) 152.

58. Marvin A. Sweeney, a Jewish biblical scholar, asks, "To what extent does Christianity have a right unilaterally to impose Jesus Christ and the New Testament on the reading of the Old Testament without acknowledging the continuing theological validity of Judaism and its reading of the biblical texts?" Review of *Prophecy and Hermeneutics: Toward a New Introduction to the Prophets* by Christopher R. Seitz in *Toronto Journal of Theology* 24.1 (2008) 115–17 at 116.

59. The Jewish theologian Michael Wyschogrod pays Barth the highest compliment: "Karl Barth is the Christian theologian of our time who is oriented toward Scripture . . . And because Barth is Scriptural, his attention turns to Israel in a rather unique way which the Jewish theologian reads with avid interest . . . [He] is, in some sense, a member of the family whom Israel cannot ignore . . . Barth, I think, does not remain a gentile, which is to say, he becomes a Christian." "Why Was and Is the Theology of Karl Barth of Interest to a Jewish Theologian?" in *Footnotes to a Theology: The Karl Barth Colloquium of 1972*, ed. H. Martin Rumscheidt (Waterloo, ON: Corporation for the Publication of Academic Studies in Religion in Canada, 1974) 95–111 at 98, 101. Robert Raphael Geis, a German rabbi forced to emigrate during the Nazi period, praised Barth for his defense of the Jews and after the war turned to him for help in returning to Germany so as to assist in its rebuilding. *Leiden an der Unerlöstheit der*

His later writings also evince a growing appreciation for the continuing role of the synagogue in God's plan for the salvation of the entire world, and after the Holocaust he categorically rejected a Christian mission to convert the Jews.[60] When Vatican II knocked down old barriers toward mutual understanding between Catholics and Protestants, Barth made this striking comment: "We should not forget that there is finally only one really great ecumenical question: our relation to Judaism."[61] During his visit to America in 1962, a panel of Jewish, Catholic, and Protestant theologians engaged Barth in dialogue at the University of Chicago. In his conversation with Rabbi Jakob Petuchowski, Barth held out the prospect of the possibility, indeed desirability, of a shared interpretation of the Old Testament/Tanakh on the part of Christians and Jews: "There is a way open for communication between Jewish theologians and Christian theologians such as myself. We have a point of contact, and a very big one, because we read the same law, the same prophets, and the same writings . . . [W]hen we read these documents now together, we should be able to arrive at a common understanding."[62] Welcoming this suggestion, Petuchowski nonetheless expressed some doubt about the feasibility of "a common understanding" given Barth's uncompromising christocentrism:

> There is a danger that we might not be able to communicate. Thus, with all of Karl Barth's appreciation of Martin Buber, Karl Barth is compelled by the logic of his position to note that even Buber has not penetrated to the idea of the Suffering Servant in the fifty-third chapter of the Book of Isaiah, as the one who has already come . . . In a word, quoting Professor Barth, "Buber has

---

Welt: Briefe, Reden, Aufsätze, ed. Dietrich Goldschmidt and Ingrid Ubershär (Munich: Kaiser, 1984) 103–7.

60. Karl Barth, *The Doctrine of Reconciliation*, vol. IV/3.2 of *Church Dogmatics*, trans. G. W. Bromiley (Edinburgh: T. & T. Clark, 1962) 876–78. There is also the appreciative yet critical study of Friedrich-Wilhelm Marquardt, *Die Entdeckung des Judentums fur die christliche Theologie: Israel im Denken Karl Barths*, Abhandlungen zum christlich-jüdischen Dialog 1 (Munich: Kaiser, 1967). After Marquardt's critique (see his foreword to *Entdeckung des Judentums*) that Barth should have taken into account Jewish self-understandings of the present day, Barth commented, "Biblical Israel gave me so much to think about and to cope with that I simply did not have the time or the intellectual strength to look more closely at Baeck, Buber, Rosenzweig, etc." Barth later thanked Marquardt for having "noted the beginning of improvement in me, or at least a serious attempt at it"; see "Letter to Dr. Friedrich-Wilhelm Marquardt," in Karl Barth, *Letters, 1961–68*, trans. Geoffrey W. Bromiley (Grand Rapids: Eerdmans, 1981) 262.

61. Bertold Klappert, *Israel und die Kirche: Erwägungen zur Israellehre Karl Barths*, Theologische Existenz Heute; n.F. 207 (Munich: Kaiser, 1980) 76.

62. "Introduction to Theology: Questions to and Discussion with Dr. Karl Barth," *Criterion* 2 (Winter 1963) 3–11, 18–24 at 19.

not penetrated to Jesus Christ." In other words, would you really expect Buber to take the position of the Ethiopian eunuch in the eighth chapter of the Book of Acts, who, you recall, was reading Isaiah 53 until Philip asked him, "Do you understand what you read?" and then Philip explained . . . that what was described in the fifty-third chapter of Isaiah had now become historical fact in Jesus . . . How would you attempt to convince *him* that revelation culminates in the existence of Jesus of Nazareth? Would that not involve you necessarily—this confrontation with a Jew—in the discussion of those very questions of history, Biblical criticism, and even world views . . . which within your own dogmatic system you have so far relegated to the background? . . . [W]ould it not be necessary, in order for us to communicate, for you to move historical questions more directly to the center of the stage?[63]

Although Barth reiterated his contention that he was not an enemy of historical-critical research as such, it is evident that Petuchowski had correctly identified the real obstacle in Barth's theology to any shared Jewish–Christian interpretation of the Bible. Barth does not allow historical-critical study to challenge the church's christological exegesis of the Old Testament. It is one thing to claim that the Old Testament is a witness to revelation. On this Jews and Christians can agree. It is quite another thing, however, to assert that God is revealed only in Jesus Christ, and that apart from this belief the Old Testament cannot be understood as a witness to revelation. Not surprisingly, Petuchowski confessed to "a certain ambivalence that must mark a Jew's approach to Karl Barth."[64]

Petuchowski's question about "history, Biblical criticism, and even world views" is the crucial one to ask in any serious effort to assess whether Barth's theology has actually succeeded in moving beyond the characteristic problems of liberal theology that he most wanted to avoid. We have to remember that Barth did not repristinate the orthodox Protestant dogma that the Bible is a supernaturally revealed book immune to historical and scientific error. If he had, there would be no point in criticizing him for not having taken historical-critical study more seriously. But since his call for a theological exegesis was meant to supplement—not to replace—the

---

63. "Introduction to Theology," 19. Interestingly, Barth had elsewhere made the suggestion that one possibility for the future of liberal theology might be to learn from the work of Buber: "If I were a liberal theologian, I should try the theology of Martin Buber . . . Liberal theology might well find new possibilities within the framework of such a pre-Messianic Judaism." Karl Barth, "Liberal Theology: Some Alternatives," trans. L. A. Garrard, *Hibbert Journal* 59 (1961) 213–219 at 217–18.

64. "Introduction to Theology," 18.

legitimate results of such study, the manner in which historical scholarship is taken up into his theological framework cannot escape the scrutiny of other interpreters of scripture who accept historical criticism yet also agree with Barth on the necessity of a theological exegesis. And here again the fundamental question is whether the entire Bible can be pressed into the service of Barth's christocentric theology without violating the integrity of the biblical text itself.

Does biblical theology really have any autonomy for Barth in relation to dogmatics? Barr thinks not.[65] Speaking as a biblical theologian, he judges that Barth's dogmatics fails to meet the criterion of exegetical appropriateness to the biblical text: "The fact is that if Barth's general lines of thinking are to be moved from the dogmatic level and restarted on the level of any sort of biblical theology, something has to be modified. *No* biblical theology has the means to agree entirely with Barth, unless it simply becomes subservient to his dogmatics."[66] Barr objects that Barth refused to take seriously the problem posed by the historical insight into the irreducible plurality of theological perspectives in scripture. Not only is there the difference between Old Testament and New Testament theology (the recognition of which led Schleiermacher and Harnack to their conclusion that the Old Testament is Jewish and hence incompatible with Christianity), but within each testament there is a diversity of theological viewpoints. This discovery poses the most serious obstacle to Barth's attempt to retrieve the scriptural principle of the Reformers. In his examination of Barth's theological method, John B. Cobb Jr. argues that "the major presupposition [of Barth's theology] . . . is the assumption of the unity of Scripture . . . It must be noted, however, that most Biblical scholars are impressed by the deep diversities of understanding that characterize the Biblical writers even on such central questions as are decisive for Barth . . . My point here is that in the formulation of the principle that guides Barth's exegesis of Scripture there is operating alongside Barth's openness to Scripture as such his hostility to some of the consequences of other interpretations of Scripture."[67] The source of the problem lies in Barth's premise that it is possible to rehabilitate the Reformers' affirmation of the scripture's unity and authority as the sole norm and source of doctrine apart from endorsing their precritical understanding of the Bible.

---

65. For Barth, "biblical theology, as something different from dogmatics, did not matter very much." Barr, *Holy Scripture*, 141.

66. Barr, *Holy Scripture*, 141, emphasis original.

67. John B. Cobb Jr., *Living Options in Protestant Theology: A Survey of Methods* (1962; reprint, Lanham, MD: University Press of America, 1986) 193–96.

This problem of theological diversity within the Bible was present, albeit in embryonic form, already during the Reformation when Luther concluded that James cannot be reconciled with Paul. If the Reformers' program was to be consistent with itself, there could be no discrepancies arising from exegesis of the Bible's literal sense with what was alleged to be its "main doctrine" (Melanchthon). Yet Luther's example raises the question how the Reformers' material principle (*sola fide*) was actually related to their formal principle (*sola scriptura*). Calvin's commitment to exegete the entire canon so as to avoid precisely the sort of problem identified by Luther led to his attempt at harmonizing the statements of Paul and James.[68] Although Barth said that the canon is not closed—thereby acknowledging the legitimacy in principle of a theological criticism of the canon (*Sachkritik*)—in practice he resisted any appeals to a "canon within the canon" as reductive.[69] But if the canon's unity was a problem before the era of historical criticism, can it really serve as the basic premise of dogmatics in our time? "If not, Barth must employ selectivity and norms based on something else than the united witness of Scripture. These principles may still be found within Scripture, but their selection must point to some preunderstanding of the man approaching Scripture. Then the question of the justification of this preunderstanding raises the whole range of issues that Barth's method is designed to circumvent . . . If this criticism is valid . . . we must say that the ideal for theology held up before us by Barth is a false ideal."[70] Barth's construal of what is purported to be the unified message of scripture is based upon

68. Calvin, *Institutes*, 3.17.11. In the Second Helvetic Confession, of 1566, the most widely received statement of Reformed faith in the sixteenth century, Calvin's exegesis of James is judged to be correct, while Luther's willingness to engage in *Sachkritik* is endorsed as a matter of principle: this means, however, that if Luther's exegesis should turn out on closer inspection to be the correct one after all, then James has got to go; see *The Creeds of Christendom with a History and Critical Notes*, 3 vols., ed. Philip Schaff (1931; reprint, Grand Rapids: Baker, 1990) 3:267–68.

69. Walter Lindemann protests, "One cannot, on the one hand, approach every single interpretation of Christian faith in the history of theology with the legitimate question whether unsuitable elements have not here been incorporated into the witness of the texts as Barth does, while exempting all such interpretations within the biblical canon from this same criticism on the other hand . . . Barth is able to exempt himself from criticism of the canon only because he does what he accuses others of doing; he too subjects the canon to a systematic principle, the doctrine of revelation . . . Moreover, the principle of trinitarian revelation is so designed that it functions rather as a harmonizing principle than as a critical principle within the canon." *Karl Barth und die kritische Schriftauslegung* (Hamburg: Reich Evangelischer, 1973) 90. For an example of Barth's trinitarian exegesis of the Old Testament, see *The Doctrine of Creation*, III/1:191–92; in his discussion about the meaning of Gen 1:26, Barth castigates historical-critical scholarship for "its arrogant rejection of the exegesis of the Early Church" (192).

70. Cobb, *Living Options in Protestant Theology*, 196–97.

a selective use of certain passages within scripture (indeed, from the New Testament!) that are taken as providing the key to the interpretation of the whole. While the consequences of this procedure for his handling of the Old Testament are apparent, Barth's exegesis of the New Testament can be seriously challenged as well.[71]

The basic problem in Barth's dogmatics, as I see it, is this relation between his theological method and his substantive interpretation of Christian faith. Although the method, according to Barth's formulation, has no independent standing apart from the material content it is designed to serve, there remains an unresolved tension between Barth's insistence upon an obedient hearing of the entire canon and his christocentric doctrine of revelation to which both testaments are supposed to bear witness. I believe that a choice has to be made: either the method needs to be modified or the theological content requires revision. If Barth were to continue to press for a method that faithfully accounts for the entire canon, he would be compelled to revise the material content of his dogmatics in order to do justice to the full range of theologies found in both testaments, including the Old Testament's nonchristological witness to God's revelation. But honest recognition of this theological plurality in the canon would force the question whether it is even possible to build a coherent theology on so diversified a collection of texts as comprise the Bible. If, however, Barth were willing to modify his method, he could still argue for a radically christocentric theology on immanent material grounds alone without insisting that the entire Bible supports this view. Barth's theology would thus remain a viable option quite apart from his statement of method. But with the acknowledgment of this distinction comes the admission that his theology is, in fact, based on

---

[71]. W. D. Davies, in his examination of the apostle Paul's relation to rabbinic Judaism, calls into question Barth's exegesis of Romans 1-2 that allegedly provides the biblical grounds for his categorical denial of "natural theology": "Paul presupposes throughout what is the Jewish equivalent of the Stoic doctrine of the Law of Nature: there had been a revelation of God's moral demands prior both to the giving of the Torah of Judaism and to the advent of the Christian Gospel. Dr. Barth's interpretation of Romans 1-2, stimulating and suggestive though it is, fails to do justice to the Rabbinic core of Paul's thought at this point—a Rabbinic core which, as we pointed out, is clothed in Hellenistic terminology but nevertheless remains central for the understanding of Paul." *Paul and Rabbinic Judaism: Some Rabbinic Aspects in Pauline Theology* (Philadelphia: Fortress, 1980) 327–28. In his controversy with Barth on this question, Emil Brunner quipped, "It seems to me a queer kind of loyalty to Scripture to demand that such a revelation should not be acknowledged, in order that the significance of biblical revelation should not be minimized." *Natural Theology, Comprising "Nature and Grace" by Dr. Emil Brunner, and the Reply "No" by Dr. Karl Barth*, trans. Peter Fraenkel (1946; reprint, Eugene, OR: Wipf & Stock, 2002) 25. If Davies and Brunner are right about Paul's meaning here, then Barth's christocentric doctrine of revelation forfeits one of its most important warrants in the New Testament itself.

a selection from the diversity of scripture and thus does not actually move beyond the characteristic questions and problems of liberal theology that he so much wanted to transcend. And in the matter of the Old Testament, it is difficult to see how the logic of his christocentric theology could escape the negative verdict of Schleiermacher and Harnack. But for Barth to have it both ways is to ensure that the method and the content of his dogmatics will move in opposite directions in spite of his claim for harmony between them.

Although Barth would not, of course, have granted the validity of the foregoing criticisms based as they are on the presupposition of a constitutive—not merely ancillary—role for historical-critical study in a theological exegesis of the Bible, we may legitimately ask what criticisms, if any, he would have taken seriously since his theological system is so thoroughly insulated against criticism from other viewpoints given its initial definition of terms.[72] Yet there is no reason why Barth's formulation of the crucial issues at stake should go unchallenged. In the final analysis, his defense of the Old Testament as Christian scripture ultimately fails to convince on account of its strained attempt to redefine the questions. By arguing for the insufficiency of historical exegesis on the grounds that it misses the true subject matter of the text which is Jesus Christ, Barth equated a theological exegesis of the Old Testament with a christological exegesis of it. Hence, before exegesis of the Old Testament can even begin its work, its sole relevant meaning has already been decided from the outset. Aside from the fact that agreement with Barth renders historical scholarship of negligible import for theological exegesis, it also precludes the possibility of any truly self-critical dialogue between Jews and Christians about the meaning(s) of their shared scriptural heritage.[73]

---

72. What Barth once said of Schleiermacher's *Glaubenslehre* could with equal justification be said of his own *Kirchliche Dogmatik*, namely, that he developed a theological system "in almost *suspiciously* brilliant fashion." Karl Barth, *The Theology of Schleiermacher: Lectures at Göttingen, Winter Semester of 1923/24*, ed. Dietrich Ritschl, trans. Geoffrey W. Bromiley (Grand Rapids: Eerdmans, 1982; reprint, Eugene, OR: Wipf & Stock, 2020) 190, emphasis original.

73. A most welcome feature of contemporary biblical scholarship is the full participation of Jews in a field hitherto dominated by Christians. Brueggemann comments: "The de-positioning of Christian interpretation and the renewed entry of Jewish interpreters into a shared interpretive conversation may be based in a now widely shared recognition that the text of Hebrew scriptures is profoundly plurivocal and does not admit of settled, enforceable larger categories." *The Book That Breathes New Life*, 132. Hence, "insofar as Old Testament theology is Christian, it is still deeply problematic to assume uncritically that the text leads directly to or can be delivered innocently for the classical formulations of Chalcedon, that is, Trinitarian and incarnational claims" (120).

OUTLINE OF AN ALTERNATIVE TO BARTH

Two conditions must be met by any systematic proposal not beholden to Barth's strictures that aims to clarify the theological significance of the Old Testament for the church and hence its inclusion within the Christian canon: first, it must fully incorporate the insights of historical-critical scholarship; second, it must not deny the legitimacy of the synagogue's right to this same body of literature (Tanakh). Since space does not permit a full elaboration of what such a proposal would entail, here it must suffice simply to outline it as an alternative worthy of further development.

Today historical-criticism has to be defended against attacks from both ends of the theological spectrum.[74] Yet historical-critical methods of biblical study pose no problem for a conception of theology that is willing to accept without reservation its own historicizing. John J. Collins has provided a cogent defense of such a conception: "The History of Religion approach . . . is not an alternative to be avoided but an ally to be utilized. While it may be difficult for any Christian to avoid dogmatic prejudices and apologetics in addressing theological questions, it is an ideal worthy of our aspirations. Such an approach will not satisfy those who see theology as an essentially confessional enterprise, but it does affirm the possibility of a Biblical Theology that is consistent with the regnant historical-critical method."[75] This model of theology has more in common with the program of Ernst Troeltsch than with that of Barth. As Troeltsch clearly appreciated, "The application of historical criticism to religious tradition must result in a profound change in one's inward attitude to it and in one's understanding of it."[76] Moreover, such a historicized approach to theology must reject Barth's sharp dichotomy between religion and revelation.

---

74. From the left, Dale B. Martin, aligning himself with postmodern theories, rejects "the notion that Christians should insist on the *necessity* of historical criticism for the interpretation of Scripture." *Sex and the Single Savior: Gender and Sexuality in Biblical Interpretation* (Louisville: Westminster John Knox, 2006) 9. From the right, Christopher R. Seitz, seeking to rehabilitate a traditional view of scriptural authority, asserts, "In my view, historical criticism plays no positive role whatsoever" in a theological interpretation of the Bible. *Word without End: The Old Testament as Abiding Theological Witness* (Waco, TX: Baylor University Press, 2004) 97. For my responses to these two scholars, see Paul E. Capetz, "Theology and the Historical-Critical Study of the Bible," *Harvard Theological Review* 104 (2011) 459-88, published under the same title as Chapter 2 in this volume (pages 70-104).

75. John J. Collins, "Biblical Theology and the History of Israelite Religion," in *Encounters with Biblical Theology* (Minneapolis: Fortress, 2005) 24–33 at 33.

76. Ernst Troeltsch, "Historical and Dogmatic Method in Theology," in *Religion in History*, trans. James Luther Adams and Walter F. Bense (Minneapolis: Fortress, 1991) 11–32 at 13.

Still, Collins's suggestion of a nonconfessional biblical theology raises the crucial question just what exactly we should understand by a "theological exegesis." As John Bright notes, the term is "open to misunderstanding." By a theological exegesis

> is *not* meant a special kind of exegesis, for example, an exegesis that is in some way controlled by the exegete's own theological presuppositions . . . Rather, by theological exegesis is meant an exegesis of the text in theological depth, an exegesis that is not content to bring out the precise verbal meaning of the text but goes on to lay bare the theology that informs the text. All biblical texts are expressive of theology in that all are animated, if at times indirectly, by some theological concern. It is incumbent upon the interpreter to seek to discover what that theological concern is. To do this is no violation of sound exegetical principles. Rather, it is the completion of the exegetical task.[77]

Properly understood, a theological exegesis is not a matter of finding a different content in the pages of the Bible than can otherwise be uncovered by historical exegesis. What makes an exegesis "theological" is the type of question being asked of the text. Schubert M. Ogden clarifies that "theological interpretation of the biblical writings is a way of understanding and explicating their meaning that is oriented by the same existential question to which they themselves intend to give answer."[78] It is thus a disciplined effort to converse with the biblical writers about the subject matter (*Sache*) of the text. Its specific task is to "clarify the meaning and truth-claims of what was thought and believed from a modern critical perspective."[79] Only so can there be a theological engagement with the Bible that respects its own integrity and does not subordinate it to dogmatics.

If, then, there is a coherent conception of theology available that is not compelled to minimize the import of historical criticism on behalf of a theological exegesis of the Bible, then the Old Testament must be interpreted for its own sake apart from any imposition of categories derived from the New Testament. Just as Barth's interpretation of the Old Testament can be challenged as to its exegetical appropriateness, its foundational christocentric

---

77. John Bright, *The Authority of the Old Testament* (Nashville: Abingdon, 1967) 170. Regarding Barth's understanding of a "theological exegesis" of the Old Testament, Bright judges, "In my opinion, 'exegesis' is the wrong word here" (170n4).

78. Schubert M. Ogden, "Theology and Biblical Interpretation," in *Doing Theology Today* (Valley Forge, PA: Trinity, 1996) 36–51 at 48. But note that this formulation of the task does not entail uncritical acceptance of the biblical writers' own answers.

79. John J. Collins, "Is a Critical Biblical Theology Possible?" in *Encounters with Biblical Theology*, 11–23 at 18.

premise can also be questioned in terms of its theological adequacy as an interpretation of the basic Christian witness. Ogden speaks for a number of theologians today in calling for a theocentric christology in place of a christocentric theology:

> To affirm, as is so often done, particularly by Protestant theologians, that the faith of the New Testament is "christocentric" is significantly to alter the New Testament's own express emphasis . . . [T]he assertion that faith is "christocentric" is at best an elliptical assertion and, like other such assertions, constantly susceptible to misunderstanding and distortion. Unless it is made clear not only that "we are Christ's," but that "Christ is God's" (1 Cor 3:23; cf. 11:3), that is, unless the *theocentric* basis and sanction of "christocentrism" is explicitly acknowledged, emphasis on Jesus Christ can be a snare and a delusion and mere travesty of authentic apostolic faith.[80]

Ogden has correctly identified what is, to my mind, the major doctrinal error giving rise to the problem that the Old Testament has posed for modern theology. By contrast, a theocentric construal of Christian faith, if pursued consistently, would reverse the order of long-standing doctrinal priorities through a revised understanding of the systematic interrelations obtaining among the doctrines of christology, soteriology, and revelation: "The New Testament sense of the claim 'only in Jesus Christ' is not that God is only to be found in Jesus and nowhere else, but that the only God who is to be found anywhere—*though he is to be found everywhere*—is that God who is made known in the word that Jesus speaks and is."[81] Interestingly, Ogden can adduce the testimony of the early Barth in support of this point:

> No one need object that this power, this meaning, this substance is to be found not only in Jesus but elsewhere. For we ourselves affirm this very thing: indeed, precisely we *can* affirm it. What is

---

80. Schubert M. Ogden, *Christ without Myth: A Study Based on the Theology of Rudolf Bultmann* (Dallas: Southern Methodist University Press, 1979) 143. James A. Sanders agrees, "The New Testament . . . presents not so much a christocentric theology as a theocentric Christology." *From Sacred Story to Sacred Text* (Philadelphia: Fortress, 1987) 41. Georg Strecker lends his support to this view: "Pauline Christology is essentially subordinationist. This corresponds to the fact that Paul thinks in a thoroughly theocentric manner . . . [I]t is God who is met in Christ." *Theology of the New Testament*, trans. M. Eugene Boring (Louisville: Westminster John Knox, 2000) 112. See also Douglas F. Ottati, *Jesus Christ and Christian Vision* (Louisville: Westminster John Knox, 1989).

81. Ogden, *Christ without Myth*, 144, emphasis orginal. See also Ogden's book, *The Point of Christology* (San Francisco: Harper & Row, 1982) for a further development of his proposal.

> known and found in Jesus is that God is found everywhere, that before and after Jesus mankind has been found by God; in him we have the criterion by which all finding and being found by God may be known as such and by which we can conceive this finding and being found as a truth of the eternal order. *Many walk in the light of redemption, forgiveness, resurrection; but that we see them walk, that we have eyes for them, we owe to one.* And that it is *the Christ* we have found in Jesus is confirmed because Jesus is the final word, which clarifies all the others and brings them to sharpest expression, of the faithfulness of God to which the law and the prophets bear witness.[82]

Accordingly, the purpose of the church's christological witness to Jesus is none other than to bear witness to the one God who is creator, judge, and redeemer of all persons.

Ogden recognizes that the canon as such cannot serve directly as the exegetical foundation of contemporary theology given its internal diversity. For him—unlike for Barth—the sense in which the Bible is authoritative can only be established critically (*Sachkritik*). While the *kerygma* provides the criterion for evaluating the adequacy of the New Testament's theologies, the proper use of the Old Testament remains to be resolved.

> The usual view on this point in recent Protestant theology is, in effect, this: just as the New Testament is to be used by theology only under the control of the New Testament message, so the Old Testament's authority for theological reflection and argument is subject to that of the New. But . . . this familiar view of the use of the Old Testament is now scarcely less untenable than the views of the Reformers and of the orthodox dogmaticians of which it is a revision. That the New Testament is to be used in theology only under the authority of the Jesus-kerygma poses no particular difficulty, since the New Testament's writings . . . expressly have to do with the subject-term of this kerygma, that is, with Jesus . . . However, we now recognize that it is historically false as well as theologically misleading to claim that the Old Testament writings, too, are expressly about Jesus.[83]

---

82. Barth, *Epistle to the Romans*, 97, cited by Ogden according to his own translation in *Christ without Myth*, 10. Ogden notes that "the position of Barth in *Der Römerbrief* is much more radical than Bultmann's in being free of any mythological claims for a unique revelation of God in Jesus Christ" (125n67).

83. Schubert M. Ogden, "The Authority of Scripture for Theology," in *On Theology* (San Francisco: Harper & Row, 1986) 45–68 at 65–66.

This observation "forces the question whether the Old Testament may be properly used as a theological authority at all."[84] Yet, in truth, an affirmative answer to it lies close at hand in the recognition that the Old Testament provides the church's *kerygma* with its indispensable presupposition of monotheism and all that is therein entailed for the understanding of human persons in the world before God. For its part, this monotheistic presupposition also serves an indispensable critical function in relation to the various theological formulations of the *kerygma* beginning with the New Testament itself.[85]

> Consequently, if theology asks, as it must, for the meaning of the Jesus-kerygma, and thus for the understanding of human existence—of ourselves, the world, and God—that the Jesus-kerygma necessarily presupposes, the answer, clearly, is that it is a certain form or development of the understanding of existence that is variously expressed in the writings of the Old Testament . . . But if this is correct, there is no doubt that the Old Testament, in its way, is also a theological authority, nor does using it as such pose any particular difficulty.[86]

This alternative construal not only has the merit that the historical sense of the Old Testament need pose no special problems for a theological exegesis of the Bible. It also redeems what I earlier indicated to be Barth's pivotal insight, namely, that the question of the Old Testament is not primarily about the formal issues of biblical authority or theological method but, rather, about the substantive meaning of the gospel.

In conclusion, we may note the pointed observation made by the Roman Catholic biblical scholar Roland E. Murphy: "It is ironic that a Protestant theology, expressly committed to the biblical word, should make an interpretation of the New Testament the arbiter of the canonical status of an earlier part of the Bible."[87] Indeed, the irony of the Reformation's legacy

---

84. Ogden, "Authority of Scripture," 66.

85. Knierim rightly asks "whether the understanding of Christ as expressed in diverse theological interpretations triggered by the New Testament is at times so controversial among Christians, today as throughout history, that they reflect a polytheistic more than a monotheistic Christology or Christianity." *The Task of Old Testament Theology*, 7n5. The decision of the church to retain the Old Testament was simultaneously a reaffirmation of monotheism as the indispensable presupposition of Christian theology. For an example of how the Old Testament functioned as a constraint upon the development of trinitarian doctrine, see Gregory of Nyssa, "Concerning We Should Think of Saying That There Are not Three Gods to Ablabius," in *The Trinitarian Controversy*, trans. William G. Rusch (Philadelphia: Fortress, 1980) 149–61 at 151.

86. Ogden, "Authority of Scripture," 67.

87. Roland E. Murphy, "Old Testament/*Tanakh*—Canon and Interpretation," in

is precisely that it resulted in an impasse for modern Protestants, who were forced to make a decision that Luther and Calvin could never have foreseen: either to accept the historical realization that the Old Testament is a Jewish book that rightly belongs to the synagogue or to minimize the import of historical study by insisting that its true theological meaning is christological. In a church defined by "scripture alone," exegesis unfettered by doctrinal restraints undermined the assumption of a single biblical theology. Although the Reformers' theological method has proven to be untenable, their endeavor to free the Bible from captivity to the church's traditions has succeeded. Herein lies Protestantism's real and enduring contribution to the question of the Old Testament. Perhaps a partial precedent can already be found in Calvin's exegesis of Ps 72: "Those who would interpret it simply as a prophecy of the kingdom of Christ, seem to put a construction upon the words which does violence to them; and then we must always beware of giving the Jews an occasion of making an outcry, as if it were our purpose, sophistically, to apply to Christ those things which do not directly refer to him."[88] One of Calvin's contemporary heirs, James A. Sanders, continues in this same spirit: "The Bible is a dialogical literature that in turn gave rise to two dialogical religions based on it . . . No closure can curb the dialogue that is inherent in a canon of scripture, which, over against the *magisteria* and *regulae fidei* that developed after closure in all the churches, mandates dialogue about its continuing relevance and authority."[89] An unparalleled opportunity is now given for both synagogue and church to engage one another in genuine dialogue about their common scriptural inheritance apart from having to regard "Judaism as the unchanged word of the Bible from which Christianity deviated, or Christianity the true fulfillment of

---

Hebrew Bible or Old Testament? Studying the Bible in Judaism and Christianity, ed. Roger Brooks and John J. Collins, Christianity and Judaism in Antiquity 5 (Notre Dame: University of Notre Dame Press, 1990) 11–29 at 22.

88. John Calvin, *Commentary on the Book of Psalms*, trans. James Anderson, in *Calvin's Commentaries*, 22 vols. (originally published in Edinburgh by the Calvin Translation Society; reprint, Grand Rapids: Baker, 1989) 5:100. Hans-Joachim Kraus, citing this passage among others, says that "Calvin reveals himself here in following the Jewish scholars as a harbinger and pioneer of lucid, relevant historical-critical research . . . Never before in all of church history has Christian theology come so close to Judaism and met so openly with it on the basis of the Hebrew Bible as in the work of Calvin." "The Contemporary Relevance of Calvin's Theology," in *Toward the Future of Reformed Theology: Tasks, Topics, and Traditions*, ed. David Willis and Michael Welker (Grand Rapids: Eerdmans, 1999) 323–38 at 330, 332.

89. James A. Sanders, "The Issue of Closure in the Canonical Process," in *The Canon Debate*, ed. Lee Martin McDonald and James A. Sanders (Peabody, MA: Hendrickson, 2002) 252–63 at 260, 262.

the prophets which the Jews rejected."⁹⁰ Rolf Rendtorff captures well the significance of this historic moment for both religions: "It is the first time in history that Jews and Christians have had the opportunity to meet on an equal level . . . The immediate question is whether we are ready and able to begin a dialogue that should have started almost two thousand years ago but now starts under fundamentally new conditions."⁹¹

---

90. Michael Hilton, *The Christian Effect on Jewish Life* (London: SCM, 1994) 2.

91. Rolf Rendtorff, "Toward a Common Jewish-Christian Reading of the Hebrew Bible," in *Hebrew Bible or Old Testament? Studying the Bible in Judaism and Christianity*, ed. Roger Brooks and John J. Collins (Notre Dame: University of Notre Dame Press, 1990) 89–108 at 84.

Index

Adams, James Luther, 7n9, 80n54, 97n116, 127n80, 165n76
Albright, William Foxwell, 72n5
Althaus, Paul, 36n65
Anderson, James, 170n88
Annas, 44
Apuleius, 97n116
Aristotle, 94, 94n109
Athanasius, 94, 128n84
Augustine, 96

Bächli, Otto, 148n24
Backus, Irena, 141n2
Baeck, Leo, 120n48, 159n60
Bainton, Roland, 47, 47n99, 48n103, 49n109, 66n157
Barr, James, 12n13, 138n110, 156, 156n52, 158n57, 161, 161n66
Barth, Karl, 4, 8, 9, 10, 12, 20-40, 20n12, 22n15, 23nn17-19, 24nn20-21, 25nn22-25, 26nn26-29, 27nn30-32, 28n14, 29n40, 30nn45-46, 31nn47-49, 34n61, 35n62, 36n63, 36n65, 36n66, 37nn66-69, 38nn72-73, 39nn75-77, 40n78, 48, 49, 49nn105-108, 50, 50nn110-111, 51, 51n112, 52, 52n115, 54, 54n120, 54n121, 56, 57, 57n127, 65, 73, 73n8, 74, 87, 87n83, 88n84, 89n87, 93n107, 106, 106n3, 115n35, 131, 134, 135, 139-68, 142nn4-5, 143n7, 144nn8-9, 145nn10-14, 146nn15-18, 147nn19-22, 148nn23-26, 149nn27-30, 150nn31-35, 151nn35-39, 152nn40-42, 154nn46-47, 155nn49-51, 156n54, 158n57, 158n59, 159nn60-62, 160n63, 161n65, 162n69, 164n72, 166n77, 168n82, 169
Battles, Ford Lewis, 45n94, 54n121, 91n97, 148n26
Baumgartner, Walter, 156n54
Beckmann, Klaus, 105-6, 106n2, 107, 112n28, 121, 124, 124n66, 124nn68-69, 125n74, 131, 134, 135, 135n103, 136, 141n3
Bellis, Alice Ogden, 115n33
Bense, Walter F., 7n9, 80n54, 127n80, 165n76
Bernstein, Richard J., 81n55
Betz, Hans Dieter, 83n61, 125n71
Bierma, Lyle D., 141n3
Bonhoeffer, Dietrich, 18, 18n7, 67
Boring, M. Eugene, 167n80
Bornkamm, Heinrich, 47, 47n101, 157n56
Bouwsma, William J., 19n9
Bowden, John, 140n2
Bowie, Andrew, 117n41
Bright, John, 166, 166n77
Bromiley, Geoffrey W., 49n105, 145n13, 148n26, 159n60, 164n72
Brooks, Roger, 170n87, 171n91
Brueggemann, Walter, 157, 157nn55-56, 164n73
Brunner, Emil, 153, 163n71

Buber, Martin, 151, 151n38, 159, 160, 160n63
Bullinger, Heinrich, 50n110
Bultmann, Rudolf, 4, 12, 20–40, 28nn35–38, 29nn40–42, 30nn43–44, 31n47, 32nn49–51, 32nn49–53, 33nn53–57, 34nn58–61, 35n62, 36n64, 37nn67–69, 38n73, 39n74, 39n77, 40n78, 51, 54n120, 56, 56n123, 57, 57nn128–130, 58, 58n131, 58n133, 59, 59nn133–134, 64, 64n150, 64n152, 65, 71n3, 83, 83n63, 88, 89, 89n87, 90, 93n107, 98, 125n70, 127, 127n79, 153, 155n48, 168n82
Bussey, O., 142n4
Buttrick, George Arthur, 79n52

Calvin, John, 5, 6, 9, 10, 12, 20, 21, 22, 26, 38, 41, 45, 45n94, 46nn96–7, 49, 50n110, 51, 51n112, 52, 54, 55, 65n155, 66, 67, 67n159, 69, 69n166, 73, 85, 89n87, 93, 94, 101n122, 140n1, 141n2, 142, 142n5, 148n26, 157n56, 162, 162n68, 170, 170n88
Cameron, Euan, 43n85
Capetz, Paul E., 54n120, 61n142, 65n155, 68n164, 87n83, 134n102, 141n3, 165n74
Chapman, Mark D., 71n3
Childs, Brevard S., 54n121, 70, 72–74, 72n5, 73nn6–10, 73nn12–13, 74nn14–17, 75n26, 78, 78n46, 79, 79nn52–53, 84, 84n68, 85, 85nn71–72, 86, 86nn74–76, 87, 87nn79–82, 88, 88nn84–86, 90, 90nn91–94, 91, 91n97, 91n100, 92, 97n117, 98, 98n117, 100, 103, 142n6, 157n56
Clark, Gordon H., 52n115
Cobb, John B., Jr., 18n6, 19, 19nn10–11, 52n116, 67, 67n161, 119n47, 161, 161n67, 162n70
Collins, John J., 104, 104n129, 134n102, 165, 165n75, 166, 166n79, 170n87, 171n91
Craig, Samuel G., 86n73

Crim, Keith R., 28n35
Cunningham, Mary Kathleen, 36n66

Dallas, A. K., 10n11
Darwin, Charles, 16
Davies, W. D., 163n71
De Grazia, Louis, 28n35
DeJonge, Michael P., 18n7
Devenish, Philip E., 35n62
Dibelius, Martin, 45n92
Dillenberger, John, 44n87
Dilthey, Wilhelm, 109n12
Doberstein, John W., 47n101
Donner, Herbert, 54n121, 78n46
Dorrien, Gary, 31n47
Dowey, Edward A., Jr., 54–55, 55n123
Duke, James, 3n1, 108n7

Ebeling, Gerhard, 41n81, 53, 53n118, 54n121, 96, 96n115
Eck, John, 54n121, 91n97
Edwards, J. W., 142n4
Eliot, George, 124n67
Erasmus, 42n84, 44n88

Fiorenza, Francis, 3n1, 108n7
Foley, Grover, 41n81
Fraenkel, Peter, 163n71
Frei, Hans W., 54n121, 78, 78n46, 131n94, 140n1
Frymer-Kensky, Tikva, 115n33
Funk, Robert W., 33n54

Gadamer, Hans-Georg, 26n26, 98
Galambush, Julie, 115n35
Gamble, Harry Y., 51, 52nn113–144, 53, 54nn119–120
Gamwell, Franklin I., 102n123
Garrard, L. A., 160n63
Geis, Robert Raphael, 158n59
Gerrish, B. A. (Brian), 42n83, 44n88, 45n91, 55, 55n124, 69n166, 101n122, 128, 128n84
Gibson, David, 24n21
Gibson, Mel, 94, 95
Gilmour, S. MacLean, 125n73
Goethe, 27n30, 154n47
Goldshmidt, Dietricch, 159n59
Green, Clifford J., 18n7

Index

Green, Garrett, 75n23
Gregory of Nyssa, 137n109, 169n85
Gritsch, Eric W., 157n56
Gritsch, Ruth C., 157n56
Grobel, Kendrick, 56n125, 89n87, 125n70
Grubenwieser, Victor, 120n48
Guder, Darrell L., 39n77
Guder, Judith J., 39n77
Gunkel, Hermann, 10n11, 102, 103n125
Gunneweg, A. H. J., 140n2
Gustafson, James M., 39n77

Hammann, Konrad, 35n62
Hanson, K. C., 10n11, 103n125
Harkness, Georgia, 61n141
Harnack, Adolf von, 93n107, 105, 126n77, 135, 141, 141n3, 142, 149, 150, 152, 153, 161, 164
Harrill, J. Albert, 63n149, 64n151
Harvey, Van A., 127n81, 138n115
Hays, Richard B., 59–61, 59n136, 60nn137–139, 61nn140–143, 62–64, 66, 68, 81, 82, 82n59, 82n60
Heidegger, Martin, 38, 38n73
Hengstenberg, Ernst Wilhelm, 141n3, 142, 156n54
Herod, 44
Heschel, Susannah, 122, 123n61
Hillerbrand, Hans J., 141n2, 151n38
Hilton, Michael, 135, 135n105, 171n90
Hodgson, Peter C., 71n3
Hofmann, J. C. K. von, 106, 124n69, 134, 135
Hofstadter, Richard, 17n5
Hollinger, David A., 5, 5n4, 6nn5–7
Hooke, S. H., 96n115
Hopkins, John Henry, 64n151
Hoppe, Joachim, 112n27
Horton, Douglas, 25n22, 144n8
Horton, Michael S., 24n21
Hoskyns, Edwyn C., 20n12, 142n5
Hunsinger, George, 131n94

James, 43, 44, 44n88, 45, 46, 49, 50n110, 162, 162n68

Jasper, David, 142n7
Jaspert, Bernd, 32n50, 34n61, 54n120
Jeanrond, Werner G., 154, 154n45
Jesus Christ, 1, 9, 36, 41n82, 44, 47, 48, 50n110, 55, 57, 58n132, 67, 86n76, 93, 97n117, 98n117, 108, 109, 111, 120, 121, 122, 122n59, 123, 124, 125, 125n73, 126, 126n75, 126n77, 127, 127n79, 127n80, 128, 129, 129n88, 130, 131, 132, 133, 134, 135, 136, 139, 141, 141n2, 143, 145, 147, 148, 149, 152, 152n42, 154, 155, 156, 157, 158n58, 160, 164, 167, 168, 168n82, 169, 169n85, 170
Job, 148
John, 41, 123, 123n63, 123n64, 124
Jonas, Ludwig, 109n12
Judas, 44
Jüngel, Eberhard, 25n25

Kaminsky, Joel S., 115n33
Kamitsuka, Margaret D., 69n164
Käsemann, Ernst, 126n76
Katzer, Ernst, 111n23
Keck, Leander E., 122n58
Keller, Roger Raymond, 149n27, 152n42
Keller, Rosemary Skinner, 61n141
Kelsey, David H., 88n84, 146n15, 153, 154n44
Klappert, Bertold, 159n61
Knierim, Rolf P., 11n12, 137n108, 156, 156n53, 169n85
Knight, Harold, 93n107, 106n3, 142n4, 145n11
Koester, Helmut, 81, 81n56
Kraeling, Emil G., 150n33
Kraft, Dieter, 151n35
Kraus, Hans-Joachim, 105n1, 170n88

Landmesser, Christof, 32n49
Lantero, Erminie Huntress, 36n64
Lao-Tse, 27n30, 154n47
Lehmann, Helmut T., 150n31
Lehmann, Paul L., 66n158
Leitch, James W., 54n121
Leith, John H., 54n121, 91n97

Levenson, Jon D., 72n4, 90, 91, 91nn95–96, 93n108, 103n127
Lindbeck, George A., 75n23
Lindemann, Walter, 36n63, 162n69
Lohse, Eduard, 56n126
Lucas, Erhard, 111n23
Luke, 41
Luther, Martin, 1, 3, 4, 5, 6, 9, 10, 11, 12, 19, 20, 21, 22, 26, 38, 39n77, 40, 41, 41n82, 42n83, 42n84, 43, 44, 44n87, 44n88, 44n89, 45, 45n93, 46, 46n95, 46n98, 47, 48, 49, 50, 50n110, 51, 53, 53n117, 54, 55, 57, 58, 65n155, 66, 66n157, 67, 68, 68n162, 68n164, 73, 85, 86n76, 89n87, 91n97, 96, 97, 97n116, 101n122, 104, 128n84, 141n2, 142, 150n31, 157n56, 162, 162n68, 170

Machinist, Peter, 83n62
Mackintosh, H. R., 55n122, 108n5
Marcion, 8, 9, 10, 105, 109, 133, 135, 137n109, 146, 150, 153, 155
Mark, 41, 44
Marquardt, Friedrich-Wilhelm, 159n60
Marsden, George M., 16n2
Marsh, John, 149n27
Martin, Dale B., 70, 70n2, 75–79, 76nn27–34, 77nn35–43, 78nn44–49, 79nn50–51, 80, 80n55, 81, 81n55, 81nn57–58, 82, 82n60, 83, 84, 84n66, 91–99, 91nn98–101, 92n102, 92n104, 93nn105–108, 94nn110–111, 95nn113–114, 98nn118–119, 98n120, 100, 101n121, 103, 134n102, 165n74
Matthew, 41, 44
McCormack, Bruce L., 36–37, 36n65, 38nn70–71
McDonald, Lee Martin, 170n89
McKeon, Richard, 94n109
McNeill, John T., 45n94, 148n26
Meckenstock, Günther, 112n27
Meeks, Wayne A., 81n56, 115n36, 116, 116nn36–37
Melanchthon, 162

Moeller, Bernd, 42n84
Mommer, Peter, 88n84, 142n6
Montague, W. J., 126n76
Montgomery, W., 7n8, 124n65
Morgan, Robert, 21n13, 111n21
Moses, 110, 113n30
Murphy, Roland E., 169, 169n87

Niebuhr, H. Richard, 39n77, 71n3, 87, 87n78, 93n107, 126, 126n78, 130, 130n91, 155n49, 155n50
Niebuhr, Reinhold, 5, 71n3, 93n107
Niebuhr, Richard R., 121n54, 152n43

Oberman, Heiko A., 42n84, 48, 48n102, 53, 53n117, 97n116
Ogden, Schubert M., 35n62, 58n132, 58n133, 59n133, 63n148, 64n153, 65nn154–155, 83n63, 90, 90nn89–90, 126n75, 128n83, 136, 136n106, 138n111, 155n48, 166, 166n78, 167, 167nn80–81, 168, 168nn82–83, 169n84, 169n86
Oman, John, 123n63
Ottati, Douglas F., 167n80
Outler, Albert C., 67n160

Parker, T. H. L., 149n27
Paul, 7, 20, 23, 24, 25, 27, 29, 30, 31, 31n47, 32n49, 32n53, 33, 34, 38, 41, 43, 44, 45, 46, 50n110, 57, 61–62, 62n145, 63, 66, 67, 82, 82n59, 88, 88n86, 93, 96, 97, 97n116, 98, 103, 104, 117n42, 142n5, 162, 163n71, 167n80
Paul, Garrett E., 25n25, 138n113
Pearl, Leonard, 120n48
Pelikan, Jaroslav, 18, 18n8, 41n82, 43n86, 47, 47n100, 48n104, 68, 68n163, 133n101, 150n31
Peter, 44
Petuchowski, Jakob, 159, 160
Philip, 160
Pickle, Joseph W., 113n29, 114n31, 117, 118n43
Pilate, 44
Placher, William C., 131n94
Plato, 7, 33n53

Preuss, Horst Dietrich, 123n64
Pronk, Pim, 62n144
Puckett, David L., 140n1, 141n2
Pye, Michael, 111n21

Rad, Gerhard von, 75
Räisänen, Heikki, 9n10
Rendtorff, Rolf, 171, 171n91
Reuchlin, Johannes, 42n84
Ricoeur, Paul, 98
Ritschl, Albrecht, 40n79
Ritschl, Dietrich, 164n72
Robinson, James M., 7n8, 27n33, 28n35, 29n40
Rosenzweig, Franz, 159n60
Rummel, Erika, 42n84
Rumscheidt, H. Martin, 158n59
Rusch, William G., 137n109, 169n85

Sanders, James A., 167n80, 170, 170n89
Saunders, Thomas Bailey, 126n77
Schaaf, James, 10n11
Schaff, Philip, 162n68
Scheible, Heinz, 73n11
Schleiermacher, Friedrich, 2–3, 3nn1–2, 5, 8–9, 10, 12, 22, 22n15, 54n122, 69n166, 71n3, 93n107, 105–38, 106n1, 107n5, 108n7, 108n9, 109nn12–14, 109n13, 110n16, 110n21, 111n21, 111nn23–24, 112nn26–28, 113n30, 114nn31–32, 117nn40–41, 117n41, 118n43, 119nn46–47, 120n49, 120n51, 121n52, 122n55, 122nn58–60, 123n63, 124n69, 125n73, 130n91, 131n93, 132n97, 132n99, 133n100, 137n107, 138n113, 141, 141n3, 142, 148n26, 149, 150, 152, 153, 155n50, 161, 164, 164n72
Schmid, Konrad, 15n1
Schoeps, Hans-Joachim, 151, 151n38
Scholz, Heinrich, 109n13
Schüssler Fiorenza, Elisabeth, 94, 94n112
Schweitzer, Albert, 7n8, 123, 124n65

Seitz, Christopher R., 70, 74–75, 74nn18–20, 75nn21–26, 78n46, 79, 83, 83n64, 84, 84n65, 84n67, 84n69, 85n70, 86n76, 92, 97n117, 98, 100, 103, 103n126, 104n128, 134n102, 158n58, 165n74
Semler, Johann Salomo, 73–74, 73n11, 91, 107
Servetus, Michael, 93
Shelley, John, 58n133
Smart, James D., 62n145
Smith, Louise Pettibone, 33n54, 36n64
Soelle, Dorothee, 58n133
Sonderegger, Katherine, 152n40
Soulen, R. Kendall, 155n50
Steely, John E., 141n3
Stendahl, Krister, 79, 79n52, 117n42
Steudel, J. C. E., 117n40
Stewart, J. S., 55n122, 108n5, 141n3
Strange, Daniel, 24n21
Strauss, David Friedrich, 124, 124n67, 124n69, 126, 135
Strecker, Georg, 167n80
Sweeney, Marvin A., 97n117, 158n58
Sykes, Stephen, 107n4

Thiel, Winfried, 88n84, 142n6
Thompson, Mark D., 24n21, 52n115
Thomson, G. T., 37nn67–69, 93n107, 106n3, 145n11
Thyen, Hartwig, 32n49
Tice, Terrence N., 109n13
Tillich, Paul, 5, 5n3, 67n161, 68n163, 69, 69n165, 71n3, 89n87, 93n107, 97n116, 131, 131nn94–87, 132, 153
Torrance, Thomas F., 148n26
Tracy, David, 33n53, 71n3, 98, 98n120
Trillhaas, Wolfgang, 112n27
Troels, Engberg-Pedersen, 116n36
Troeltsch, Ernst, 7, 7n9, 71n3, 80, 80n54, 82n60, 87, 93n107, 104, 104n128, 110n21, 118n44, 127n80, 138, 138nn112–114, 165, 165n76

Ubershär, Ingrid, 159n59

Van Til, Cornelius, 24n21
Verheyden, Jack C., 125n73
Vriend, John, 62n144

Warfield, Benjamin Breckenridge, 86n73
Weder, Hans, 32n49
Welch, Claude, 127, 127n82
Welker, Michael, 170n88
Wernberg-Möller, P., 155n51
Wesley, John, 5, 66, 67, 67n160
Wilcox, Donald J., 46n98

Wildman, Wesley J., 129–30, 129n88, 130nn89–90
Williams, Daniel Day, 64n152
Williams, Michael A., 45n92
Willis, David, 170n88
Wolfes, Matthias, 115n34
Wright, G. Ernest, 72n5
Wurm, Theophil, 40n78
Wyschogrod, Michael, 158n59

Yeago, David S., 75n26

Zwingli, Huldrych, 49, 50n110

Printed in the USA
CPSIA information can be obtained
at www.ICGtesting.com
JSHW021202221023
50376JS00004B/163